Third Edition

CONTENT AREA READING

An Integrated Approach

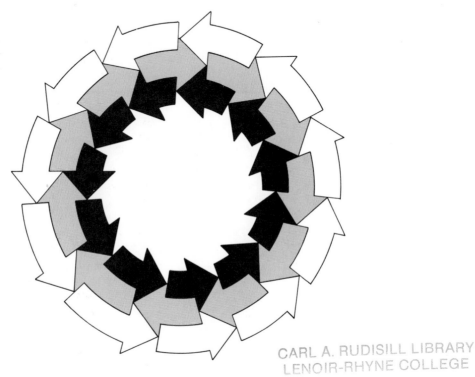

John E. Readence
Louisiana State University

Thomas W. Bean
University of Hawaii at Hilo

R. Scott Baldwin
University of Miami, Florida

KENDALL/HUNT PUBLISHING COMPANY
2460 Kerper Boulevard   P.O. Box 539   Dubuque, Iowa 52004-0539

【H】
THE KENDALL/HUNT
LEARNING THROUGH READING SERIES

Lyndon W. Searfoss,
Consulting Editor

Contents

Preface

The third edition of CONTENT AREA READING: AN INTEGRATED AP-PROACH presents preservice and inservice teachers with theory and related teaching strat-egies to aid students in reading and learning from their textbooks. In this third edition we have attempted to integrate the current state of the art in content area reading with some new ideas of our own. Additionally, this edition differs from previous editions in two main ways. First, we have included a chapter on writing in the content areas as a further step in integrating all language processes to help students learn from text. Second, the text has been reorganized into three new sections, each of which is described below. Thus, the book pro-vides teachers with a comprehensive examination of content area reading in order to make them better teachers of content, rather than teachers of reading.

Part A of this book includes four chapters that introduce content area reading and learning from text. Chapter 1 provides a rationale and description of the philosophy behind content area reading. Chapter 2 follows with an examination of the reading process and lays the foundation for the strategies recommended in this book. Chapter 3 discusses attitudes and interests, with an emphasis on strategies for developing students' interest in subject matter areas. Chapter 4 concludes this section of the book with a discussion of methods for the evaluation of classroom textbooks and ways to introduce them to students.

Part B consists of four chapters of strategies for teaching and learning in the content areas. Chapters 5, 6, and 7 discuss strategies for vocabulary development, comprehension instruction, and writing, respectively. Finally, Chapter 8 examines study strategies for moving students toward independence.

Part C provides two chapters that discuss the assessment and accommodation of stu-dent differences. Chapter 9 describes diagnostic strategies to assess students' reading abil-ities in the content classroom, while Chapter 10 offers instructional suggestions for accommodating individual differences.

Each chapter, in turn, has certain unique features that should enhance teachers' com-prehension of the concepts presented. First, an *anticipation guide/reaction guide* opens and closes each chapter. This aid offers teachers the opportunity to react to a series of statements before and after they read about concepts related to those statements. In addition, a *rationale* for each chapter is provided, as well as *objectives* for teachers to accomplish based upon the reading of the chapter. The beginning of each chapter then closes with a *graphic organizer*, a visual display of pertinent vocabulary terms and their interrelated concepts designed to provide teachers with a chapter overview. *Activities* are interspersed throughout each chapter to afford teachers additional exposure to the new concepts discussed. At the end of each chapter, in addition to the reaction guides, suggested *miniprojects* allow teachers to apply their newly learned information from the chapter. *Additional readings* are recommended to extend and refine the information presented. Finally, a *glossary* serves as a ready reference for italicized vocabulary terms encountered in each chapter of the text.

Through the use of such unique features, each chapter is offered as a model for the strategies advocated by this book. We are attempting to "practice what we preach" by making the entire book a model that reinforces concepts and demonstrates that suggested techniques and strategies **can** work. Hopefully, pre-service and in-service teachers using this book will then have an example as they construct lesson plans and apply the suggested strategies in their own classrooms.

J. E. R.
T. W. B.
R. S. B.

Learning from Text

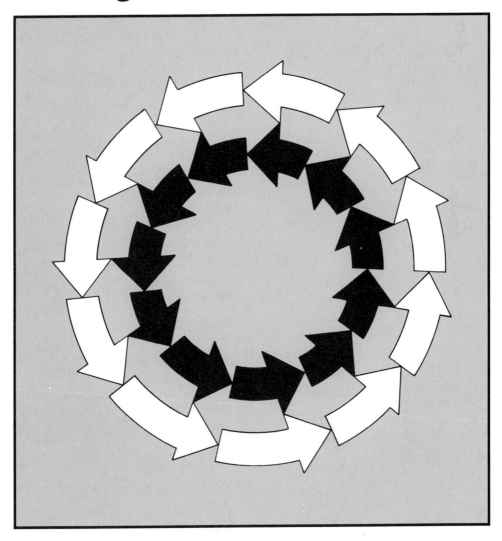

1

Anticipation Guide/Reaction Guide

Directions: Before you begin reading this chapter, take a moment to put a check mark by any of the statements with which you agree. Use the column entitled "Anticipation."

Anticipation   **Reaction**

_____ 1.   _____ 1. Every teacher should be a teacher of reading.

_____ 2.   _____ 2. A content teacher's prime responsibility is to deliver subject matter information.

_____ 3.   _____ 3. Reading instruction should be left to reading teachers.

_____ 4.   _____ 4. Providing students with a purpose for reading will improve their reading abilities.

_____ 5.   _____ 5. Upon leaving elementary school, students should have mastered the skills necessary for content reading.

Content Area Reading: A Rationale

Rationale

Parents Call for Higher Standards
High School Graduation Requirements Increase
Student Sues School Administration
National Panels Call for High School Improvement
State Mandates Minimal Competency Testing

In her stage theory of reading development, Chall (1983) has argued that high school reading ability is necessary for a minimal level of proficiency in coping with the increasingly complex reading tasks of our technological age. Yet thousands of students leave high school not knowing how to read at all; many more thousands depart with reading skills so inadequate that they can't hope to survive the demands of our print-bound, technological culture. And the public impression appears to be that these problems are getting worse, not better! Whether or not the public is correct, we are still faced with massive literacy problems to which there are no simple solutions.

This text is based on the notion that America's literacy dilemma is ultimately solvable and that each and every teacher can play a major role in the resolution. In fact, we believe that expensive remedial programs are inferior to programs in which each teacher (K-12) is committed to making students literate in the context of the materials they are reading. In essence, content reading is the domain of all teachers.

Reading instruction has been the traditional interest of the elementary school, the assumption being that normal students in normal programs SHOULD enter subject matter classrooms knowing how to read. If reading is defined in terms of elementary tasks, e.g., basic decoding skills, the assumption is reasonable. In contrast, the assumption is pure fantasy if reading is defined in terms of subject matter tasks, e.g., expanded homework and independent reading assignments, required notetaking in class, and vastly increased dependence upon textbooks with varied and complex organizational patterns. It does not make sense to assume that students will automatically modify elementary reading skills to suit these subject matter reading demands. In fact, we will argue that such reading requirements should be met with specific instructional strategies that are tied directly into the source of potential reading difficulties, the textbooks and supplemental materials that are used in subject area classes on a daily basis. Moreover, we will argue that subject matter specialists are best qualified to implement these strategies, not because they will make students better readers in general, but because they will convert students into more efficient learners in specific science, math, English, and social studies classes and more adept consumers of information in our technological society.

The present chapter will explore the role of content area reading in learning from a text and will provide a rationale for its implementation. Additionally, the chapter investigates the general reluctance of content teachers to accept any reading-oriented responsibilities in the light of standard misconceptions about content area reading.

Chapter Objectives

After reading this chapter, you should be able to:

1. Understand why it is important to help students read and learn effectively from their textbooks.
2. Provide a description and justification for a content reading emphasis.

Graphic Organizer

The following graphic organizer is provided to give you some advance structure for new vocabulary and concepts that will be presented in this chapter.

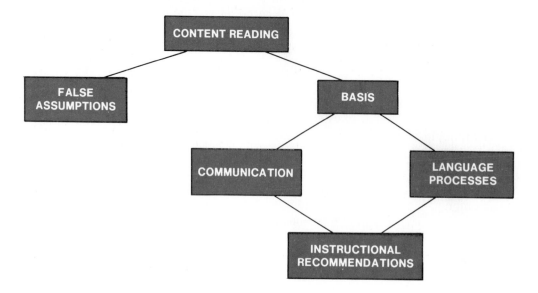

Some Historical Perspective

Enhancing students' ability to read and learn from a given text is not a current phenomenon; rather, it has long been a concern of educators at all levels. In fact, the current emphasis on content area reading instruction can be traced back to early writings of this century. For instance, Gray (1952) pointed out that the importance of providing guidance in reading in all subject matter areas was first emphasized nationally in a 1925 report of the National Committee on Reading.

Moore, Readence, and Rickelman (1986) examined the literature on content area reading. They identified a number of distinct emphases that emerged from the first half of this century and have continued to exert an impact on reading instruction in the content areas. Included among these are emphases on:

1. Comprehending text information (Huey, 1908; Thorndike, 1917);
2. Study (Yoakam, 1928);
3. Reading demands of various subjects (McCallister, 1936); and,
4. Improving the reading abilities of older students (Center & Persons, 1937).

Assumptions and Misconceptions

Although content area reading instruction has been with us for a number of years, content teachers have been reluctant to accept an instructional emphasis that fuses reading with content. Why? To begin with, there seem to exist a variety of false assumptions about reading instruction in general and students' ability to read upon entering subject matter classrooms. The following are some of these assumptions:

1. Students have learned to read in elementary schools.
2. Students have sufficient prior knowledge to cope effectively with the important information in content textbooks.
3. The processes involved in reading and comprehending efficiently in content textbooks are identical to those utilized in reading from basal readers in elementary school.
4. Remedial reading classes will provide those individual students having skill deficiencies with the necessary reading skills for success in subject-matter reading.
5. Subject matter specialists often believe that content reading means teaching phonics and other skills not directly related to their subject areas.
6. Subject matter specialists view themselves as information dispensers.

Belief in these assumptions presupposes that students have mastered the processes necessary to enable them to glean essential information from reading, regardless of writing style and content. It also presupposes that students can meaningfully blend new information with prior knowledge and efficiently utilize textbook aids designed to refine and extend important concepts. A close examination of these assumptions reveals how wrong they are.

Activity

Read the following paragraph from Sartre (1948) and summarize it in your own words from recall.

We are completely in agreement with him on this point: That symbolization is constitutive of symbolic consciousness will trouble no one who believes in the absolute value of the cartesian cogito. But it must be understood that if symbolization is constitutive of consciousness, it is permissible to perceive that there is an immanent bond of comprehension between the symbolization and the symbol. (p. 65)

Did you have difficulty reading the passage? If you were familiar with existential philosophy and Sartre, you might have breezed right through it. However, if this material was foreign to your own personal experiences, adequate comprehension probably proved elusive. In addition, the burden of many new terms and concepts may have caused the passage to seem obscure.

In order to learn to read this passage with full understanding, you would have to be provided background knowledge in the subject area and introduced to its new vocabulary and concepts. Even then the long, complicated sentences could prove tedious and confusing.

Such are some of the difficulties inherent in reading from textbooks. You now have some sensitivity for the demands placed on young students in reading their subject matter materials. Students usually lack experiential background and are unfamiliar with the vocabulary and concepts in social studies, science, or any other content areas. It is presumptuous, and possibly damaging, to expect students to perform well with subject-matter texts that are too hard, or too easy. Moreover, this is true for bright students as well as slow learners. If students are given a textbook that does not contain new concepts and unfamiliar vocabulary, the students probably don't need to read the book in the first place.

Complicating matters further are teachers' expectations that remedial reading classes will provide the necessary help students must have to cope successfully with their textbooks. Such programs are of questionable value (Allington, Stuetzel, Shake, & Lamarche, 1986). Remedial reading classes usually focus on decoding skills, which emphasize phonics instruction and pre-packaged comprehension skills programs. This focus often has little relevance to what is being studied in content area classrooms, especially when such reading instruction is poorly coordinated with subject-matter curricula. Such programs perpetuate the notion that reading takes place only in reading class and that content teachers have no responsibility for helping students read and learn from their textbooks. Unfortunately, when reading programs extend beyond the elementary school, remedial reading programs, rather than content reading programs, are emphasized.

Most remedial reading classes emphasize an elementary/clinical approach, in which reading instruction is "warmed-over" elementary reading. Such a model of secondary reading can be described as a *closet-clinician model,* in which the reading teacher attempts to remediate reading deficiencies through phonics and isolated skill drills that are in actuality divorced from the "real" school curriculum of textbooks and subject matter. Instruction that centers on giving older readers the same type of instruction they had in elementary school over and over again does not seem to make much sense, especially considering the fact that these remedial students have failed with that instruction previously.

Yet, can we fault reading teachers who work with older students for this emphasis? Certainly some fault must lie with the teacher training programs in which they were prepared for their jobs. These programs again emphasize a traditional skills approach to the teaching of reading. With such a model it is no wonder the emphasis taken in reading in our schools! Though teacher training programs are beginning to recognize their responsibility in content area reading, the existing reading model in our universities provides a poor example for content teachers. Teacher training programs for content area teachers, additionally, are not oriented toward reading in the content areas. Teachers in preparation are taught with a mind set to convey their body of information to students. Unfortunately, for some teachers, this mind set continues once they leave the university. For instance, Hinchman (1985), in a qualitative study of secondary teachers' plans and conceptions of reading, found that teachers consider reading as a means of "covering the course content" (p. 254). Reading was viewed as a way to dispense information, rather than as a means to read and learn from the textbook. Additionally, Goodlad (1984), in a comprehensive study of schooling in America, confirmed the notion that some teachers see their role as that of an information dispenser. He found that:

> . . . about 75% of class time was spent on instruction and that nearly 70% of this was "talk"— usually teacher to student. Teachers out-talked the entire class of students by a ratio of about three to one . . . the bulk of this teacher talk was instructing in the sense of telling. Barely 5% of this instructional time was designed to create students' anticipation of needing to respond . . . when a student was called on to respond, it was to give an informational answer to the teacher's question. The two activities, involving the most students, were being lectured to and working on written assignments. (pp. 229–230)

Thus, many teachers, both preservice and inservice, are not even aware of content reading and the potential this emphasis would have for aiding students in reading and learning from their textbooks.

Perhaps a final complication to utilizing content reading in subject-matter classrooms is the well-intended, but detrimental, slogan that "every teacher is a teacher of reading." Tell social studies teachers, for instance, that they are teachers of reading and you may understand how receptive they would be to content reading. If apoplexy does not occur, their certain retort will be that they are teachers of social studies, not reading! The reading model content teachers usually witness, emphasizing the previously mentioned skills characteristics, will not encourage them to attend to the reading needs of their classes. Moreover, their resolve that they are subject-matter specialists first is a valid one.

A Basis for Content Area Reading

Singer (1979) surveyed the attitudes of subject matter teachers toward teaching reading in the content areas. Where previously such groups of teachers were less than enthusiastic toward the slogan "every teacher is a teacher of reading," Singer found favorable attitudes by such teachers when asked their opinion concerning the statement that "every teacher teaches students to learn from texts." This statement connotes a model of reading instruction that focuses on aiding students in learning from text rather than learning isolated skills.

The authors agree with this reemphasis. Content reading currently has too many prior associations with learning to read, skills instruction, and the closet-clinician model. Under this reemphasis, content teachers are considered catalysts for learning, whose responsibility it is to aid students in reading and learning from text. The focus of content reading instruction is on reading to learn, not on learning to read.

Let's examine in depth the roles of the teacher, the reader, and the textbook as each relates to success in learning. First, if texts were meant to be read in isolation, there would be little, if any, need for someone called a teacher. Similarly, if texts are so easy to read that a reader needs little or no help to learn the material, a teacher, again, would be superfluous. Yet, as our Sartre quotation illustrated, such is not normally the case with text materials. Texts are usually challenging and present students with a myriad of problems.

Second, it makes sense to describe content reading as a means of improving communication. There is sort of a "long-distance" communication that materializes between an author of a text and a reader attempting to comprehend it. The reader is, in effect, trying to communicate with authors of texts by constructing a meaning from their words and thoughts. Given, then, the goal of the reader and the difficulty of texts, a facilitator is needed to promote this interaction between reader and text. Indeed, this should be the role of the teacher.

If teachers consider themselves to be information dispensers, then there is no need for textbooks. Teachers who make text reading assignments and then go over in class exactly what is in the text not only make class boring but also encourage students to neglect to read their assignments (Alvermann, Dillon, O'Brien, & Smith, 1985). This type of teacher is certainly not encouraging the development of independent readers who can take their place as useful citizens and lifelong learners in our society. A teacher who focuses only on the content ignores the processes needed by students to comprehend the content in immediate and future reading situations.

Thus, we must conceive of texts as information dispensers, and the reader's task is to acquire that information, even if that may be a challenge because of the way the text has been written. The teacher's role in this communication effort is to encourage the thinking processes essential to understanding, i.e., to facilitate learning from text. Teachers, then, can promote this interaction if they conceive of themselves as facilitators of the learning process in that they have inherent advantages over textbooks or any other information dispensing device. Schallert and Kleiman (1979) have cited four skills that teachers can exercise that a text cannot: 1) tailoring the message; 2) activating prior knowledge; 3) focusing attention; and 4) monitoring comprehension.

Teachers can tailor the message by adapting their presentations to the needs, abilities, and experiential backgrounds of their students. They already know what students know and do not know and can interact with them during their presentations. Second, teachers can activate prior knowledge by reminding students of what they know and how it relates to what they are to learn. Third, teachers focus attention by increasing students' interest and motivation to learn new material and by directing them to pay attention to selected pieces of the text. Finally, teachers can monitor comprehension by checking to see if students understand important parts of a text presentation. Clearly, texts cannot accomplish any of these tasks.

Nevertheless, while it is true that textbooks cannot do these things, it is also true that textbooks are not designed to do this. They are designed to give information. Materials don't do the teaching; teachers, by definition, do the teaching and this teaching entails helping students acquire the processes necessary for successful learning. Thus, we have a student-centered curriculum in which the teacher's role is to instruct students in the processes involved in comprehending textual material, rather than a subject-centered curriculum in which the textual information is of the utmost importance.

Instructional Recommendations

Just what goes on in the name of instruction in a student-centered curriculum? What differentiates a student-centered curriculum from a subject-centered one? How does one "facilitate learning from text"?

The following recommendations are ones that the authors consider appropriate when a teacher wants to emphasize content area reading. Specific guidelines for the implementation of these recommendations are provided in later chapters.

1. *Present content and processes concurrently.* Moore and Readence (1986) described several possible approaches to learning from text. Among those discussed were: a) presenting isolated skills; b) aiming toward content; and, c) presenting content and processes concurrently.

a. *Presenting isolated skills* is typical of a closet-clinician model of reading. The method consists of the direct teaching of skills, with no consideration for content. Students use special materials or workbooks not related to the texts students are assigned to learn in their regular classes. For instance, students may be taught how to detect the sequence when their reading assignment requires the interpretation of graphs. Though the teacher may intend that the students will transfer their newly acquired skills, this approach, like most skill-centered remedial programs, fails because students also need to be taught how to transfer skills from one material to another. More importantly, they fail to see any purpose in learning skills divorced from content.

b. *Aiming toward content* focuses on acquiring content versus *how* to acquire that content. In other words, the teacher sets purposes for reading and during a follow-up discussion checks to see if the purposes were met. However, this method also is unsuccessful because there is no instruction in how to extract the information from the text. Students are told what to do but not how to do it. Thus, students are not provided the means to complete their assigned tasks; telling students what to do is not synonymous with instruction and is not sufficient to improve students' reading abilities.

c. Students learn best and acquire content most successfully when their attention is focused directly on the material to be learned. *Presenting content and processes concurrently* does this by providing direct instruction in the processes necessary to acquire content in addition to pointing out what content is to be acquired. For example, if the content to be learned is organized into a cause-effect format, the teacher would first present a lesson on organizing content according to that format before giving students the actual content in which they would use their knowledge of that process. Thus, text information is stressed alongside the processes needed to attain it. Specifying *what* should be attained without specifying *how* to do it is pointless. Taking "process" into account as well as "content" acknowledges that: 1) reading is indispensable to the successful learning of all academic subjects, and 2) content as specified in a text is only one part of the dynamic interaction between reader, text, and teacher in classroom learning situations. As a consequence, the learning of content and the teaching of processes to help learn it become **integrated** within a total lesson framework.

2. *Provide guidance in all aspects of the instructional lesson—before, during, and after reading.* Learning content is not simply reading the assigned pages, answering the end-of-chapter questions, and listening to the teacher present what has already been read. Generally, students need to be prepared to read a text, need guidance in reading for selected ideas, and need reinforcement to retain the material learned.

More specifically, before reading, students need to be aware that using their prior knowledge and having purposes for reading aids the comprehension process. In addition, teachers can explicitly demonstrate to students how to learn from text through *modeling*. In this technique, teachers become a role model by explaining how they comprehended something; i.e., a reporting of the mental operations involved in their comprehension of a particular text. Students can then repeat the process in order to comprehend on their own.

During the reading, students are searching for information to satisfy the purposes set by the teacher and/or themselves. The teacher may use some adjunct material to guide the students' search. After reading, teachers check to see if preset purposes have been attained.

One useful way to give feedback to students is to have a *debriefing* session, which includes self-reports, introspection, and hindsights by students. Debriefing does not cover content alone, but also entails checking out the processes students used to comprehend the text in relation to what was modeled for them. As students become more adept, the demonstration and guidance teachers provide should be faded, or withdrawn, so students can be moved toward independence in their reading and learning. Thus, helping students learn content is **integrated** throughout all phases of the instructional lesson.

3. *Use all language processes to help students learn from text.* The authors believe that all language processes, not just reading, can be utilized as a means to approach learning from text. While reading will undoubtably remain the major means of dealing with text, other language processes can play key roles in helping students learn content. Indeed, Postman (1979) suggested that all teachers become "language educators" and consider using all language processes to enhance students' ability to cope successfully with subject matter materials. Recent research on writing (e.g. Tierney and Pearson, 1983) has further pointed out the interconnections between reading and writing and has suggested that reading be viewed as a composing process. In effect, writing, listening, and speaking become additional tools to teach more content.

It is our belief that the receptive language processes of reading and listening should be **integrated** with the expressive processes of writing and speaking to promote thinking and learning with content materials. The integrative aspects of reading and the other language processes are shown below:

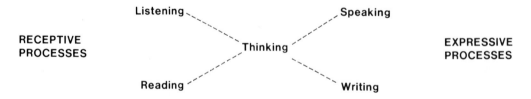

In a system such as this, content reading takes on the larger notion of "content communication" by emphasizing those teaching practices which integrate language processes and thinking as one learns content.

4. *Use small groups to enhance learning.* Wood (1987) has pointed out that while the lecture method is the dominant means of instruction in our classrooms, one of the most effective is small group instruction. Additionally, Johnson, Maruyama, Johnson, Nelson, and Skon (1981) synthesized the literature on cooperative versus competitive instructional efforts. They found that when students were encouraged to work collaboratively with peers,

productivity and achievement were enhanced. We realize that the lecture method is prevalent in teaching, yet many of the strategies advocated in this text are best used with, or even require, small group instruction. We recommend such strategies because they promote active learning situations and emphasize peer interaction.

Initial attempts at small group instruction may be chaotic and create management problems; however, this is only part of learning to interact within a group for both the students and the teacher. Once both are accustomed to such instruction, we feel that this method will pave the way for greater output in learning content, both in depth of understanding and in breadth of cognitive and affective experiences. Thus, teachers become cost-efficient when they **integrate** small groups into their teaching; i.e., they enhance the learning environment through good teaching practices which, in turn, create more knowledgeable students.

5. *Be patient in strategy implementation.* Don't expect instant results the first time you use a strategy recommended in this text. First attempts at strategy implementation are fraught with errors; as with any new learning, becoming an "expert" at using a strategy requires time and patience. Try a strategy out three or four times before you render a final decision on its utility.

As you begin trying a new method, keep in mind the following model of strategy implementation (Readence, Baldwin, & Dishner, 1980). Implementating strategies in the classroom entails movement through five developmental stages: a) awareness; b) knowledge; c) simulation; d) practice; and e) incorporation. Awareness is necessary before one would seek knowledge about a strategy. In this case, awareness is simply recognizing that content learning and reading texts requires a special knowledge base for efficient processing.

Knowledge occurs when teachers acquire insights about specific strategies that will help students learn from text. Simulation occurs when teachers experiment with specific strategies outside the classroom. They try out strategies on other teachers to obtain preliminary feedback and modify procedures to suit their students' needs. Practice entails the actual use of a strategy with students. This step also entails experimentation and modification. Finally, at the incorporation stage, a strategy becomes an automatic part of a teacher's instructional repertoire and a natural part of teaching.

The general recommendations cited above give you an overview of our philosophy in writing this text. To give you more of a flavor of the specifics that surround our recommendations, examine the list of practices below. These will be expanded upon in later chapters. For any immediate clarification of terminology used in this list, consult the glossary.

Activity

These practices are recommended for enhancing reading and learning in the content areas. If you are an inservice teacher, circle the appropriate number showing how much you do each of these. If you are a preservice teacher, observe a content area teacher to see which practices are used.

1—Almost always	3—Sometimes	5—Never
2—Most of the time	4—Seldom	

Recommended Practices for Teaching in Content Areas

1. The teacher utilizes all language processes to enhance students' learning from text.   1 2 3 4 5
2. The reading levels of the students are known by the teacher.   1 2 3 4 5
3. The readability level of the text has been determined by the teacher.   1 2 3 4 5
4. The teacher has evaluated the text for the presence or absence of characteristics which make a well-organized text.   1 2 3 4 5
5. Materials for instruction, including the textbook, are chosen to match the reading levels of the students.   1 2 3 4 5
6. Books and other materials are available for students who read below and above the readability level of the text.   1 2 3 4 5
7. Textbook aids, such as illustrations, maps, and graphs, are explained or called to the attention of the students.   1 2 3 4 5
8. Class time is spent discussing how to read the text effectively.   1 2 3 4 5
9. The special vocabulary of the text has been located.   1 2 3 4 5
10. The teacher has identified the special processes necessary for completing the reading assignment.   1 2 3 4 5
11. The teacher presents the special vocabulary and concepts introduced in the text materials assigned for reading in the context of a well-planned lesson.   1 2 3 4 5
12. Prior knowledge of the text concepts is activated before reading the text.   1 2 3 4 5
13. Purpose is provided for each reading assignment.   1 2 3 4 5
14. Assignments are stated clearly and concisely.   1 2 3 4 5
15. The teacher integrates special reading processes into subject matter lessons.   1 2 3 4 5
16. The teacher makes differentiated text assignments according to the ability levels of the students.   1 2 3 4 5
17. The teacher asks questions designed to promote thinking at all levels of comprehension.   1 2 3 4 5
18. The teacher provides some form of guide or outline to aid in study.   1 2 3 4 5
19. The course content requires more than reading a single textbook.   1 2 3 4 5
20. A variety of reference materials is made available.   1 2 3 4 5
21. Students are taught to use appropriate reference materials.   1 2 3 4 5
22. Students are encouraged to read widely in materials related to the text.   1 2 3 4 5
23. Small group instruction is used where appropriate.   1 2 3 4 5

Summary

The present chapter has sought to provide a rationale for content area reading. Assumptions and misconceptions presently surrounding content area reading have been enumerated and discussed. Content reading as an *INTEGRATED* communication process has been offered as a viable means by which to emphasize learning from text. Some general recommendations for instruction have been offered and an overview of the textbook has been provided in the form of a list of instructional practices advocated by the authors to be explored in later chapters.

Now go back to the anticipation guide at the beginning of this chapter. React again to the statements as you did before, but this time record your answers in the column entitled "Reaction." Compare your responses with those you made earlier.

Miniprojects

1. Make a copy of the short selection from Sartre and ask other teachers from various content areas to perform the same task asked of you. Summarize your findings and compare these with other class members.
2. Write a sentence or paragraph using the technical vocabulary from your own content field. Exchange this with a class member from a different subject-matter area. Can you understand each other's passage? Why or why not? What might help you increase your understanding?

Additional Recommended Readings

Bean, T. W., & Readence, J. E. (1988). Content area reading: The current state of the art. In J. Flood & D. Lapp (Eds.), *Content area reading and learning: Instructional strategies.* Englewood Cliffs, NJ: Prentice-Hall.
   Discusses the current status of content area reading and the issues surrounding it and describes how this approach assists in the development of a literate society.
Conley, M. W. (1986). Teachers' conceptions, decisions, and changes during initial classroom lessons containing content reading strategies. In J. A. Niles & R. V. Lalik (Eds.), *Solving problems in literacy: Learners, teachers, and researchers* (pp. 120–126). Thirty-fifth Yearbook of the National Reading Conference. Rochester, NY: National Reading Conference.
   Documents the decisions and changes teachers make when first attempting to implement content area reading strategies.
Dishner, E. K., Bean, T. W., Readence, J. E., & Moore, D. W. (Eds.). (1986). *Reading in the content areas: Improving classroom instruction* (2nd ed.). Dubuque, IA: Kendall/Hunt Publishing Company.
   Chapter one of this book of readings presents a number of articles which provide a rationale for content area reading instruction.

Gee, T. C., & Rakow, S. J. (1987). Content reading specialists evaluate teaching practices. *Journal of Reading, 31,* 234–237.

> Provides a listing of rank-ordered teaching recommendations for consideration and use by content area teachers.

Samuels, S. J., & Pearson, P. D. (Eds.). (1988). *Changing school reading programs: Principles and case studies.* Newark, DE: International Reading Association.

> Chapters in this text by Singer & Bean and by Santa present case studies about establishing content reading programs in classrooms and schools.

Siedow, M. D., Memory, D. M., & Bristow, P. S. (1985). *Inservice education for content area teachers.* Newark, DE: International Reading Association.

> Contains numerous suggestions for content area teachers to improve their effectiveness in teaching their subject matter.

References

Allington, R., Stuetzel, H., Shake, M., & Lamarche, S. (1986). What is remedial reading? A descriptive study. *Reading Research and Instruction, 26,* 15–30.

Alvermann, D. E., Dillon, D. R., O'Brien, D. G., & Smith, L. C. (1985). The role of the textbook in discussion. *Journal of Reading, 29,* 50–57.

Center, S. S., & Persons, G. L. (1937). *Teaching high school students to read: A study of retardation in reading.* New York: Appleton-Century.

Chall, J. S. (1983). *Stages of reading development.* New York: McGraw-Hill.

Goodlad, J. I. (1984). *A place called school.* New York: McGraw-Hill.

Gray, W. S. (1952). Progress achieved and the tasks faced in improving reading in various curriculum areas. In W. S. Gray (Ed.), *Improving reading in all curriculum areas* (pp. 6–11). Supplemental Educational Monographs No. 76.

Hinchman, K. (1985). Reading and the plans of secondary teachers: A qualitative study. In J. A. Niles & R. V. Lalik (Eds.), *Issues in literacy: A research perspective* (pp. 251–256). Thirty-fourth Yearbook of the National Reading Conference. Rochester, NY: National Reading Conference.

Huey, E. B. (1908). *The psychology and pedagogy of reading.* New York: Macmillan.

Johnson, D. W., Maruyama, G., Johnson, R., Nelson, D., & Skon, L. (1981). Effects of cooperative, competitive, and individualistic goal structures on achievement: A meta-analysis. *Psychological Bulletin, 89,* 47–62.

McCallister, J. M. (1936). *Remedial and corrective instruction in reading: A program for the upper grades and high school.* New York: Appleton-Century.

Moore, D. W., & Readence, J. E. (1986). Approaches to content area reading instruction. In E. K. Dishner, T. W. Bean, J. E. Readence, & D. W. Moore (Eds.), *Reading in the content areas: Improving classroom instruction* (2nd ed., pp. 36–41). Dubuque, IA: Kendall/Hunt Publishing Company.

Moore, D. W., Readence, J. E., & Rickelman, R. J. (1986). An historical exploration of content area reading instruction. In E. K. Dishner, T. W. Bean, J. E. Readence, & D. W. Moore (Eds.), *Reading in the content areas: Improving classroom instruction* (2nd ed., pp. 4–27). Dubuque, IA: Kendall/Hunt Publishing Company.

Postman, N. (1979). *Teaching as a conserving activity.* New York: Delacorte Press, 1979.

Readence, J. E., Baldwin, R. S., and Dishner, E. K. (1980). Establishing content reading programs in secondary schools. *Journal of Reading, 23,* 522–526.

Sartre, J. (1948). *The emotions: Outline of a theory.* New York: Book Sales.

Schallert, D. L., & Kleiman, G. M. (1979, June). *Some reasons why teachers are easier to understand than textbooks* (Reading Educ. Rep. No. 9). Urbana: University of Illinois, Center for the Study of Reading.

Singer, H. (1979). Research: Slogans and attitudes. *Journal of Reading, 22,* 756–757.

Thorndike, E. L. (1917). Reading as reasoning: A study of mistakes in paragraph reading. *Journal of Educational Psychology, 8,* 276–282.

Tierney, R. J., & Pearson, P. D. (1986). Toward a composing model of reading. In E. K. Dishner, T. W. Bean, J. E. Readence, & D. W. Moore (Eds.), *Reading in the content areas: Improving classroom instruction* (2nd ed., pp. 64–75). Dubuque, IA: Kendall/Hunt Publishing Company.

Wood, K. D. (1987). Fostering cooperative learning in middle and secondary level classrooms. *Journal of Reading, 31,* 10–18.

Yoakam, G. A. (1928). *Reading and study: More effective study through better reading habits.* New York: Macmillan.

2

Anticipation Guide/Reaction Guide

Directions: Before you begin reading this chapter, take a moment to put a check mark by any of the following statements with which you agree. Use the column entitled, "Anticipation".

Anticipation   **Reaction**

_____ 1.   _____ 1. You need to have some prior knowledge about a topic in order to understand what you are reading.

_____ 2.   _____ 2. Comprehending text material is a creative, constructive process.

_____ 3.   _____ 3. Rote memorization is an efficient method for learning and remembering content material.

_____ 4.   _____ 4. Making students aware of an author's text structure is important for comprehension.

_____ 5.   _____ 5. Whole class discussion discourages wide student participation.

The Reading Process

Rationale

The uniquely human act of reading has intrigued psychologists and linguists alike since the early part of this century. The pioneering studies of the reading process by Huey (1908) and others stand as a departure point for current investigations of reading comprehension. Indeed, Huey's (1908) opening comments in his text, written over 80 years ago, are still valid today.

> And so to completely analyze what we do when we read would almost be the acme of a psychologist's achievements, for it would be to describe very many of the most intricate workings of the human mind, as well as to unravel the tangled story of the most remarkable specific performance that civilization has learned in all its history. (p. 6)

Our understanding of the reading process has been expanding rapidly since Huey's landmark efforts. Although systematic study of the reading process is likely to continue for many years, there is a great deal that we currently know. More importantly, this existing body of knowledge should influence teaching and learning in the content classroom since effective instruction integrates theory and practice.

Contemporary studies of the reading process from the perspective of cognitive psychology and linguistics highlight the complex nature of text reading. Cognitive psychologists are interested in describing the processes by which we acquire, store, retrieve, and employ knowledge, and the role language plays in this process. Linguists and sociolinguists are primarily concerned with exploring the abstract quality of language in a variety of cultural contexts. Reading, encompassing both psychological and linguistic components, has become a focal point for cognitive inquiry (Anderson & Pearson, 1984; Singer & Ruddell, 1985; Smith, 1982). From cognitive science, we can gain some useful insights about the reading process to serve as guideposts for content teaching.

The following chapter will provide an introduction to our current understanding of the reading process and will focus on how this information relates to reading content material. At the close of this chapter you should have a good foundation for future chapters on text selection and teaching strategies.

Chapter Objectives

After reading this chapter, you should be able to:

1. Understand the cognitive factors that influence reading comprehension.
2. Understand the linguistic factors that influence reading comprehension.

Graphic Organizer

The following graphic organizer is provided to give you some advance structure for new vocabulary and concepts that will be presented in this chapter.

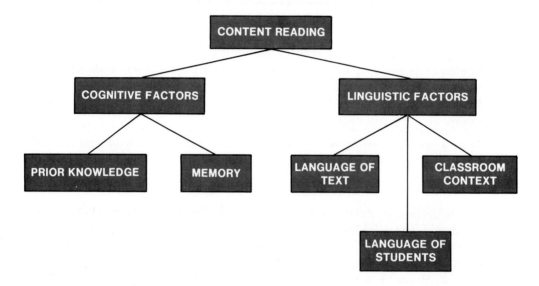

Cognitive Factors

Prior Knowledge and Reading Comprehension

One of the most universal findings to emerge from cognitive research is the marked degree to which a learner's *prior knowledge* of a topic facilitates future comprehension. In fact most contemporary definitions or descriptions of comprehension allude to the role of prior knowledge as a pathway to understanding new ideas. For example, Adams and Bruce (1982) assert that "language is, at best, a means of directing others to construct similar thoughts from their own prior knowledge" (p. 3). Text comprehension is a tacit contract between author and reader. Smith (1982) regards comprehension as "an interaction between a reader and a text" (p. 11).

In the particular case of reading, a student uses prior knowledge of a topic to comprehend textual information. Experiments conducted by cognitive scientists provide us with an explicit demonstration of just how prominent a role prior knowledge plays in text comprehension. As an example, read the following sentence and see if you can figure out what it is referring to.

THE PHOSCHECK DROPPED LEFT OF THE CAT.

If you were informed prior to reading this sentence that the topic concerned fire fighting (specifically methods of controlling forest and brush fires), that knowledge might have increased your comprehension of this otherwise ambiguous sentence. In firefighting operations, "phoscheck," a fire retardant, is dropped from helicopters. The term "cat" refers to a Caterpillar tractor cutting a fire line near where the chemical fire retardant is being dropped.

Bransford (1982, p. 65) provides the following letter to illustrate the value of shared prior knowledge between author and reader.

Activity

Read the following letter and see if you can write a short summary of it.

Dear Jill,

Remember Sally, the person I mentioned in my letter? You'll never guess what she did this week. First, she let loose a team of gophers. The plan backfired when a dog chased them away. She then threw a party but the guests failed to bring their motorcycles. Furthermore, her stereo system was not loud enough. Sally spent the next day looking for a "Peeping Tom" but was unable to find one in the yellow pages. Obscene phone calls gave her some hope until the number was changed. It was the installation of blinking neon lights across the street that finally did the trick. Sally framed the ad from the classified section and now has it hanging on her wall.

Please write soon.

Love,
Bill

Despite the fact that you can "read" all the words in this letter, your understanding of it may be less than satisfying. Sally's behavior is certainly bizarre, and while Jill must know why, we do not. As it turns out, Sally is attempting to intimidate a pesky neighbor into moving. We can infer from the last sentence that she was ultimately successful.

Although these contrived examples, culled from various psychology experiments, display the value of prior knowledge, how does this rather commonsense finding relate to text comprehension in content material? Moreover, can it be shown that readers who possess prior knowledge of a content topic achieve better comprehension than students who do not have this knowledge? Finally, if prior knowledge is valuable, how can we develop this knowledge in our classrooms?

Classroom studies show that students' prior knowledge enhances text comprehension. For example, Stevens (1982) provided students in social studies with background information on the Texan War. Another group received a prereading lesson on the unrelated U.S. Civil War. When both groups read a test passage on the Battle of the Alamo, students with prior knowledge about the Texan War answered significantly more test questions correctly than their peers in the uninformed group. Another study by Crafton (1983) involved a group of students who read a text passage on sociobiology followed by a second passage on the same topic. Another group read a passage unrelated to sociobiology followed by the target sociobiology text. As you might guess, the group of students who developed some prior knowledge of the topic produced greater recall of the test passage than their less informed peers.

These two studies demonstrate the importance of students' existing knowledge about a content topic. The Stevens study shows that a content teacher's effort to provide background information has a positive effect on students' subsequent comprehension of related material. In chapters five and six we will demonstrate a number of strategies you can use to enhance students' prior knowledge.

The Crafton study illustrates the value of reading as a way of acquiring prior knowledge. Certainly silent reading of a general introductory passage before delving into more detailed challenging text is a good way to build prior knowledge. In chapter eight we introduce a number of student-centered study strategies that you can weave into your content instruction.

As you can see, our instructional intuition and recent classroom studies confirm the importance of prior knowledge. Theories from cognitive science provide a picture of how this knowledge is organized in memory. An understanding of this organization will enable a teacher to appreciate individual differences in reading comprehension.

The Organization of Prior Knowledge in Memory

Cognitive structure is a term used to describe the way in which an individual stores experiences and concepts. In such structuring, each individual forms a system of categories based largely on common cultural and experiential patterns. For example, Eskimo culture specifies a rich category system for the quality of snow. In Hawaiian culture that category is virtually nonexistent. Such categories serve to aid an individual in organizing and understanding experiences by promoting an efficient memory search of prior experiences during problem-solving tasks. The following diagram depicts a portion of a possible category system for classifying various kinds of mammals.

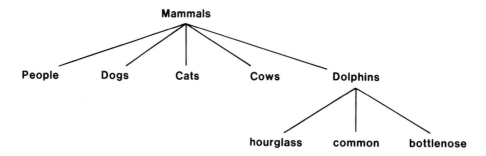

A category system such as the one above functions as a representation of knowledge in memory that can be searched to make sense of the surrounding environment. In general, information located at a high level (e.g. mammals) in our cognitive structure is more easily retrieved than lower level details such as hourglass or bottlenose dolphins (Norman, 1976). For example, although the category "dolphin" is readily accessible when we see a dolphin or a picture of one, the more than 50 types of dolphins would be much harder to recall. The accessibility of subsets of a category is highly dependent on individual differences with respect to one's past experience, culture, and interests. A student who was raised near the sea and has a strong interest in marine biology may have a readily accessible and highly detailed cognitive structure for the category "dolphins," while the general population of students possess a much less elaborate network for this category.

It should be evident at this point that prior knowledge constitutes an important individual difference in our students. Richness of prior knowledge in part, therefore, determines the extent to which a given text can be comprehended by a given individual. In future chapters we will introduce specific strategies for determining and enhancing students' prior knowledge of a topic they encounter in content text material. The next section of the present chapter will explore how an individual's organization of prior knowledge interacts with content text material to facilitate or inhibit reading comprehension.

The Influence of Prior Knowledge on Reading Comprehension

As a student moves into the secondary grades, an ever-expanding wealth of prior knowledge is available to cope with the flood of new information introduced in the content areas. While the concept of cognitive structure explains how this prior knowledge is organized in memory, *schema theory,* patterned after Piaget's formulation, provides a more detailed explanation of comprehension (Anderson & Pearson, 1984; Rumelhart, 1981; Rumelhart & Norman, 1981).

Schema theory attempts to describe the comprehension process in terms of how we cope with familiar, new, or discordant information. Clark and Clark (1977) defined schema as a "kind of mental framework based on cultural experience into which new facts are fitted" (p. 168). For example, we can easily understand familiar situations like registering for classes at the university because we have a well-developed schema for this task (Rumelhart, 1981). Similarly, secondary students often have elaborate, in-depth schemata for motorcycles, cars, computers, skateboards, clothes, and other topics of interest to them.

Based on schema theory, Rumelhart and Norman (1978) outline three essential ingredients for the comprehension process. First, an individual must have a category system containing information about the surrounding environment. Rumelhart & Norman term this category system *schemata* (the plural of schema). Next, two alternative processes, determined by an individual's existing schemata, are involved in comprehension. The first alternative process, *assimilation,* fits new information into existing schemata. The second alternative, *accommodation,* involves adjusting or modifying existing schemata to accept radically new or discordant information. Of course there is a third possibility—students can simply ignore or reject information that fails to fit their prevailing view of the world.

Assimilation relies on the reader's rich cognitive structure to allow interpretation and shading-in of missing information in text. The following activity illustrates the role of your existing schemata in the assimilation of incomplete information.

Activity

Read the following passage and answer the question that follows (Christen, Searfoss, & Bean, 1984).

The Herpetologist

The scrawny boy in faded jeans raised his thumb in one last weary attempt to get a ride. Today was a disaster; no one wanted to stop and darkness was only a short time away. Suddenly, a grey van, splashed with primer paint squealed to a stop and a smile told the boy he was welcome. After a few miles of small talk, life seemed once again better and the boy fell asleep, bone-tired and relieved to find a safe place to sleep for a while.

His ankle moved! No, something pushed gently against it. The boy, barely awake, reached carefully down and felt it move, smoothly and slowly past his leg.

"Quiet!" said the face with a smile, "she won't hurt you if you move slowly, at least until after her dinner." (Christen, Searfoss, & Bean, 1984, p. 33)

Question: What is "smooth and moving" by the boy's leg?

Although the story never explicitly mentions a snake, your prior knowledge of things that slither undoubtedly helped you assimilate this text into your existing schemata. Or, perhaps you knew that a "herpetologist" is a zoologist specializing in the study of reptiles.

A person's schema or knowledge structure can be regarded as the central guidance system in the comprehension process. An individual searches existing schemata to make sense of incoming information from the text. The degree to which this incoming information is consistent with the expectations generated from existing schemata determines the presence or absence of comprehension.

Since schemata represent individual perceptions and beliefs concerning more general, universal concepts, it's entirely possible to have an incomplete schema for some events. For example, Rumelhart and Norman (1978) suggest that an individual growing up in an urban environment may have a schema for farming based largely on childhood nursery rhymes. Such a schema would be inadequate for understanding the workings of a modern farm environment involving the use of technologically advanced harvesting equipment and procedures. Indeed, modifications would have to be made in this person's existing nursery rhyme schema to accommodate information about a contemporary farm operation.

The schema that we all have for mammals provides another example of how existing knowledge guides and influences our comprehension of new information. Our schema for mammals constitutes a fluid network of categories into which we can assimilate new and exotic varieties of mammals if they meet our criteria for category membership. For instance, within our schema for mammals most of us have a subset of knowledge about attributes for specific mammals such as cats. We have a schema for cats that may look something like the one that follows.

Our schema for cats, though not as elaborate as that of a true cat afficionado, allows us to routinely identify and comprehend cats in real and fantasy settings. We can easily assimilate most cats and kittens into our existing, albeit limited, notion of cats. But what happens when we are confronted with a friend's cat named "Fifty" who possesses a defining attribute not contained in our schema for cats? Specifically, "Fifty" does not have a tail, yet he is surely a cat since he possesses all the other essential features.

If we take the trouble to ask our friend about Fifty's missing tail we discover that Fifty is a Manx cat. Now we have a label but still lack an in-depth understanding of this particular tailless cat. Our friend comes to the rescue with a "compendium of cats" and we do some reading about the Manx. We discover that it is tailless because of a mutant gene. Moreover, there are different types of Manx cats including some with stubby tails called "stumpies." We decide to adjust our schema for cats to include this tailless attribute and the Manx category. Our schema for cats would now look like the following graphic organizer.

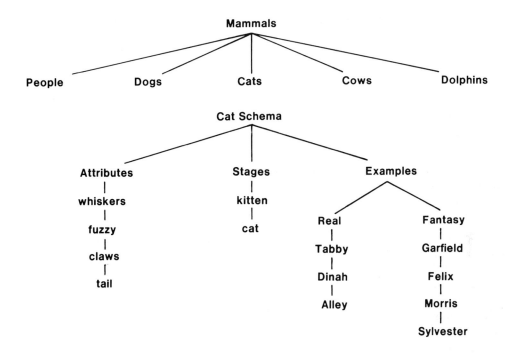

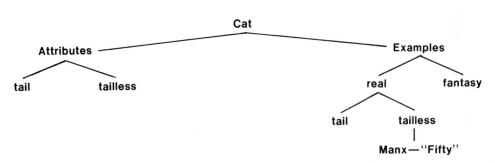

Modification of our existing schema is the essence of accommodation. However, concept learning in many content fields is often more complex than Piaget's assimilation and accommodation processes imply. Although these labels are useful for describing the end result of a learner's effort to understand information in a text, more recent descriptions of concept learning try to explain the struggle learners go through as they attempt to jettison misconceptions and restructure faulty schemata in light of new, sometimes discordant concepts. In the section that follows, we want to consider recent work in concept learning that charts the often rocky road to attaining knowledge.

Concept Learning in Content Areas

Take a moment and consider each of the following statements:

---

1. All bees sting.
2. If you are bitten by a tarantula in the hills of southern California, you might as well be dead.
3. The earth is flat.

Each of these statements comprise erroneous knowledge structures or schemata that students sometimes stubbornly cling to, despite a teacher's best efforts to convince them otherwise (Bean, Singer, Cowen, & Searles, 1987). Indeed, the first two misconceptions may be consistent with your schema for bees and tarantulas. Yet a male bee does not have a stinger—you can hold a male bee in your hand without any fear of injury. And, although tarantulas are poisonous and even deadly in South America, the southern California variety are not deadly. Finally, at the secondary and college levels, students generally know that the earth is not flat and it does not look like a frisbee.

If we define learning as the accumulation of ever more rich knowledge structures in science, social science, physical education, English, and the arts, how is it that students manage to dispense with misconceptions they may have staunchly held for many years? Recent discussions of concept learning have their roots in Piaget's notions of assimilation and accommodation, but they attempt to capture the slowly evolving nature of knowledge acquisition. For example, Vosniadou and Brewer (1987) argue that while Piaget's broad learning categories of assimilation and accommodation are indeed powerful, we need to examine how students progress from novices to experts within specific subject area domains such as science and social studies. Based on their studies of young children's developing view of the earth as a sphere, they find that Rumelhart and Norman's (1981) three-category view of concept development best explains the slow, cumulative process by which a learner acquires new concepts.

Rumelhart and Norman use the terms *accretion, tuning,* and *restructuring* to chart the course of concept learning. *Accretion,* much like assimilation, simply involves the accumulation of facts within existing schemata. Thus, in physics, a student may hold theories resembling those of Aristotle (i.e., the earth is flat), rather than Newton (i.e., the earth is round). Confronted with counterevidence in the form of models, films, teacher explanation, and so on, a student may modify this flat earth schema slightly, concluding that the earth is a flat disk like a frisbee. This gradual change in an erroneous concept is called *tuning.* Finally, given enough instruction and counterevidence, a learner may progress to a radical *restructuring* of erroneous concepts, concluding that the earth is indeed a sphere.

Without adequate teacher guidance, students' stubborn misconceptions may override information presented in a text. Alvermann, Smith, & Readence (1985) found that middle grade students' existing misconceptions in science caused them to ignore incompatible information presented in a text about the sun. Thus, you need to take the time to informally assess students' preconceived notions about topics when you suspect their understanding may be erroneous or only partially adequate.

Despite potential problems with misconceptions, linking new concepts to some familiar, existing concept remains a powerful strategy we can use to advantage in content teaching. Indeed, perhaps the most prominent way in which a learner attempts to cope with new information, such as the structure and function of a cell in science, is through a comparison to some existing knowledge (Bean, Singer, & Cowan, 1985; Rumelhart & Norman, 1981). For example, a beginning biology student with little knowledge of a cell's features might benefit from seeing how a cell's parts and functions are analogous to the parts and functions of a factory. The factory analogy acts as a catalyst in forming a new, separate schema for a cell. Teachers routinely resort to verbal analogies when they see students looking perplexed. Sometimes these analogies are successful and at times they fail to connect with students' experiences, especially if students are approaching English as a second language. Thus, as a content teacher, you need to identify students' existing knowledge and provide experiences in reading, listening, speaking, and writing that help them progress smoothly through tuning and restructuring knowledge. Activities such as the anticipation guide and brainstorming, especially reflective written brainstorming in a dialogue journal, provide us with some sense of students' prior knowledge. We can then anticipate misconceptions that may arise as students read and take measures to help them modify existing information that may be naive or in error. In later chapters we will introduce specific strategies aimed at exploring students' concept development through reading and writing.

Prior Knowledge of a Topic and Reading Interest

Contemporary models of the reading process present comprehension as a complex interaction of reader knowledge and text variables. In addition to these critical variables, there is a growing interest in affective features of text comprehension, particularly reader attitude and topic interest. In Spiro's words: "Constructed meaning is the interactive product of text and context of various kinds, including linguistic, prior knowledge, situational, attitudinal, and task contexts, among others" (1980, p. 246). The section that follows provides a sketch of the slowly evolving work on reader interest and its effect on comprehension.

Studies indicate that a strong relationship exists between reading interest and comprehension (Wigfield & Asher, 1984). Not surprisingly, students comprehend reading material better if it concerns a topic they like to read about (Asher, 1980; Baldwin, Peleg-Bruckner, & McClintock, 1985). For example, Belloni and Jongsma (1978) found that reluctant readers achieved significantly higher comprehension scores on stories dealing with topics of individual preference compared to topics of low interest. Asher, Hymel, and Wigfield (1978) reported similar findings. In a refinement of this first study, Asher (1980) had students respond to a 25 item picture rating scale featuring cars, sports, and other topics of potential high or low interest. Students displayed greater comprehension of passages that most closely corresponded to the picture they assigned a high interest rating.

More recently, Baldwin, Peleg-Bruckner, and McClintock (1985) determined that topic interest was not simply a reflection of prior knowledge. Their study showed that topic interest, especially among boys, makes a substantial contribution to students' comprehension even when prior knowledge of a topic is low.

Not only the topic, but also the manner of presentation can affect comprehension. Graesser (1981) found that students' self-selected reading material seemed to indicate a preference for narratives. However, content area reading assignments often entail reading expository material, which may depart from a student's preferred interests. Therefore, a content teacher needs to carefully guide students' understanding of the text by building their prior knowledge and generating topic interest. In later chapters we will be introducing some systematic procedures for discovering students' reading preferences. More importantly, we will introduce techniques a content teacher can employ to insure that our students become life-long readers.

Motivation to Learn from Content Texts

When students are confronted with expository textbooks that seem to hold little intrinsic appeal, their motivation for reading and learning may sink to a low ebb. Without adequate teacher guidance and ingenuity, students in content fields such as science and social science may sluggishly go through the motions of learning, dispensing only minimal effort. Recent discussions of motivation suggest that the effort a person is willing to expend on a task is a product of (1) the degree to which the individual expects to perform successfully if they try reasonably hard, and, (2) the degree to which they value the available rewards for success (Good & Brophy, 1987). Thus, if you lecture, assign text reading, and ask students only low level factual questions that encourage memorization and forgetting, students are likely to lapse into a reluctant, sluggish mode of participation. If you want to encourage students to actively link new knowledge to their existing background knowledge, to critically evaluate ideas advanced in your class texts and discussions, and to value their growing concept knowledge, the following general principles are important (Good & Brophy, 1987).

You need to provide a supportive, well-structured classroom environment and assignments that are challenging but not frustrating. Your learning objectives should be those worth pursuing rather than busy work that merely encourages memorizing facts and copying text-based definitions. For example, if you are studying a unit on the Constitution with a focus on the Bill of Rights, you might engage students in a disucssion of student rights as a prelude to their text reading.

Slicing the complexity of lengthy tasks into manageable increments that students can accomplish in a short period of time helps reduce that feeling of helplessness and inertia associated with tasks students perceive to be beyond their capacity. Similarly, teaching students to set their own realistic learning goals may help reduce frustration. These goals may be in the form of reading a small section of a chapter or answering a specific, reasonable portion of the chapter questions. Along with reducing the scope of a task, providing immediate feedback and rewarding success through pleasurable activities, points, or simply praise will go a long way toward helping students' motivation and interest in your content area.

Finally, opportunities for active student responses to text concepts are crucial to enthusiasm for content learning. Projects, experiments, discussions, debates, role playing, and computer simulations all contribute to students' interest in learning content that could otherwise be potentially dull fare. Classroom activities that place students in cooperative learning dyads and triads with their peers, especially if they are engaged in solving problems or grappling with higher order questions, also enhance motivation. In addition, if you provide immediate feedback on how students are succeeding or experiencing difficulty, this too will help them see the value in their efforts. Finally, when students have opportunities to complete finished products, whether they be in the form of essays, reports, models, a play, artwork, or a gourmet meal, they have a vivid and tangible record of their efforts (Good & Brophy, 1987). We can all remember, possibly in some detail, those learning situations in which we produced something of intrinsic value. You need to strive for lessons that capture these principles. In subsequent chapters we will introduce specific strategies designed to involve students actively in content learning. Additionally, we will consider those students for whom content learning is especially challenging because of a persistent cycle of failure. We offer some strategies for coping with the wide-ranging individual differences typical of our content classrooms.

Characteristics of Memory

This section introduces some important concepts concerning human memory. Since a student's prior knowledge is represented in memory, it is essential that you understand how memory aids or disrupts the efficient use of prior knowledge in the comprehension process.

Cognitive psychologists typically differentiate three aspects of memory. These are sensory store, short-term memory, and long-term memory. In reality, these three terms represent hypothetical constructs about memory rather than particular locations in the brain. The following diagram illustrates the flow of information as it is processed by our memory system.

Sensory store, the first channel in our memory system, rapidly transmits auditory and visual information from the environment to the brain. Although sensory store is of theoretical interest to some cognitive psychologists, it has very little impact as far as content teaching is concerned since there is nothing we can do to improve the sensory store. In contrast to sensory store, the concepts of short- and long-term memory both have important implications for content teaching.

Short-term memory is often called "working memory" because it holds information on a temporary basis until the information is either processed into long-term memory or erased to accept more incoming information (Brainerd, 1983). Short-term memory contains traces of the most recent information we are attending to at any given moment.

The single most important feature of short-term memory is its limited capacity for storing information. In a now widely quoted paper on memory research, Miller (1956) showed that the short-term storage capacity for individual items of information was seven, plus or minus two. Your struggle to retain a new friend's phone number is a concrete example of Miller's seven, plus or minus two principle in operation. Including the area code, a phone number such as 618–296–9149 exceeds the storage capacity of short-term memory (Smith, 1982). Fortunately, there is a way to circumvent the seven, plus or minus two limitation. Miller used the term *chunking* to describe the recoding of information into fewer, more manageable units. Using a chunking strategy, the phone number 618–296–9149 can be held in short-term memory as three, rather than ten, discrete items (i.e., [618][296][9149]). However, short-term memory has a second limitation that even chunking cannot overcome.

The second important feature of short-term memory is its fleeting nature. Information such as a new friend's phone number must be constantly rehearsed if it is to remain available in short-term memory for longer than a few seconds. If attention is diverted for even a moment to something else, the limited storage capacity of short-term memory will be overloaded and the phone number erased to accept the new, incoming information. Both the fleeting duration of short-term memory and its limited storage capacity have important implications for the reading process in general and content teaching in particular.

In terms of the reading process in general, if a student plods along in print at a laborious pace attempting to "sound-out" every unfamiliar word, short-term memory will be overburdened. The result of this word-by-word reading is that students can forget the beginning of a sentence before they get to the end. Students must learn to read text material, including unfamiliar words, in the most efficient way possible to overcome the limits of short-term memory. In a later chapter we will introduce some decoding strategies that encourage fluent reading.

In the content areas, some modes of presenting unfamiliar material may inadvertently impose excessive demands on students' short-term memories (Rohwer & Dempster, 1977). The oral presentation of a large amount of new information in social studies or science may exceed the capacity of students' short-term memories. Problem-solving tasks in mathematics present similar problems. Word problems, which involve the temporary storage of one part of the problem while the student simultaneously processes additional information, place excessive demands on the limited storage capacity of short-term memory (Brainerd, 1983). Finally, the processing limitations of short-term memory suggest that rote memorization of content material is likely to be an ineffective study strategy.

The processing limitations of short-term memory should be kept in mind when a teacher plans or analyzes content teaching and learning tasks. Fortunately, *long-term memory,* or "permanent" memory, plays an important role in compensating for the limitations of short-term or "working" memory.

In contrast to short-term memory, long-term memory seems to have an infinite capacity for storing information. Long-term memory is the storage system for all our prior knowledge. It comprises our individually complex schema of the world, shaped by cultural experiences and beliefs. As such, long-term memory is a highly organized system. Indeed, the ease with which we can retrieve information from long-term memory is directly related to how well the information was organized at the time of initial processing from short-term memory.

One of the most powerful ways to encode information in long-term memory is through writing. Increasingly, writing is seen as a learning strategy that teachers should integrate across content areas (Bean, 1989). In chapter seven we offer a number of specific writing-to-learn approaches you can weave into your own teaching repertoire to enhance students' comprehension and long-term retention of concepts.

Long-term memory does have one limitation. The rate at which information can be processed into long-term memory is relatively slow (Craik & Lockhart, 1972). However, the ease with which information is processed into long-term memory depends in large measure on how meaningful the information is in terms of the student's prior knowledge. The more meaningful the information, the easier it will be processed.

The following chart summarizes the two major aspects of memory treated in this section.

Characteristics	Short-term Memory (Working Memory)	Long-term Memory (Permanent Memory)
Capacity	Limited	Practically Unlimited
Persistence	Very Brief	Practically Unlimited
Retrieval	Immediate	Depends on Organization
Input	Very Fast	Relatively Slow

Thus, in general, content teachers should acknowledge the importance of prior knowledge and meaningful organization in long-term memory information processing in their teaching. Students will be able to comprehend new information in a content area if you take time to demonstrate how the new information builds upon and extends what they already know about the topic. And, students will be able to retrieve information from long-term memory if you model and encourage meaningful organization of new information when it is first presented to the class.

Summary of Prior Knowledge, Interest, and Memory Factors

A student's existing knowledge of a topic constitutes one of the most important cognitive factors in reading comprehension. Such prior knowledge of a topic is organized according to individual cultural experiences. Therefore, you must take the time to appraise your students' existing knowledge of a topic before you assume they can cope with it in your classroom discussions and reading assignments. More importantly, the activities you provide to prepare your students to read text material will contribute profoundly to their reading comprehension. Along with prior knowledge, you must also consider and foster student interest in a topic as you develop a content area lesson. Boredom and poor comprehension go hand in hand.

The characteristic limitations of short-term memory also require special attention as you prepare and develop a content area lesson. Since the limited storage capacity of short-term memory is easily overloaded, you must insure that your students use efficient reading strategies, particularly when confronted with unfamiliar words. Furthermore, the fleeting nature of short-term memory implies that new material must be presented in an organized fashion that integrates new concepts with existing knowledge. If new material is presented in an organized fashion, it will be more easily processed into long-term memory where it will be available for recall in the comprehension of future, related information.

Linguistic Factors

Although cognitive factors play a major role in reading comprehension, linguistic factors also influence the reading process. In this section we will describe and demonstrate specific linguistic aspects of written language that interact with cognitive factors to aid or inhibit reading comprehension.

The Language of Text

Authors of stories and even challenging scientific text use predictable organization patterns or *text structures*. For example, stories usually begin with a setting and one or more characters. The reader follows the main character's attempts to solve a problem or achieve a goal. This familiar text structure makes it relatively easy for a reader to make predictions about story events (van Dijk & Kintsch, 1983). Even more difficult expository text in science has an identifiable pattern of organization. For example, biology texts usually inform the reader about properties and functions of a topic such as carbohydrates or enzymes.

A text's pattern of organization is the larger ideational framework that binds together its complex system of paragraphs. This *macrostructure,* which may range from a cause-effect discussion of the Sherman Anti-Trust Act in history to an informational description of photosynthesis in science, is integral to expository text (Meyer & Rice, 1984). Similarly, the relationships that bind together individual sentences in a text into a coherent structure comprise a text's *microstructure.* Microstructure and macrostructure features of text become important as you attempt to gauge how friendly or unfriendly a text is for students. In chapter four we introduce a process for evaluating a text along these dimensions.

Students who are made aware of the overall structure of a particular text can use this knowledge in comprehending, studying, and discussing key concepts. Moreover, a text that provides a discernible organizational pattern places fewer demands on the limitations of short-term memory than poorly structured text (van Dijk & Kintsch, 1983). In chapter six we discuss text structure in detail and introduce comprehension strategies that capitalize on this important linguistic aspect of text.

Fluent readers are sensitive to the overall structure of a text and to the words and sentences that combine to create this structure (Stanovich, 1980). However, texts can be "friendly" or "unfriendly" at the word, sentence, and paragraph levels (Singer, 1986). This linguistic aspect of text has been studied in detail over the years by observing the *miscues* readers make (Goodman & Goodman, 1977). Miscues are substitutions and omissions for words in a text. For example, a reader who substitutes "car" for "cat" has made a miscue that disrupts meaning. Some miscues do not disrupt meaning. For example, substituting "a" for "the" may not interfere with comprehension.

In familiar material, readers can focus on the author's message. Conversely, in highly technical material that is unfamiliar, greater attention must be devoted to an accurate determination of the meaning of individual words and sentences. This is especially crucial for second language learners. The following activities provide a demonstration of fluent reading in friendly text and difficult technical material. Your content text is probably somewhere between these two extremes for most students.

Activity

Give yourself no more than five seconds to read "The Boat in the Basement" selection below (Goodman, 1977). Write a single sentence summary of what you remember.

The Boat in the Basement

A man was building a boat in his basement. When he had finished the
the boot, he discovered that it was too big to go though the door. So he
had to take the boat a part to get it out. He should of planned ahead.

At the word and sentence level there are five miscues in this selection. Probably the only miscue you detected was the substitution of "boot" for "boat" since this is the only miscue that seriously disrupts meaning, with the possible exception of "though" for "through." Even given the miscues, your written summary is undoubtedly an accurate account of the story line since its pattern is a predictable narrative. You have just demonstrated the fluent reading process by using selected features of print to predict and construct meaning.

The "Boat in the Basement" is very friendly story material. What happens to the fluent reading process when a reader is confronted with highly technical material that is anything but friendly? The following activity provides some clues.

Activity

Give yourself as much time as you need to read this selection. Jot down the steps you take to figure it out and write a one sentence summary of the author's main idea.

> The six year old was brought in with polydypsia and polyuria. It was anorectic. After the work-up, it was found to have toxic neutropis, a left shift.

In this case, knowing that this is a veterinarian's report about a sick dog won't assuage your lack of familiarity with the vocabulary. Moreover, this is scientific writing, which prevents using the surrounding context as an alternative means of grasping the author's main idea. Here's a translation that may help, but some of the precision inherent in scientific prose is lost in the process.

> A six-year-old dog was brought into the vet. The dog had been drinking a lot of water and urinating frequently. It was not eating. After the lab tests it was found to have an increase in white blood cells caused by an infection. Immature cells are also being pumped out due to infection.

These two examples illustrate that fluent content area reading is an interactive process. Word and sentence level features of text and text structure patterns of organization combine to make a text friendly or unfriendly. Fortunately, teachers can provide direct instruction in both these linguistic features as an integral part of content instruction. In chapters five and six we introduce strategies designed to help students regard even challenging text as reasonably "friendly."

The Language of Students

In addition to those features of texts that make them friendly or unfriendly, students' language facility plays a powerful role in comprehension. You are likely to have a fair number of second language learners in your content classroom. If the texts students must read are very distant from their native language, second language students may have difficulty forming the mental pictures necessary for concept learning to occur (Perez, 1982). For example, the following sentence, adapted from Laird and Jossen (1983, p. 10) illustrates the frustration a second language learner may experience in text material containing vocabulary that is largely unfamiliar.

> "Oh! Dakine mea'ai stay so ono," said Wili Wai Kula.

If readers must translate every work of a text with a dictionary or a laborious search through memory, they will have little attention left for comprehension. Moreover, integration of ideas across words and sentences becomes impossible. Contrast the above example with Laird and Jossen's (1983) original text, *Wili Wai Kula and the Three Mongooses,* a Hawaiian version of the familiar *Goldilocks and the Three Bears.*

> "Oh! The *mea'ai* smells so *ono,*" said a hungry Wili Wai Kula. She tasted the rice and sausage on the biggest plate. It was too hot. Next, she tasted the rice and sausage on the medium-sized plate. It was too cold.

In this instance, some of the vocabulary is unfamiliar. However, your prior knowledge of the original fable, combined with some vocabulary knowledge and context clues should help you comprehend "mea'ai, a Hawaiian word for meal, and "ono," which means good. Krashen and Terrell (1983) recommend that text for second language learners strike a delicate balance between familiar and unfamiliar vocabulary. Visual aids and pre-reading guides that help students see how their prior knowledge is related to concepts in the text help students use semantic cues. Otherwise, there is a real tendency for these students to read in a word-by-word fashion or to decode accurately without really comprehending what they have read. Notice that once you see a bridge between the familiar Goldilocks story and the Hawaiian version you can comprehend the selection despite not knowing all the vocabulary. In content areas, students' background knowledge is not likely to be quite this direct. But you can try to select texts that capitalize on familiar topics while adding new information to students' concept learning. In addition, the guide material discussed in chapters five and six can go a long way toward unlocking text concepts in the target language.

The Classroom Context

Finally, in addition to cognitive and linguistic factors, the social context of a classroom has its own linguistic conventions and features. *Sociolinguistics* is the study of language in a cultural context. A number of recent studies, stemming from the anthropological tradition of intensive participant observation, provide us with an emerging picture of teacher-student and student-student interaction that belies a simplistic view of content teaching. The goal of intensive observational study is to uncover the social patterns that influence teacher and student success in constructing meaning (Bloome, 1987; Green & Bloome, 1983).

Classroom interaction patterns are, at least on the surface, usually orchestrated by the teacher and based on an intuitive or conscious theory of learning. Thus, teachers instruct, question, praise, and monitor students' comprehension in observable patterns that reveal their particular view of reading comprehension. This may range from simply assigning text reading, questioning students orally and giving a test, to the more carefully guided approach we are advocating.

In Goodlad's (1984) massive observational study of classrooms across the country, he found student passivity to be the norm. More recently, Bloome (1987) speculated that cross-cultural differences between students and teachers may result in some students' unwillingness to risk a public display of their knowledge. This reticence may be misinterpreted by the teacher who might well believe a student lacks knowledge of the topic at hand.

In a classroom that follows our model of content teaching, an observer would expect to see various forms of pre-reading strategies in use (e.g., Anticipation Guides), small group discussion of text concepts using the guides, and post-reading Reaction Guide discussion.

Yet even with this guided approach, the classroom remains a social environment with its own "hidden curriculum" that is shaped by social as well as academic factors (Hamilton, 1983).

For example, in an effort to go beyond such oversimplified measures of content learning as "time on task," Bloome (1983) observed four junior high classes for six months. He took field notes of classroom discussions as well as audio and video recordings. He found that students often seemed to be "on task" when they were actually doing something else. The "something else" ranged from reading a friend's note to daydreaming while simultaneously feigning attention and accurately responding to the teacher's questions through the adroit use of cues from a friend.

Bloome (1987) finds that a typical classroom reading and discussion pattern contains the following dimensions. Students are required only to produce text reproductions that merely reiterate text content. Amidst such low level discussions, they become skilled at procedural display—looking as if they are doing the work and participating while simultaneously carrying on other, more personally interesting and rewarding activities. Thus, a teacher-dominated discussion of text concepts produces an overly passive style of student thinking and participation.

In our view, a classroom content lesson coexists with the larger context of the school and the sociolinguistic context of students' lives. A content lesson competes for students attention amidst other, often more compelling interests. It is likely to compete successfully if most students have adequate opportunities to participate. Yet, most classroom discussions take place with the whole class bidding for a brief turn at question answering. The following diagram illustrates the usual flow of discussion in this structure. Searfoss and Readence (1989) term this a "ping pong" exchange since the flow of discussion is from teacher-to-student-to teacher.

The level of questions students are asked also exerts a strong influence on their interest and attention to a discussion. For example, questions that are text explicit and so trivial that only the teacher has the answer tend to produce low student attention and performance (Green & Bloome, 1983). Text-explicit comprehension involves getting the facts as stated by the author. In contrast, text-implicit and experience-based questions usually generate high student interest and performance. Text-implicit comprehension requires the reader to infer what the author meant. Finally, experience-based comprehension is derived almost exclusively from previous knowledge.

The field notes that follow, charting a whole group classroom discussion in 10th grade world history, help illustrate the effect of group structure and level of questioning. Students' homework reading involved a chapter on Sparta. The discussion focuses on Sparta's culture in comparison to Viking culture. The "hidden curriculum" competing for students' attention involved an ongoing candy sale to raise funds for a trip. The notes are line numbered and questions are coded to reflect the level of thinking and source of information required to generate a response (i.e. TE=text-explicit; TI=text-implicit; and, E=experience-based).

We can characterize a vibrant discussion as one in which students' interest and participation is high (Bean, 1985). As you read the field notes depicting this discussion try to decide whether or not this discussion qualifies as a "vibrant discussion."

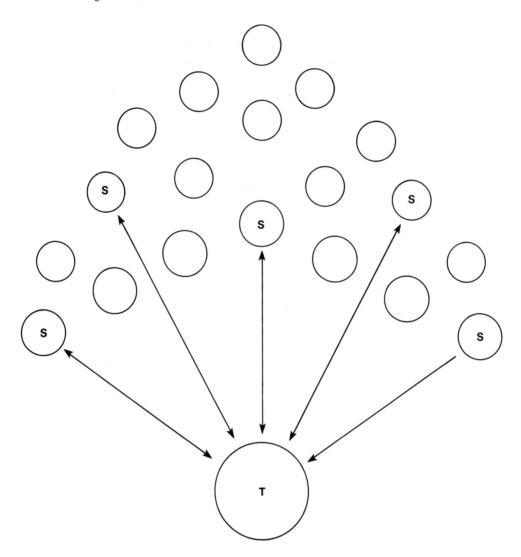

Tenth Grade World History Discussion on Sparta

The discussion took place in second period following an announcement about yearbook photos. Students had been selling candy as part of a fund raising activity and their enthusiasm for this comprised a strong undercurrent throughout much of the period.

01 Teacher (hereafter T): What were the Hellots? (TE)
02 Todd: Peasants (TE)
03 T: Lisa—anything else? (TE)
04 Lisa: They were conquered and became slaves of Spartans. (TE)
05 T: How did the threat of revolt change Spartan life? (TE)
06 Mica: They built an army. (TE)

07 T: Specifically? (TE)

08 Gary: They became more militaristic, they didn't trade, they were isolationist. (TE)

09 John: They attacked the Hellots every year. (TE)

At this point, some students were negotiating sales of candy rather than participating. The teacher admonished them saying, "Calm down today!"

Not surprisingly, one of the drawbacks of large group discussion in a class of 25 or more students is limited turn-taking opportunities. How many students participated in the discussion up to this point? Five. What was their motivation for participating? Teacher questions. A flow chart of the discussion illustrates this nicely:

01 (TEACHER QUESTION)→02 (Todd's Answer)→
03 (TEACHER QUESTION)→04 (Lisa's Answer)→
05 (TEACHER QUESTION)→06 (Mica's Answer)→
07 (TEACHER QUESTION)→08 (Gary's Answer)→
09 (John's Answer)

The teacher generated four of the nine utterances. This teacher dominated pattern began to change as students reconstructed ideas from their reading. Notice that Gary's answer (line 08) stimulated John's (line 09) desire to add further foundational information. Moreover, five of the 25 students responded, indicating a balanced system of turn-taking is in operation, carefully orchestrated by the teacher. Yet, student answers are brief and much less elaborate than their animated dialogues about the candy sale before class.

After watching a filmstrip on the Vikings, the following whole group discussion occurred. Compare the level of questioning and flow of turn-taking in this discussion to the previous nine utterances.

01 Teacher: Are the Vikings similar to Sparta? (TI)

02 Nikki: Yes (TI)

03 T: Who determines right and wrong? (E)

04 Jodi: Your conscience. (E)

05 T: Have you read Antigone? (E)

06 West: No (E)

07 T: Culture also determines behavior. (E)

08 T: What's the role of the aged in Viking culture?
    (TE/filmstrip)

09 Mike: Unimportant. (TE)

10 T: What about African society? (TI/linking back to chapter 1 in their text)

11 Erica: It's different—the elders are valued. (TI)

12 T: Any generalizations about cultures? (E)

13 Kenny: They change. (E)

14 Teresa: They are all different. (E)

15 West: Each one abides by its own laws. (E)

16 T: Why are old people in Viking society not valued yet they are valued in African
    society? (TI)

17 Bob: Because of the work involved in the Viking society. (TI)

18 T: Where were the Vikings? (TE)

19 Susanna: Scandinavia. (TE)

20 T: What accounts for the poor treatment of old people in the Viking culture? (TI)
21 West: They can't fight. (TI)
22 Susanna: They can't travel in the snow. (TI)
23 Mike: Climate. (TI)

In contrast to the previous, text-explicit discussion, this one based on a filmstrip leads students to higher implicit and experience levels of thinking. However, the flow of discussion remains teacher directed. Of the 23 utterances, 10 are teacher generated.

We might question the degree to which the above teacher directed dialogue qualifies as a true discussion. Based on an eighteen-month observational study of twenty-four science, social studies, literature, health, and human development classes, Alvermann, Dillon, and O'Brien (1987) make a useful distinction between recitation and discussion. Recitation usually consists of a teacher-directed question and answer sequence to review, drill, or quiz lesson content. In contrast, a discussion features three distinguishing characteristics: (1) the discussants present multiple points of view and may change their perspective on a topic after hearing convincing counterarguments; (2) students must interact with each other and the teacher is largely in the background; and (3) students' verbal utterances must be longer than two or three word phrases typical of recitation.

Teacher-student interaction patterns influence students' comprehension and attitude toward the content being studied (Bloome, 1983). Collaborative, small group discussion using pre- and post-reading strategies such as Anticipation/Reaction guides are a good alternative to teacher-centered discussion. We are not suggesting that there is anything wrong with whole group lectures and discussions. But we do believe that small, problem-solving groups can afford greater opportunities for student participation if they are focused on an important topic with clear task guidelines.

In chapter six, on comprehension, we consider strategies that you may wish to adopt to enhance students' critical reading and discussion. Reflective writing can also form a basis for student-centered sharing and discussion of ideas and issues. These elements of content reading will be elaborated in subsequent chapters.

Summary

The present chapter introduced a variety of psychological, linguistic, and sociolinguistic factors that influence content area reading. Among the psychological factors, we considered the influence of prior knowledge, interest, and memory on students' comprehension. Linguistic factors included cue systems in print, text structure, and the influence of classroom context.

Now that you have a fairly comprehensive view of the reading process, go back to the anticipation/reaction guide at the beginning of this chapter. React again to the statements as you did before reading. This time, record your answers in the column entitled, "Reaction." Compare your latest responses with those you made before reading the chapter.

Miniprojects

1. Choose any one of the illustrative experiments introduced in the Prior Knowledge and Reading Comprehension section of chapter two (e.g. "The Boat in the Basement," "Dear Jill," etc.). Try this experiment with at least three people of various ages and backgrounds. Summarize your findings and compare these with other class members.
2. List at least three methods you currently use, or plan to use, to mobilize students' existing knowledge of topics in your particular content area. Compare your compilation with listings produced by other class members.
3. Visit a classroom of your choice. Based upon your observation notes, analyze the interaction pattern that occurs and determine the level of comprehension emphasized.

Additional Recommended Readings

Crafton, L. K. (1983). Learning from reading: What happens when students generate their own background information? *Journal of Reading, 26,* 586–592.
    This article provides a clear demonstration for the value of pre-reading instruction.

Dishner, E. K., Bean, T. W., Readence, J. E., & Moore, D. W. (Eds.). (1986). *Reading in the content areas: Improving classroom instruction* (2nd ed.). Dubuque, IA: Kendall/Hunt Publishing Company.
    Chapter 2 provides a number of articles that shed further light on the content area reading process.

Hamilton, S. F. (1983). Socialization for learning: Insights from ecological research in classrooms. *The Reading Teacher, 37,* 150–156.
    This article provides a good introduction to sociolinguistic studies of classroom interaction.

Singer, H., & Ruddell, R. B. (Eds.). (1985). *Theoretical models and processes of reading* (3rd ed.). Newark, DE: International Reading Association.
    This 960-page volume offers a compendium of past and recent thinking about the reading process.

Smith, F. (1982). *Understanding reading* (3rd ed.). New York: Holt, Rinehart and Winston.
    A more detailed explication of many of the ideas advanced in this chapter.

References

Adams, M., & Bruce, B. (1982). Background knowledge and reading comprehension. In J. A. Langer & M. Smith-Burke (Eds.), *Reader meets author/bridging the gap: A psycholinguistic and sociolinguistic perspective* (pp. 2–25). Newark, DE: International Reading Association.

Alvermann, D. E., Dillon, D. R., & O'Brien, D. G. (1987). *Using discussion to promote reading comprehension.* Newark, DE: International Reading Association.

Alvermann, D. E., Smith, L. C., & Readence, J. E. (1985). Prior knowledge activation and the comprehension of compatible and incompatible text. *Reading Research Quarterly, 20,* 420–436.

Anderson, R. C., & Pearson, P. D. (1984). A schema-theoretic view of basic processes in reading. In P. D. Pearson (Ed.), *Handbook of reading research* (pp. 255–292). New York: Longman.

Asher, S. R. (1980). Topic interest and children's reading comprehension. In R. J. Spiro, B. C. Bruce, & W. F. Brewer (Eds), *Theoretical issues in reading comprehension* (pp. 525–534). Hillsdale, NJ: Erlbaum.

Asher, S. R., Hymel, S., & Wigfield, A. (1978). Influence of topic interest on childrens' reading comprehension. *Journal of Reading Behavior, 10,* 35–47.

Baldwin, R. S., Peleg-Bruckner, Z., & McClintock, A. (1985). Effects of topic interest on childrens' reading comprehension. *Reading Research Quarterly, 20,* 497–504.

Bean, T. W. (1985). Classroom questioning: Directions for applied research. In A. C. Graesser & J. Black (Eds.), *Psychology of questions* (pp. 335–358). Hillsdale, NJ: Erlbaum.

Bean, T. W. (1989). Writing in the content areas. In L. W. Searfoss & J. E. Readence (Eds.), *Helping children learn to read* (2nd ed.), Englewood Cliffs, NJ: Prentice-Hall.

Bean, T. W., Singer, H., & Cowan, S. (1985). Analogical study guides: Improving comprehension in science. *Journal of Reading, 29,* 246–250.

Bean, T. W., Singer, H., Cowen, S., & Searles, D. (1987, December). *Acquiring concepts from biology text: A study of text-based learning aids and reader-based strategies.* Paper presented at the National Reading Conference, St. Petersburg, FL.

Belloni, L. F., & Jongsma, E. A. (1978). The effects of interest on reading comprehension of low-achieving students. *Journal of Reading, 22,* 106–109.

Bloome, D. (1983). Reading as a social process. In B. A. Hutson (Ed.), *Advances in reading/language research* (pp. 165–196). Greenwich, CT: JAI Press.

Bloome, D. (1987). Reading as a social process in a middle school classroom. In D. Bloome (Ed.), *Literacy and schooling* (pp. 123–149). Norwood, NJ: Ablex.

Brainerd, C. J. (1983). Working-memory systems and cognitive development. In C. J. Brainerd (Ed.), *Recent advances in cognitive development theory* (pp. 167–236). New York: Springer-Verlag.

Bransford, J. D. (1982). Prerequisites for comprehending prose. *Fforum, 3,* 65–66.

Christen, W., Searfoss, L. W., & Bean, T. W. (1984). *Improving communication through writing and reading.* Dubuque, IA: Kendall/Hunt Publishing Company.

Clark, H. H., & Clark, E. C. (1977). *Psychology and language: An introduction to psycholinguistics.* New York: Harcourt Brace Jovanovich.

Crafton, L. K. (1983). Learning from reading: What happens when students generate their own background information? *Journal of Reading, 26,* 586–592.

Craik, F. I., & Lockhart, R. S. (1972). Levels of processing: A framework for memory research. *Journal of Verbal Learning and Verbal Behavior, 11,* 671–684.

Good, T. L., & Brophy, J. E. (1987). *Looking in classrooms* (4th ed.). New York: Harper & Row.

Goodlad, J. I. (1984). *A place called school.* New York: McGraw-Hill.

Goodman, K. S. (1977). *The boat in the basement.* From a paper presented at the Center for the Study of Reading, University of Illinois.

Goodman, K. S., & Goodman, Y. M. (1977). Learning about psycholinguistic processes by analyzing oral reading. *Harvard Educational Review, 47,* 317–333.

Graesser, A. C. (1981). *Prose comprehension beyond the word.* New York: Springer-Verlag.

Green, J., & Bloome, D. (1983). Ethnography and reading: Issues, approaches, criteria, and findings. In J. A. Niles & L. A. Harris (Eds.), *Searches for meaning in reading/language processing and instruction* (pp. 6–30). Thirty-second Yearbook of the National Reading Conference. Rochester, NY: National Reading Conference.

Hamilton, S. F. (1983). Socialization for learning: Insights from ecological research in classrooms. *The Reading Teacher, 37,* 150–156.

Huey, E. B. (1908). *The psychology and pedagogy of reading.* New York: Macmillan. Reprinted by the MIT Press, Cambridge, MA: 1968.

Krashen, S. D., & Terrell, T. D. (1983). *The natural approach: Language acquisition in the classroom.* Hayward, CA: Alemany Press.

Laird, D. M., & Jossen, C. (1983). *Wili Wai Kula and the three mongooses.* Honolulu, HI: Barbaby Books.

Meyer, B. J. F., & Rice, G. E. (1984). The structure of text. In P. D. Pearson (Ed.), *Handbook of reading research* (pp. 319–351). New York: Longman.

Miller, G. A. (1956). The magical number seven plus or minus two: Some limits on our capacity for processing information. *Psychological Review, 63,* 81–96.

Norman, D. A. (1976). *Memory and attention.* New York: John Wiley and Sons.

Perez, S. A. (1982). Visual imagery instruction to improve reading comprehension. In C. Carter (Ed.), *Non-native and nonstandard dialect students* (pp. 69–71). Urbana, IL: National Council of Teachers of English.

Rohwer, W. D., & Dempster, F. N. (1977). Memory and education. In R. V. Kail Jr., & J. W. Hagen (Eds.), *Perspectives on the development of memory and cognition* (pp. 407–436). Hillsdale, NJ: Erlbaum.

Rumelhart, D. E. (1981). Schemata: The building blocks of cognition. In J. T. Guthrie (Ed.), *Comprehension and teaching: Research reviews* (pp. 3–26). Newark, DE: International Reading Association.

Rumelhart, D. E., & Norman, D. A. (1978). Accretion, tuning, and restructuring: Three modes of learning. In J. W. Cotton, & R. L. Klatzky (Eds.), *Semantic factors in cognition* (pp. 37–53). Hillsdale, NJ: Erlbaum.

Rumelhart, D. E., & Norman, D. A. (1981). Analogical processes in learning. In J. R. Anderson (Ed.), *Cognitive skills and their acquisition* (pp. 335–359). Hillsdale, NJ: Erlbaum.

Searfoss, L. W., & Readence, J. E. (1989). *Helping children learn to read* (2nd ed.). Englewood Cliffs, NJ: Prentice-Hall.

Singer, H. (1986). Friendly text: Description and criteria. In E. K. Dishner, T. W. Bean, J. E. Readence, & D. W. Moore (Eds.), *Content area reading: Improving classroom instruction* (2nd ed., pp. 112–128). Dubuque, IA: Kendall/Hunt Publishing Company.

Singer, H., & Ruddell, R. B. (Eds.). (1985). *Theoretical models and processes of reading* (3rd ed.). Newark, DE: International Reading Association.

Smith, F. (1982). *Understanding reading* (3rd ed.). New York: Holt, Rinehart and Winston.

Spiro, R. J. (1980). Constructive processes in prose comprehension and recall. In R. J. Spiro, B. C. Bruce, & W. F. Brewer (Eds.), *Theoretical issues in reading comprehension* (pp. 245–278). Hillsdale, NJ: Erlbaum.

Stanovich, K. E. (1980). Toward an interactive-compensatory model of individual differences in the development of reading fluency. *Reading Research Quarterly, 16,* 32–71.

Stevens, K. C. (1982). Can we improve reading by teaching background information? *Journal of Reading, 25,* 326–329.

van Dijk, T. A., & Kintsch, W. (1983). *Strategies of discourse comprehension.* New York: Academic Press.

Vosniadou, S., & Brewer, W. F. (1987). Theories of knowledge restructuring in development. *Review of Educational Research, 57,* 51–67.

Wigfield, A., & Asher, S. R. (1984). Social and motivational influences on reading. In P. D. Pearson (Ed.), *Handbook of reading research* (pp. 423–452). New York: Longman.

3

Anticipation Guide / Reaction Guide

Directions: Before you begin reading this chapter, take a moment to put a check mark by any of the statements with which you agree. Use the column entitled ''Anticipation.''

Anticipation	**Reaction**	
_____ 1.	_____	1. Pleasure reading teaches specific reading skills.
_____ 2.	_____	2. Some students have failed for so many years that it is all but impossible to motivate them.
_____ 3.	_____	3. Males do not like to read about romance.
_____ 4.	_____	4. Unfortunately, school library collections in content areas consist primarily of textbook-type materials that are inherently boring.
_____ 5.	_____	5. Reading instruction is only effective if it creates readers who can read and who do read.

Attitudes and Interests

In the box below are six figures. Three represent houses and three represent utilities: gas, water, and electricity. Your task is to connect each utility to each house. If you are successful, you will have drawn nine lines. Observe the following rules:

1. No lines may cross.
2. You may *NOT* run a line through any house or utility in order to reach another house or utility.
3. This is strictly a two-dimensional problem; that is, you are *NOT* allowed to draw dotted lines to indicate "digging" beneath houses, utilities, or other lines.
4. You *MAY* spatially rearrange the houses and utilities any way you like.

Continue working this problem on scrap paper until you reach a solution or are willing to admit that you can't figure it out.

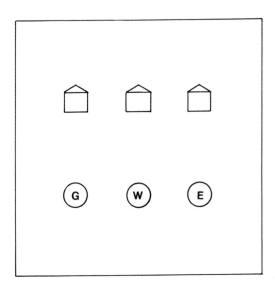

"I have a vivid memory of Daisy calling me a (expletive deleted) on my very first day of classes. Needless to say, our junior high school had its share of discipline problems. Some of these 'children' were merely recalcitrant, others were outright hostile, a few precipitated violence on a regular basis. Many of these students were virtual denizens of the principal's foyer.

In an effort to reduce undesirable traffic through the main office, our principal instituted 'temporary placement' (TP). Under TP, all students ejected from classes during any given period went to one room in the building; and each teacher surrendered one planning period per week to supervise TP. I was unfortunate enough to draw TP on Friday afternoons.

I dreaded TP duty—also referred to as 'herding the animals.' I used to wake up every Friday morning with a rock in my stomach. The students were difficult to control, and I often had to contend with twenty or more. These kids desperately needed something to do, but they seemed incapable of focusing their attentions on anything more constructive than throwing chalk or taunting each other.

One Friday, in an act of desperation, I took a twenty-dollar bill from my wallet and pinned it to the bulletin board. I told the students that I had a puzzle for them and that the first person to arrive at the solution would get the twenty dollars. The problem is to draw one line from each

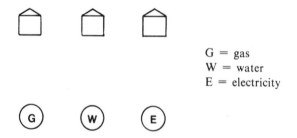

G = gas
W = water
E = electricity

utility to each house without crossing any lines or going through one figure to get to another. I strongly suspected that the problem was insoluble, but I lied to the students in order to maintain control over them.

The students worked at a feverish pace, each and every one of them. Kids who hadn't read a page or lifted a pencil in weeks struggled like demons, their faces flushed with anticipation, their index fingers white from the pressure of continuous writing; I was astonished.

When the buzzer sounded the end of the period, all but one or two were still struggling with the problem, reluctant to give up. Finally, having experienced one more deception on the part of the school, a group of disappointed students vacated the room, leaving me alone with my guilt. It was one of my most painful lessons that year, but it taught me that none of my students were completely beyond motivation." (Anonymous)

For the sake of discussion, suppose the teacher had given the TP students this very same house-utility puzzle *every* Friday. What would have happened? Our own prediction is that interest would have faded quickly after the initial session and finally extinguished itself completely. Sooner or later each student would come to see the puzzle as an impossible task, and only a fool works on impossible tasks. The analogy to school behaviors is straightforward. Students who have been academic losers year in and year out come to believe that reading and textbook assignments are also impossible tasks. Moreover, the longer the history of failure, the more difficult it becomes to r ve to students that textbooks can be managed, that reading can be intrinsically rewarding, and that libraries actually contain books worth reading. Negative attitudes toward textbooks, reading, and school in general are often the nastiest problems teachers have to face.

This chapter will explore the affective dimension of content area reading. You will learn to encourage students to broaden their reading interests and improve their attitudes.

Chapter Objectives

After reading this chapter, you should be able to:

1. Explain how interests and attitudes can influence comprehension and achievement.
2. Implement a Sustained Silent Reading program.
3. Develop an interest inventory for your own content area.

Graphic Organizer

The following graphic organizer is provided to give you some advance structure for new vocabulary and concepts that will be presented in this chapter.

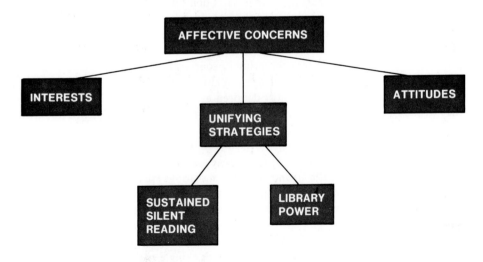

Affective Concerns of Content Reading

In our desire to increase reading comprehension and achievement test scores, we often forget that there are reasons for reading that extend beyond the realm of the textbook. Building instructional programs that teach young people how to read is a powerful and obviously legitimate concern. As such, most reading programs are, in one way or another, designed to prevent or alter illiteracy. However, there is also an affective dimension to reading that concerns itself with another problem, that is, knowing how to read, but choosing not to for some reason. Being turned off about reading (or never having been turned on in the first place) is a major problem in our culture. For example, it has been estimated that half of all adult Americans have never read a book the whole way through (Spiegel, 1981). Consequently, all types of reading programs should emphasize strategies for producing graduates who are not only capable of reading, but who choose to do so on a regular basis, for recreation, to satisfy a curiosity to learn, or for self-improvement. It is a waste of time to drag students to the means of learning only to find out that they do not wish to partake.

The ultimate goal of content area reading should be to create students who:

1. Process information efficiently.
2. Have positive attitudes toward books.
3. Possess broad reading interests.
4. Have acquired a taste for quality literature and learning.

Reading Attitudes

Attitudes may be defined as those feelings that cause a reader to approach or avoid a reading situation. A student's attitude toward reading is a critical determinant for effective learning. Therefore, it is not surprising that unfortunate attitudes usually accompany poor reading ability (Athey, 1985). In some cases it may be that the unfortunate attitudes cause the reading failure. However, it is far more often true that continuous and painful failure over long periods of time leads to understandably negative attitudes toward reading. It's hard to like something you're not good at! Reading difficulties which were originally a matter of "I can't do it" mutate with the passing years into "I don't want to do it and I don't need it." Under these conditions, reading instruction that is adequate to remedy specific skill weaknesses will fail miserably because the students no longer care to learn!

A second reason for negative reading attitudes rests in the reward system for reading. Mathewson (1985) has observed that the primary source of motivation to read is external, e.g., grades or other school-induced pressures. What Mathewson suggests is that this external reward system works well for most children as long as they are in school; however, once they graduate, the external stucture is withdrawn and young people are left with no reason to read.

Coping with impoverished attitudes toward reading requires instructional tactics that do two things: (1) They allow students to experience success in reading textbooks and other school materials (Helmstetter, 1987); and (2) They encourage students to generate their own intrinsic (internal) reward system for reading, i.e., to discover that reading can be a pleasure in and of itself, and a means to satisfy the mind's curiosity and the longings of the heart (Baldwin, 1986).

Also integral to attitude and attitude development are interests and self-concept. Students' *interests,* or what they like to read, may be the single most important influence on attitudes toward reading. It may be that as interests develop, attitudes will develop accordingly. This relationship, however, may be a positive or a negative one. Those students who are less interested in reading, or unrewarded by it, are less likely to feel positively toward it. Conversely, if students are stimulated or rewarded by reading, they are more likely to have a disposition to read. Additionally, experiential background is intimately bound up in interests, and therefore, attitudes (Wigfield & Asher, 1984).

Past experiences also have a tremendous impact on *self-concept* (Stanovich, 1986). Students react to their perceptions of their reading performance and to how others view them. If peers, parents, or teachers do not value reading performance very highly, this will become a factor in the future reading behavior of students. Conversely, a valued performance could enhance self-concept and change one's attitude toward reading. Though there may be few studies which directly explore the relationship of self-concept to attitude, there seems to be little doubt that such interplay exists. Therefore, the authors view the whole area of the affective domain—attitudes, interests, and self-concept—as being intimately bound together, and the effects of one variable may cause changes in other affective variables.

Concern, therefore, should be given by all teachers to the affective domain. The authors feel all content teachers should make thorough attempts to encourage the growth of positive attitudes toward reading in their content areas. Planning for such a venture should be based upon some type of formal or informal assessment.

Assessment. The assessment of reading attitudes should be an important part of any reading program. If schools are to produce lifetime readers and independent learners, they must of necessity encourage students to seek personal meaning and pleasure in reading. Poor attitudes are inconsistent with meaningful pleasurable experiences.

There are a number of methods for assessing reading attitudes, including personal interviews and behavior checklists (Summers, 1977). The most common method is the self-report questionnaire. The following reading attitude survey (Baldwin, Johnson, & Peer, 1980) was designed for use with middle and secondary school students.

BJP Middle/Secondary Reading Attitude Survey*

Directions: This survey tells how you feel about reading and books. The survey is not a test, and it is anonymous. It will not affect your grades or progress in school, but it will help your school to create better programs. Answer as honestly as you can by circling the letter or letters which tell how you feel about each statement.

SA = Strongly agree
 A = Agree
 D = Disagree
SD = Strongly disagree

1. Library books are dull.	SA	A	D	SD
2. Reading is a waste of time.	SA	A	D	SD
3. Reading is one of my hobbies.	SA	A	D	SD
4. I believe I am a better reader than most other students in my grade.	SA	A	D	SD
5. Reading is almost always boring.	SA	A	D	SD
6. Sometimes I think kids younger than I am read better than I do.	SA	A	D	SD
7. I enjoy going to the library for books.	SA	A	D	SD
8. I can read as well as most students who are a year older than I am.	SA	A	D	SD

9. I don't have enough time to read books.   SA   A   D   SD
10. I believe that I am a poor reader.   SA   A   D   SD
11. I would like to belong to a book club.   SA   A   D   SD
12. I like to take library books home.   SA   A   D   SD
13. Teachers want me to read too much.   SA   A   D   SD
14. You can't learn much from reading.   SA   A   D   SD
15. Books can help us to understand other people.   SA   A   D   SD
16. I almost always get A's and B's in reading and English.   SA   A   D   SD
17. I like to have time to read in class.   SA   A   D   SD
18. Reading gets boring after about ten minutes.   SA   A   D   SD
19. Sometimes I get bad grades in reading and English.   SA   A   D   SD
20. I like to read before I go to bed.   SA   A   D   SD

Scoring: The positive items are 3, 4, 7, 8, 11, 12, 15, 16, 17, 20. Give four points for a *SA,* three points for an *A,* two points for a *D,* and one point for a *SD.* For the negative items, 1, 2, 5, 6, 9, 10, 13, 14, 18, 19, score four points for a *SD,* three for *D,* two for *A,* and one for *SA.* Scores can range from 20 to 80.

60–80 = Good
40–59 = Fair
20–39 = Poor

This attitude survey, or others like it (Tullock-Rhody & Alexander, 1980), may be used as a pre/post-test for determining the affective impact of programs. It is also possible to look at specific areas of reading attitude. For example, in the BJP Survey:

Items 1, 7, 12 = Attitude toward libraries
Items 4, 6, 16, 19 = Reading self-concept
Other items = General attitude toward reading

It is standard procedure for individual scores to be recorded for purposes of counseling students with bad attitudes. We recommend that this **not** be done. Students with negative attitudes toward reading are not necessarily unintelligent. As a consequence, if they have any reason to think that they will be singled out and/or questioned because of their negative attitudes, they will take the only intelligent option and lie on the survey. The technical name for this is *response bias,* writing down what one believes the examiner wants rather than what the test taker really believes. A second reason for not generating individual scores is that students whose attitudes toward books and reading are so bad that they need counseling are painfully conspicuous most of the time, and no test is needed to identify them. On the other hand, trying to determine whether or not a program has created a positive change in group attitudes requires some objective measure. Therefore, we recommend that attitude surveys be anonymous and that class, grade, and school averages be used to assess groups rather than individuals.

Activity

Take the BJP attitude survey. How good is your reading attitude? Be honest!

Once data have been gathered concerning the attitudes of students, attention should be given to promoting reading related to content areas. Suggestions are presented below to develop or maintain positive attitudes toward reading. These suggestions will be related to teacher behaviors and practices, instructional practices, classroom organization, and student self-concept. Most of these suggestions are easy to accomplish but should constantly be evaluated in terms of their effectiveness in promoting attitudinal change.

Promoting Positive Attitudes Toward Reading in Content Areas

Teachers who do not read or do not value reading may pass this negative attitude on to their students. Rieck (1977), in a study investigating teacher and student attitudes toward reading, described how content teachers "telegraphed" messages against reading. Approximately 300 students from the classrooms of 14 teachers responded "no" to a question concerning whether or not students read their assignments. These same students then responded to a series of additional questions. Below are the questions and the student responses (p. 647):

Question	Response
1. Do you like to read?	52%—Yes
	38%—No
	10%—No response
2. Do you read your assignments in this class?	15%—Yes
	81%—No
	4%—No response
3. Do your tests mainly cover lecture and discussion, or reading assignments?	98%—Lecture and discussion
4. Are you required to discuss your reading assignments?	23%—Yes
	73%—No
	4%—No response
5. Does your teacher give you a purpose for reading or are you only given the number of pages to read?	95%—Pages
	5%—Purpose
6. Does your teacher bring in outside material for you to read and recommend books of interest for you to read?	5%—Yes
	95%—No
7. Does your teacher like to read?	20%—Yes
	33%—No
	47%—Don't know

The results of this study are, needless to say, very revealing and have important implications for the attitudinal environment content teachers create in their classrooms. Teachers are telling students they are required to read; yet, they are really communicating to their students:

> "You really don't have to read the assignments because you aren't tested on them and probably won't have to discuss them. You should read x number of pages, but there is no real reason to do so. Reading really isn't important. Outside reading is of little value in this class. My students will have no way to tell whether or not I like to read." (p. 647)

While this message may not be characteristic of all content teachers, the response it generates does point out the importance of teacher attitude. Teachers are models of reading behavior for their students. If teachers show students they value reading, they will motivate students to read. Conversely, teachers can also model a negative attitude toward reading. As it has been stated countless times before, teacher attitude is contagious!

Readence and Baldwin (1979) have described the instructional climate teachers should establish in their classroom to convey a positive model for reading to students. To enhance any instructional strategy dealing with reading assignments, teachers should communicate to students that they have the "right to be involved" and "the right to be wrong" in reading-related classroom discussions. In this way students will realize that they can interact with print or with the teacher without fear of negative consequences and that they are free to respond without reprisal even if they should disagree with the text author or the teacher. A classroom conducted with this rationale effectively demonstrates to students that they should have a questioning mind as they read or discuss material; that the teacher values such behavior; and that they, too, have a voice in decision-making regarding daily reading assignments. Teachers, thus, are not placed in the position of having either a student-centered or a subject-centered environment. Teachers can utilize the best of both environments by actively involving the students in the learning of subject matter. In this way students will see that teachers view reading as important and that their reaction to reading is valued, also. The authors view the instructional atmosphere created by teachers as essential to fostering positive attitudes toward reading.

A number of other suggestions for promoting favorable attitudes toward reading are offered by Cooter and Alexander (1984) and Rieck (1977). Many of these suggestions reemphasize the importance of the teacher presenting an effective model for reading to students.

1. **Encourage Students to Read.** Communicate this to students by sharing reading materials related to your content area. Read them interesting, thought-provoking items. Use materials relevant to the daily experiences of students, and above all, let them see you reading. One effective strategy for accomplishing this is Sustained Silent Reading (McCracken, 1971), during which class time is set aside for everyone, including the teacher, to read, and later, to share their reading experiences. Establishing Sustained Silent Reading programs will be discussed later in this chapter.
2. **Use Appropriate Instructional Materials.** When planning reading activities, consider materials which will interest students. Use multiple materials appropriate for your students' individual strengths and weaknesses in reading and within which they can succeed. Communicate to them the usefulness of reading for success in school and out-of-school activities.
3. **Plan for Effective Instruction.** Make the task of reading clear. Students should know what is expected of them in the reading task; they must know what to do before beginning to read; and, they must be able to associate their prior knowledge with the present reading task in order to enhance learning (Baldwin and Readence, 1979). Provide a purpose for reading, and follow up the reading with a reinforcing activity after the material has been discussed.
4. **Be Enthusiastic.** Show students you enjoy your subject. Read widely in your field to keep informed, and recommend books students will enjoy reading. Bulletin board displays of pertinent materials will also enhance your enthusiasm about your subject. Above all, be positive in your teaching approach. Providing successful experiences for all students should be one goal of instruction.

Reading Interests

If we are to create positive attitudes toward reading, it is necessary, in addition to making reading successful, to make reading pleasurable (self-rewarding). And this, in turn, requires finding out what internal needs and interests will motivate young people to read. The following principles should guide the assessment and use of individual reading interests.

1. All students can learn to enjoy reading if teachers are capable of helping them find sufficiently interesting materials and are willing to give them the time to read. In essence, there are no students who can read that won't read. This may seem to contradict what has been said up to this point; however, there is a difference between students who refuse to read materials normally given to them in school (i.e., "the boring stuff") and students who refuse to read anything, no matter how juicy it is. In some cases the range of materials acceptable to students will be extremely narrow, e.g., only stories about boxing, only science fiction, etc. Nevertheless, given the right materials and an opportunity to read them, virtually all students will read.

2. Individual patterns of reading interests can't be predicted on the basis of sex, age, or ethnic origin. Research on reading interests (Carter & Harris, 1982; Wolfson, Manning, & Manning, 1984) has consistently revealed that these variables are useful in predicting group interests; for example, adolescent males would rather read about sports than romance, and the reverse is true for females. However, it is also true that such generalizations are virtually useless in predicting the reading preferences of a given individual. Attempting to do so is to engage in the worst of stereotyping. Among adolescents and adults, individual interests are so diverse that it is all but impossible to predict them on the basis of group membership.

Activity

In a college class with about equal numbers of men and women, have students identify their favorite type of pleasure reading. How are the reading interests of men and women different?

---

3. Children and young people move through stages of literary appreciation, and it makes no sense to try to force them to enjoy literature that is beyond their stage of development (Carlsen, 1967). If a student has never read anything except Spiderman and Incredible Hulk comics, it is folly to think the youngster can appreciate *Don Quixote* or *Crime and Punishment*. For this reason, "quality" in literature is relative and not as absolute as some of us were led to believe by our previous K-12 experience. For teachers who are concerned with developing positive attitudes and getting kids to read, quality literature is anything you can get the students to read, critics notwithstanding. If students become avid readers, they will eventually seek literature that appeals to their intellect. If young people are to develop positive attitudes toward reading, it is essential to let them select their own reading material. This does not mean that their selections must be made in the absence of guidance, merely that final decisions regarding pleasure reading materials should be made by the students.

Assessment. The most useful type of interest assessment is one that permits the teacher to match specific interests with specific materials. For example, if a student indicates an interest in dogs and western and frontier life, *Old Yeller* would seem to be a good match of interests. The general interest inventory is the most common type of interest assessment, and an example of one follows.

General Interest Inventory

Directions: The purpose of this inventory is to find out what kinds of things you and your classmates are interested in reading. After every topic there is a blank space. On each space give a grade of A, B, C, D, or F based on how much you would like to read about the topic. An *A* means "It's wonderful; I love it!" An *F* means "It's terrible; take the topic away and bury it, quick!"

Sports _____	Animals _____
Science fiction _____	Fantasy _____
Folklore _____	Romance _____
Cars _____	Adventure _____
Humor _____	Mystery _____
War _____	The Arts _____
Supernatural _____	Foreign Lands _____
Science _____	History _____
Poetry _____	Family Life _____
Plays _____	Human Drama _____
Mathematics _____	Health Sciences _____

It is, of course, possible to create interest inventories with varying degrees of specificity; for instance, sports can be subclassified into baseball, basketball, football, tennis, curling, etc. Baseball could be subdivided into fiction stories, nonfiction books about pitching or hitting, and so on. In much the same manner it is possible to create an interest inventory for a specific content area. This type of inventory can provide information about group interests as well as guide outside reading for individuals. The following U.S. history interest inventory is merely one example in an endless chain of possibilities.

U.S. History Interest Inventory

Direction: Everyone in your class is going to be doing some outside reading related to American history. The purpose of this inventory is to help you find books that are actually interesting to *you*. After every topic there is a blank space. On the space next to the topic you would *most* like to read about, put a 1. Place a 2 on the space for your next choice. Place a 3 on the third best choice, and so on until you have evaluated every topic. Do *NOT* use any number more than once.

The Colonial Period (1600–1760)

    Biography _____

    Human Drama _____

    Family Life _____

    Freedom and Justice _____

The Revolutionary War Era (1760–1785)

    Biography _____

    Politics _____

    War _____

The Civil War Era (1850–1876)

    Slavery _____

    Famous Battles _____

    Politics _____

    Biography _____

    Human Drama _____

Western and Frontier Life

    Pioneers _____

    American Indians _____

    Tales of the Wild West _____

World War II (1939–1945)

    Battles in the Pacific _____

    Military Planes _____

    The War in Europe _____

    Atomic Weapons _____

    Freedom and Justice _____

Post World War II America _____

    Civil Rights _____

    Women's Liberation _____

    American Foreign Policy _____

    The Presidency _____

    Biographies of Black Leaders _____

It should also be pointed out that teachers can modify the above interest inventory to fit the needs of their teaching objectives. For instance, students might rank each general topic area (e.g., The Colonial Period) 1, 2, 3, 4 instead of ranking all topics at once. This may enable teachers to find appropriate material for each general topic area as it is encountered.

Unifying Strategies

Traditionally, the reading process has been viewed as a hierarchy of skills, that is, a bottom-up model of the reading process. And this, in turn, has resulted in strict skills-based reading programs, the theory being that reading is composed of specific skills that can be identified and taught to students directly, e.g., phonics, vocabulary, and various comprehension skills. Moreover, it is assumed that mastery of all individual skills will produce good readers in spite of the fact that it is absurd to think that all of these skills are known, let alone teachable. For example, McConkie and Rayner (1976) have provided evidence that eye movements during reading are ballistic. Just as ICBM's are programmed in advance to land at some strategic point, so also are the eyes programmed by the mind to land (fixate) on the line of print some distance to the right. The grammatical patterns of the sentence, prior knowledge of the topic, and information acquired from peripheral vision may all combine to determine where the eyes will go from moment to moment. No one knows precisely how the mind of the fluent reader accomplishes this task. Therefore, it is quite impossible to directly teach others how to do it. Yet it is a skill which fluent readers must acquire. Clearly, there are some skills that readers must teach themselves; and we would contend that this takes place naturally as a function of practice.

The importance of practice in the reading process can hardly be overestimated. Not only are some skills self-taught through practice, but common sense dictates that practice is a prerequisite to proficiency in almost everything. Moreover, there is consensus in the field of reading that regular practice with pleasurable materials is one of the best means of improving reading comprehension (Carver, 1987).

Sustained Silent Reading (SSR)

Uninterrupted Sustained Silent Reading (Hunt, 1971), *Sustained Silent Reading* (McCracken, 1971), and Sustained QUIet Reading Time (Cunningham, Arthur, and Cunningham, 1977) all refer to a systematic program that establishes regular reading times for students. Its fundamental objective is to provide students with an opportunity to practice their reading skills using pleasurable and self-selected content-related materials. There are two separate phases in SSR: instructional readiness and the reading activity itself.

Instructional Readiness. Discuss SSR with students. Let them know how the activity will be carried out and why they are doing it. Emphasize that SSR is supposed to be a pleasurable activity. Tell them that they will *not* be graded or asked comprehension questions over what they read.

Since the stated purpose of SSR is to provide pleasurable practice in reading, the students should be informed that certain types of materials are inappropriate. Textbooks, magazines, comics, and newspapers *should not* be used. Textbooks are seldom pleasure reading, newspapers make noise, and comics and magazines lend themselves to "picture looking" rather than reading. This may seem to contradict previous arguments that students should be able to read what they want to read; however, successful implementation of SSR is dependent on sustained *silent* reading. Textbooks, newspapers, comics, and magazines certainly do not lend themselves to such behavior.

Students should be responsible for selecting a book and then having it with them for SSR. Unfortunately, once newspapers, comics, and magazines are ruled out, some students will have absolutely no idea of how to choose a book. The teacher can help by administering an interest inventory and then, perhaps with the cooperation of the school librarian, assisting students in their attempts to locate a good book. If students are given systematic guidance, it is much more likely that they will find compelling and readable literature, particularly if teachers wish to create favorable attitudes toward reading content-related literature.

The Reading Activity.

1. *Everyone must read,* and this includes the teacher. SSR is not a mini-study period for students, and it is not a break or prep period for teachers. Doing homework, getting coffee, grading papers, etc., are "verboten!" It is essential that the teacher model SSR by reading right along with students.
2. *SSR should be uninterrupted.* Let students know that they are not to sharpen pencils, gossip, or ask questions, e.g., "Ms. _____ , what's this word mean?" In addition, colleagues should know that they are not to disturb a class during SSR. Lunch counts, calls on the "squawk box," and other minor irritations will occur. They should be minimized. It may be worthwhile hanging a sign on the door: "SSR IN PROGRESS. DO NOT DISTURB!"
3. *The SSR period* should be set at the beginning of class in order to insure that the activity is accomplished. It also has a settling effect on a class. Ideally, SSR should occur once a day or as often as the class meets, if at all possible. However, you may wish to initiate SSR less frequently, e.g., every other day. The authors strongly encourage the use of SSR as often as it is realistically possible in your classroom. Trying to do SSR for an entire class period once a week will do little to instill the reading habit and will become very tedious for less mature or reluctant readers. Distributed practice for short periods of time each day will have the desired effect.
4. *The time limits for SSR* will need to vary according to the age and general maturity of the class. We recommend beginning with five minutes and then gradually increasing the time as students adjust to the routine and develop a capacity to attend to reading for more than brief periods of time. Be careful not to increase the time too quickly, perhaps a minute every week or two. Each teacher should judge the amount of time to be allocated to SSR based upon student abilities and curricular demands.

   In addition, be certain to keep the SSR interval regular. Three minutes one day, ten the next, and two the next day will not work. Smooth, progressive increments (e.g., 5, 5, 5, 5, 5, 6, 6, 6, 6, 6, 7, . . .) will gradually accustom students to the rigors of sustained silent reading. The authors are aware that taking time for SSR during class will take away from your instructional time. However, the benefits that can be gained from reading pleasurable content-related material will augment your instruction, particularly if students are reading material related to the topic under discussion. It is suggested that coupling the findings of the interest inventory previously administered with the time to read those materials during SSR in your classroom will be most beneficial and rewarding for future learning of subject matter material.

5. *Time SSR with care.* We suggest using a kitchen timer placed on your desk and facing away from the students so they won't stare at it. For the same reason, wall clocks make bad timing devices as some students become clock watchers. Avoid using your wristwatch since that encourages students to ask you about time remaining. Simply tell them that the kitchen timer will always indicate when SSR is over for the day.

6. *Avoid doing SSR immediately prior to tests* since it will be difficult—maybe even painful—for students to concentrate knowing that a quiz or test is imminent. On test days, shift SSR to some later part of the class period.

7. *Problem students* can be handled in the following manner. You may have some students whose aversion to reading is so profound that they will refuse, initially, to participate in SSR. The very idea of reading for fun will be totally foreign to some students. Do not badger or pressure them. You can force people to do something, but you can't make them like it. Let problem students "sleep," just as long as they don't bother the group. As these students see others enjoying SSR, they should come to find reading preferable to inactivity.

Let your class know that misbehavior and intentional disruption will result in termination of SSR for the day. If a student does something that causes half the class to stop reading, simply say "I'm sorry, but our SSR is over for today. Put your books away and begin _____ ." Move right along to the next scheduled activity without acknowledging the culprits or their actions. Because SSR is fun, peer pressure should serve to reduce individual disruptions.

Library Power

Many students think of school libraries as receptacles for rotting textbooks, a relatively unimportant part of the school. This sort of attitude is indeed unfortunate. In reality, most school libraries contain thousands of fascinating novels, biographies, periodicals, and reference works, all waiting to be discovered. The unfortunate thing is that many students *never* discover the pleasures and satisfactions of the library. When students are reluctant to ask questions of the librarian and when their teachers fail to introduce them systematically to the library, the students often come to the distressing conclusion that there isn't anything in the school library worth reading. One of the strategic goals of every reading teacher and every content area teacher should be to expand the reading horizons of students by introducing them to the wealth of the school library. The following guidelines suggest some of the ways in which content teachers can make the most of the library or media center.

Meet the Librarian and the Library. It makes sense that before teachers can guide students in the uses of the library, teachers need to familiarize themselves with its organization and resources. Find out what periodicals, reference works, films, etc., are available for your subject area. Most librarians are anxious to help faculty members identify, catalogue, and order materials.

Library Orientation. The school librarian or media specialist is an expert in locational skills (finding information). Take advantage of those skills by setting up library orientations for groups of students. Even in senior high school, many students will not know how to use the card catalog. Some students will not be able to find a work of fiction. The librarian can provide this basic information as well as answer questions about library hours and special rules.

A Case in Point. Imagine that you are an eighth-grade American history teacher. You want your students to read beyond the class textbook, and you want them to enjoy their outside reading as much as possible. In order to meet this objective you do the following things:

1. You create a list of broad topics from American history, for example, "Family Life During the Colonial Period" or "Civil Rights in Post World War II America."
2. With the help of the librarian, you catalogue the titles in the school library that fit each topic. (Obviously, the difficulty of the task is determined by the size of the library, the number of topics you want books for, and the number of books you require for each topic.)
3. Create an interest inventory which reflects the original topics, in this case the "U.S. History Interest Inventory" cited previously.
4. Administer the inventory to students and then recommend specific titles to individual students on the basis of expressed interest.
5. The procedure can be made more sophisticated by establishing the readability of each book on the list. By doing so, one could avoid recommending a book written on a twelfth grade level to a student reading on a sixth grade level.

The following titles reflect topics on the "U.S. History Interest Inventory." These books would be appropriate for junior high students who read on a sixth or seventh grade level.

Brothers and Sisters, by Adoff, Arnold.
A collection of stories about Black Americans' experiences in Harlem, the Bayou country, and other parts of the United States.

Johnny Reb, by Allen, Merritt P.
Ezra Todd, a 16-year-old orphan, pins his fortune to a Civil War general and suffers through four years of deadly warfare.

Two Sieges of the Alamo, by Alter, Robert E.
Jack is a young pilot on a Mississippi riverboat until he discovers a runaway slave. After that he and three others decide to go to Texas to join the revolt against Mexico. Jack arrives in time to fight in the first siege of the Alamo.

Saddles and Sabers: Black Men in the Old West, by Anderson, Laverne.
Fascinating brief biographies of Black cowboys, lawmen, and cavalrymen who helped settle the West during the latter half of the nineteenth century.

Sounder, by Armstrong, William.
The story of a black sharecropper family. The oldest son and his dog, Sounder, spend many years searching for the boy's father, who has been unjustly sent to prison.

On the Frontier with Mr. Audubon, by Brenner, Barbara.
This is Joseph Mason's description of the 18-month trip that he and John James Audubon took down the Mississippi River.

Lexington and Concord, 1775: What Really Happened, by Colby, Jean P.
An account of the famous confrontations between British soldiers and American rebels in the early stages of the Revolutionary War.

Women's Rights: The Suffrage Movement in America, 1848–1920, by Coolidge, Olivia.
>   The history of the women's rights movement, from the Seneca Falls Convention of 1848 to the ratification of the 19th amendment to the Constitution in 1920.

The Salem Witchcraft Delusion, 1692, by Dickinson, Alice.
>   The history of the witch hunts, unwarranted prosecutions, trials, and hangings that occurred in Salem, Massachusetts, in 1692.

George Midgett's War, by Edwards, Sally.
>   A 14-year-old boy and his father risk everything to get supplies to George Washington's men at Valley Forge.

Redcoat in Boston, by Finlayson, Ann.
>   The story of a thirteen-year-old boy who enlists in the King's army and is shortly thereafter accused of the murder of a colonist.

Anne Frank: The Diary of a Young Girl, by Frank, Anne.
>   The touching record of a two-year period in the life of a young Jewish girl. Two families spent those two years in an attic hiding from the Nazis, and despite the constant terror, Anne had moments of happiness and hope for the future.

Which Way Freedom? by Hansen, Joyce.
>   Historical fiction about a young black man's search for freedom during the Civil War.

D-Day: The Invasion of Europe, by Hine, Al.
>   The story of the Allied Invasion of Europe on June 6, 1944, when the largest amphibious force ever assembled assaulted the beaches of Normandy.

Indian Warriors and Their Weapons, by Hofsinde, Robert (Gray-Wolf).
>   A detailed description of the charms, clothes, weapons, and fighting strategies of the Iroquois, Sioux, and other American Indian tribes.

Across Five Aprils, by Hunt, Irene.
>   A touching story of a boy named Jethro who grows up and assumes the responsibilities of a man during the five years of the Civil War.

The Scarlet Raider, by Icenhower, Joseph B.
>   Tim Morgan is too young to join the Confederate Army so he helps by running contraband through the Northern lines. When Tim is eventually able to join Captain Moseby's forces, he is thrilled and content; that is, until he is captured by a Yankee.

Louis Armstrong, by Iverson, Genie.
>   The incredible story of a man called "Satchmo"—Louis Armstrong, the King of Jazz. He was born in New Orleans and was sent to the Colored Waif's Home when he was twelve. There he learned to blow his horn—the rest is jazz history.

The Black Man in America: 1861–77, by Jackson, Florence.
>   An account of black contributions, aspirations, and suffering during the Civil War and Reconstruction, with reproductions of old photographs and drawings.

Longhouse Winter, by Jones, Hettie.
>   Four tales about people becoming animals in the spirit of the Iroquois Indians, who had an interest in storytelling.

Edge of Two Worlds, by Jones, Weyman.
>   The only survivor of a wagon train massacre encounters a Cherokee Indian who helps him reach his home and family.

Touchmark, by Lawrence, Mildred.
> Nabby Jonas, an orphan, wants very much to become a pewterer. However, in Revolutionary War times, this was not considered a proper field for a female.

Growing Up Indian, by Wolfson, Evelyn.
> Fascinating information about the social life and customs of American Indians.

A knowledge of reading interests, readability, and library resources can combine with your desire to stimulate meaningful outside reading in your content area. Given a library, some ingenuity, and a willingness to work hard, there is no limit to strategies for developing the learning habits and interests of young people.

Summary

In this chapter we have discussed the significance and assessment of reading attitudes and interests in the content classroom. Sustained Silent Reading and Library Power were presented as strategies responsive to many of the affective and cognitive needs of the content classroom. In addition, the importance of teachers modeling reading and positive attitudes toward reading, books, and libraries was emphasized throughout the chapter.

Return to the anticipation guide at the beginning of the chapter. React to the guide statements again, but this time record your answers in the column entitled "Reaction." Compare your responses with those you made in the Anticipation column.

Miniprojects

1. Create a reading interest inventory for your content area.
2. Administer Rieck's survey or the attitude inventory presented in this chapter to a group of middle or secondary students. Summarize the results.

Additional Recommended Readings

The following sources will provide useful lists of good books to read.

Agee, H. (1984). *High interest easy reading for junior and senior high school students* (4th ed.). Urbana, IL: National Council of Teachers of English.

Carter, B., & Abrahamson, R. F. (1986). The best of hi/lo books for young adults: A critical evaluation. *Journal of Reading, 30,* 204–211.

Christensen, J. (1983). *Your reading: A booklist for junior high students.* Urbana, IL: National Council of Teachers of English.

Cianciolo, P. (1985). *Adventuring with books: A booklist for pre-k–grade 6.* Urbana, IL: National Council of Teachers of English.

Donelson, K. L. (1985). *Books for you: A booklist for senior high students.* Urbana, IL: National Council of Teachers of English.

Dreyer, S. S. (1985). *The bookfinder: A guide to children's literature about the needs and problems of youth ages 2 to 15.* Circle Pines, MN: American Guidance Service.

High interest low readability booklist (1985). Chicago, IL: American Library Association.

Wolff, K., Fritsche, J. M., Gross, E. N., & Todd, G. T. (1983). *The best science books for children.* Washington, DC: American Association for the Advancement of Science.

References

Athey, I. (1985). Reading research in the affective domain. In H. Singer and R. B. Ruddell (Eds.) *Theoretical models & processes of reading* (3rd ed., pp. 527–559). Newark, DE: International Reading Association.

Baldwin, R. S. (1986). When was the last time you bought a textbook just for kicks? In E. K. Dishner, T. W. Bean, J. E. Readence, & D. W. Moore (Eds.), *Reading in the content areas: Improving classroom instruction* (2nd ed., pp. 323–328). Dubuque, IA: Kendall/Hunt Publishing Company.

Baldwin, R. S., Johnson, D., & Peer, G. (1980). *Bookmatch.* Tulsa, OK: Educational Development Corporation.

Baldwin, R. S., & Readence, J. E. (1979). Critical reading and perceived authority. *Journal of Reading, 22,* 617–622.

Carlsen, G. R. (1967). *Books and the teen-age reader.* New York: Harper & Row.

Carter, B., & Harris, K. (1982). What junior high students like in books. *Journal of Reading, 26,* 42–46.

Carver, R. P. (1987). Should reading comprehension skills be taught? In J. E. Readence & R. S. Baldwin (Eds.), *Research in literacy: Merging perspectives* (pp. 115–126). Thirty-sixth Yearbook of the National Reading Conference. Rochester, NY: National Reading Conference.

Cooter, R. B., & Alexander, J. E. (1984). Interest and attitude: Affective connections for gifted and talented readers. *Reading World, 24,* 97–102.

Cunningham, P. M., Arthur, S. V., & Cunningham, J. W. (1977). *Classroom reading instruction: Alternative approaches.* Lexington, MA: D. C. Heath.

Helmstetter, A. (1987). Year-long motivation in the 8th grade "reluctant" class. *Journal of Reading, 31,* 244–247.

Hunt, L. C. (1971). Six steps to the individualized reading program (IRP). *Elementary English, 48,* 27–32.

Mathewson, G. C. (1985). The function of attitude in the reading process. In H. Singer & R. B. Ruddell (Eds.), *Theoretical models and processes of reading* (3rd ed., pp. 841–856). Newark, DE: International Reading Association.

McConkie, G. W., & Rayner, K. (1976). Identifying the span of the effective stimulus in reading: Literature review and theories of reading. In H. Singer & R. B. Ruddell (Eds.), *Theoretical models and processes of reading.* Newark, DE: International Reading Association.

McCracken, R. A. (1971). Initiating sustained silent reading. *Journal of Reading, 14,* 521–524, 582–583.

Readence, J. E., & Baldwin, R. S. (1979). Independence in critical reading: An instructional strategy. *Educational Considerations, 6,* 15–16.

Rieck, B. J. (1977). How content teachers telegraph messages against reading. *Journal of Reading, 20,* 646–648.

Spiegel, D. L. (1981). *Reading for pleasure: Guidelines.* Newark, DE: International Reading Association.

Stanovich, K. E. (1986). Matthew effects in reading: Some consequences of individual differences in the acquisition of literacy. *Reading Research Quarterly, 21,* 380–407.

Summers, E. G. (1977). Instruments for assessing reading attitudes: A review of research and bibliography. *Journal of Reading Behavior, 9,* 137–165.

Tullock-Rhody, R., & Alexander, J. E. (1980). A scale for assessing attitudes toward reading in secondary schools. *Journal of Reading, 23,* 609–614.

Wigfield, A., & Asher, S. R. (1984). Social and motivational influences on reading. In P. D. Pearson (Ed.), *Handbook of reading research* (pp. 423–452). New York: Longman.

Wolfson, B. J., Manning, G., & Manning, M. (1984). Revisiting what children say their reading interests are. *Reading World, 24,* 4–10.

4

Anticipation   **Reaction**

—————— 1.   —————— 1. Most content teachers know the difficulty levels of their textbooks.

—————— 2.   —————— 2. Publishers provide reliable indications of the grade level difficulty of their texts.

—————— 3.   —————— 3. Students understand the use of textbook aids such as the table of contents and index.

—————— 4.   —————— 4. Sentence length is the most reliable indicator of textual difficulty.

—————— 5.   —————— 5. Students should have a voice in the text-selection process.

Evaluating and Introducing Textbooks

Rationale

For a number of years educators at all levels have shared a common interest in predicting the approximate difficulty of instructional materials. Ideally, the level of text material can be matched to the appropriate reading level of students. In reality, though, the selection of a core text has been largely based on teacher intuition. Usually, content area teachers choose text materials based primarily on an analysis of the text content. While the content of a core text is certainly important and should reflect a teacher's instructional objectives, there are additional features of the text that merit careful consideration.

The evaluation of printed material can be a highly refined and systematic process given our current understanding of those features that make textbooks understandable and useful as learning tools. Indeed, some striking features of textbooks do increase or diminish the likelihood of student understanding. Therefore, in order to match the difficulty level of the text to the reading level of students, both quantitative and qualitative factors of text material must be evaluated. *Quantitative factors* include such language variables as word and sentence length. These factors can be counted and measured with a formula to estimate the grade level designation of text difficulty. *Qualitative factors* are more difficult to determine and include such elements as prior knowledge of the reader, organization of the text, student interest, and a myriad of other important considerations.

In this chapter we will examine both quantitative and qualitative factors a content teacher needs to consider in the evaluation of text material. In addition, we will demonstrate a strategy for introducing students to an unfamiliar text.

Chapter Objectives

After reading this chapter, you should be able to:

1. Understand which quantitative and qualitative factors make a text more easily understood.
2. Apply a readability graph to a textbook.
3. Employ a checklist of quantitative and qualitative factors to evaluate a textbook for use in your classroom.
4. Conduct a text preview to acquaint students with the essential learning aids in a text.

Graphic Organizer

The following graphic organizer is provided to give you some advance structure for new vocabulary and concepts that will be presented in this chapter.

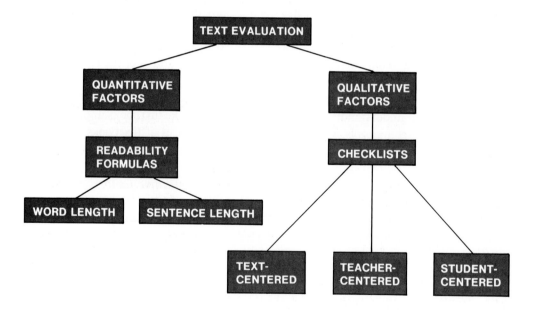

Text Evaluation

Quantitative Factors in Readability Measurement

There are a number of different approaches designed to help the content area teacher estimate the difficulty level of text material. Each approach has inherent advantages and limitations. For example, a teacher can simply guess the grade level of a text (Klare, 1974–1975). Unfortunately, this approach, while attractive in its speed and simplicity, has not proven to be very reliable. In a study of 180 secondary teachers' ability to rank order the difficulty level of text selections representing five content areas, Palmatier and Strader (1977) found that teachers were generally unsuccessful at this task.

A second, more attractive approach to a reliable estimate of text difficulty involves the administration of one or two informal tests based on a portion of the text. These procedures will be described in detail in chapter nine. In this section we will explore a third approach to predicting the difficulty of text material, the use of readability formulas.

Readability formulas are mathematically derived indices of text difficulty based on an analysis of language variables. Over 30 different readability formulas and graphs have been developed, including specialized formulas for appraising foreign language texts (Klare, 1984). While none of the formulas are absolute measures, they all share some common features that are useful in obtaining a rough estimate of a textbook's readability.

The two most common language variables accounted for in the majority of readability formulas are word and sentence length, and sentence length is thought to be the more reliable of the two (Klare, 1984). In addition to these two variables of word and sentence length, there are extensive compilations of commonly occurring words which can be used to rate the relative difficulty of a text. Words in the text that are not represented on the master list increase the difficulty rating of the text being considered. Formulas based on extensive word lists lend themselves to computer application. Indeed, they can be quite frustrating to compute using manual methods. We will explore a quick classroom method that retains the reliability of more elaborate computerized formulas. (For those interested in a closely related microcomputer formula, see Kretschmer, 1984.)

The Raygor Readability Estimate

Recently, Alton Raygor (1977) devised a readability formula specifically for middle/secondary level text material. The *Raygor Readability Estimate* is both simple to use and reliable because it eliminates a common source of error found in many readability formulas. While counting sentences in a text sample presents little difficulty, formulas that combine this measure with a syllable count (e.g., the Fry Readability Graph, 1978), introduce a moderate potential for error. Two or more evaluators are likely to arrive at divergent answers for the number of syllables in the same text sample. The individual dialects of evaluators and the inherent difficulty in defining exactly what a syllable is, both contribute to unreliable syllable counts among evaluators. A good alternative to a syllable count is determination of the proportion of words with six or more letters in a 100-word text sample (Raygor, 1977). In a study comparing the Fry and Raygor formulas, Baldwin and Kaufman (1979) found that teachers were able to complete text evaluations with greater ease and rapidity using the Raygor Readability Estimate. In addition, the Raygor formula retained the high reliability attributed to the Fry Graph.

Following are the directions and the accompanying graph for the Raygor Readability Estimate. The activity that follows will give you some initial, guided experience with this formula.

1. Count out three 100-word passages at the beginning, middle, and end of a textbook selection. Count proper nouns but not numbers.
2. Count the number of sentences in each 100-word passage, estimating to the nearest tenth for partial sentences.
3. Count the number of words with six or more letters.
4. Average the sentence length and word length measures over the three samples and plot the average on the graph. The grade level nearest the spot marked is the best estimate of the difficulty of the selection.

THE RAYGOR READABILITY ESTIMATE
Alton L. Raygor—University of Minnesota

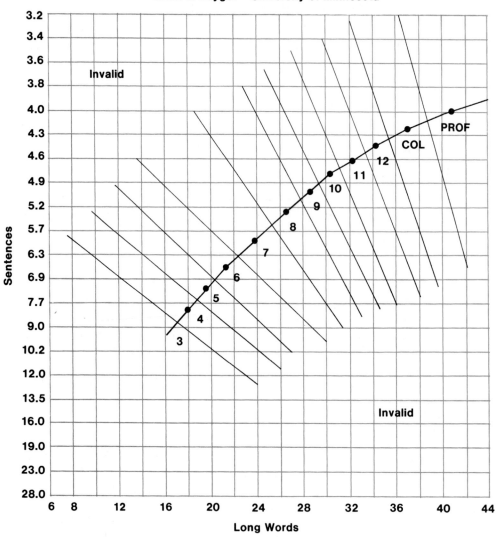

Activity

Directions: Apply the Raygor Readability Estimate to one 100-word passage from this chapter. The passage starts on page 61, paragraph 1, and begins, "For a number of years. . . ."

Locate and write in the needed information in the blank to the left of each step in the Raygor formula outlined below. Check your answers when you are finished to insure that you know how to operate the Raygor estimate and graph. When you are finished, turn to the end of the chapter for the answers.

_____ 1. The 100-word passage beginning on page 61 ends with the word "_____."

_____ 2. The 100-word passage contains _____ sentences to the nearest tenth. (Note: There are 29 total words in the last sentence which you divide into 2 from the last part of the 100-word sample, e.g., $2/29 = .1$.)

_____ 3. There are _____ words with six or more letters in the sample. (Put a check over words containing six or more letters and total these.)

_____ 4. With three 100-word samples you would average the figures for sentence and word length and enter the graph on the previous page. In the present example, simply enter the graph with the values from steps 2 and 3 respectively to determine the approximate difficulty of this 100–word sample. Record your answer in the blank.

Using the Raygor Readability Estimate will provide readability estimates that are accurate within a range of plus or minus one year. In this way you will have a realistic idea of the difficulty level of the text and can begin to judge how effective it may be with your students.

Qualitative Factors in Text Evaluation

While readability formulas are useful as one component in the analysis of text material for adoption, they do have some inherent limitations that need to be mentioned. Readability formulas provide an estimate of the linguistic features of print that may influence text difficulty. These surface features typically include the average number of polysyllabic words and the average number of sentences taken from three sample passages in a text. Unfortunately, such measures are not applicable to poetry or the symbolic discourse of such disciplines as mathematics and chemistry. Thus, a number of additional, text-centered factors need to be considered in a comprehensive evaluation of a text.

Text-Centered Factors

In a concise discussion of readability and comprehension, Marshall (1979) enumerated many of the variables that need to be considered in an analysis of text material. The quality of the writing style needs to be given careful consideration. Marshall noted that scrambling the word order of a selection would not materially alter the readability rating. Indeed, the scrambled passage would receive the same rating as a passage with acceptable syntax. Therefore, readability formulas are universally insensitive to writing style.

Some readability formulas imply that short sentences are easier to understand than longer sentences. This is certainly not the case since grammatical structures can aid or disrupt important semantic relations. Pearson (1974–1975) found that grammatical complexity aided middle-grade students' comprehension of sentence level information. In the illustration below, example one would be easier to understand than example two, yet readability formulas that use sentence length as an index of difficulty would rate the second example as the less difficult structure.

1. Marvin slept late because he was lazy.
2. Marvin slept late. He was lazy.

Sentence one is easier to comprehend because the causal relation in the sentence is made explicit by the author's use of the word "because." Conversely, example two disrupts the causal relation, requiring the reader to employ inference in order to establish the implied connection between the two events.

The criticism of short sentences may also be applied to short words. For instance, in the sentence, "The dog the cat bit died," not only is the sentence short but also the words are short. Yet, the sentence will provide some difficulty for students because of the imbedded idea and the unusual grammatical structure. Therefore, the length of words is not necessarily an indicator of easier understanding.

Other text-centered factors, in addition to those already mentioned, also deserve careful consideration in the text evaluation process. The abstract concepts and technical vocabulary an author uses are often complex, particularly in content areas such as science. Nelson (1978) noted that the explanations of complex concepts, such as the process of photosynthesis in science, may require longer sentences in order to preserve important meaning relationships. Furthermore, since concept load and technical vocabulary are closely related in the content areas, reducing the use of technical terms would dilute important concepts essential to a discipline. One indication of conceptual difficulty in a text is the degree to which technical terms can be translated to more commonly occurring synonyms. For example, the word "compression" is easily substituted using the more familiar term "squeezed." In contrast, a highly specific technical term like "photosynthesis" will undoubtedly require a good deal of teacher explanation if students are to cope with this concept in their reading.

Although readability formulas have been used to rewrite text material, Marshall (1979) cautioned against the practice of mechanically reducing sentence and word length in a selection. While the rewritten version may be easier to read on a surface level than the original, important meaning relationships may be disrupted, making the rewritten version more difficult to comprehend. Readability formulas make no distinction between conceptually important information and trivial ideas. Nor do readability formulas differentiate between coherent writing that flows logically from one idea to the next and incoherent, disorganized prose.

Davison and Kantor (1982) compared high school passages that were rewritten to lessen the vocabulary load with the original, presumably more difficult text passages. They found the rewritten versions often disrupted explicit connections among ideas in the original sentences. At the sentence level, a modest amount of incoherence rarely presents much difficulty. However, if this incoherence extends across sentences, the text may present comprehension problems. For example, consider the following brief text.

Reggie wanted to sleep late but John woke him up early for their trip to the north shore. Just as they were ready to leave, Reggie's girl friend June arrived. She wanted to go shopping. THEY took the Toyota.

Now answer the following questions:

1. Who went shopping?
2. Who took the Toyota?

Pronouns are notorious for the potential comprehension problems they can cause when antecedents are unclear. However, readability formulas are not intended to measure these more subtle features of a text.

On the other hand, readability formulas do provide a measure of vocabulary difficulty. Vocabulary difficulty undeniably influences students' comprehension, even when the writing is coherent (Freebody & Anderson, 1983). Consider the following passage:

Nadine perused the grocery shelves, carefully scrutinizing each jar of peanut butter as if they were rare, prehistoric bones. She systematically ignored the organic products in favor of the more familiar brands. Her ARACHIBUTYROPHOBIA had been getting worse lately. She finally chose a jar of creamy style peanut butter, knowing it would never be opened once she got it home.

If the main idea of this passage is at all obscure it is because of the technical, polysyllabic word "arachibutyrophobia." This word may look like it should be fear of spiders, but it actually means "fear of getting peanut butter stuck on the roof of the mouth"! Notice that a single, precise term like arachibutyrophobia is extremely economical for a writer, in this case encompassing 12 short words.

Pearson and Camperell (1981) reported that readers often rely on an author's organizational structure in their attempts to recall important information. Moreover, some organizational patterns such as comparison-contrast were more conducive to long-term recall than less cohesive patterns such as simple listing. Readability formulas are not yet sophisticated enough to account for the influence of these higher level features of text on students' comprehension. For these reasons, readability formulas must be used in combination with other qualitative considerations in order to develop a comprehensive approach to the evaluation of instructional materials.

Readability formulas like the Raygor can only hint at potential problems in text. As you examine texts in your content area, consider how well the author weaves ideas together within and across sentence and paragraph boundaries. Also examine technical vocabulary that may present potential problems.

One way to analyze text is to consider the decisions a writer must make in creating a text that will succeed in transmitting ideas. Anderson and Armbruster (1984) offered the following "maxims" from the perspective of an author (pp. 378–379):

1. *Structure:* Choose a pattern of organization that best conveys the informative purpose.
2. *Coherence:* Make relationships among ideas clear enough so that there is logical connection or "flow of meaning" from one idea to the next.
3. *Unity:* Address one purpose at a time; do not stray from the purpose by including irrelevant and distracting information.
4. *Audience Appropriateness:* Make sure the text fits the knowledge base of the reader.

These four AUTHOR maxims are certainly worth considering in the evaluation of a text. But even if a text adheres to these maxims, it should still challenge students' existing knowledge and misconceptions about a topic. Thus, you will need to guide students toward successful comprehension, regardless of a text's positive and negative features.

Teacher-Centered Factors

Contemporary texts supply an abundance of student aids designed to enhance comprehension. These include visual aids such as photographs, line drawings, graphs, tables, and diagrams. Other aids might include pre- and post-questions or questions interspersed within a chapter. Some authors also use *metadiscourse* (Crismore, 1984), or text intrusions in which the author talks directly to the reader about the information in the text, to aid students in comprehending. In addition, a glossary can be valuable in helping students cope with difficult technical vocabulary. Some contemporary texts also include supplemental films, filmstrips, and cassette tapes.

All of these devices can be valuable aids to students' understanding; however, none are substitutes for carefully guided instruction. Indeed, the very nature of content learning and content texts implies knowledge to be acquired in conjunction with a course of study. Thus, teacher-centered factors are likely to influence students' comprehension more than all the text-centered factors combined. Content texts are simply not designed to be read and comprehended in isolation, independent of a carefully guided course of instruction. The degree to which a teacher provides a bridge between what the students currently know about a topic and new conceptual information is undoubtedly the essential ingredient in the teaching and learning process. The amount of instructional guidance you provide before, during, and after reading text assignments will significantly affect students' comprehension of even the least challenging text. For example, Bean, Singer, Cowen, and Searles (1987) have shown that teacher-provided metadiscourse enhanced secondary students' ability to learn basic biology concepts. In the chapters that follow, a number of teaching strategies will be introduced to help you improve students' understanding of text concepts.

Student-Centered Factors

Finally, student-centered factors, also play a prominent role in content area learning. Two important student-centered factors are the prospective readers' prior knowledge and interest in a course topic. Students generally have a preconceived notion about particular courses and books. Therefore, it is a good practice to have students representing various levels of subject interest and reading achievement directly involved in the text evaluation process. Their opinions and recommendations often provide a "naive" perspective on the text, a perspective which you might find difficult to achieve since your prior knowledge and interest is extensive.

Text Evaluation Guidelines and Checklists

In general, students profit from text that adheres to classical principles of good writing. They can best comprehend authors who use frequent examples and graphic aids while avoiding unnecessary jargon (Pepper, 1981). The following procedure for evaluating text material is designed to combine a quantitative measure of readability with additional qualitative factors, including student-centered information.

A number of different guidelines and related checklists for evaluating text material have been advanced recently (e.g., Clewell & Cliffton, 1983; Singer, 1986). While all of these guidelines and checklists are intuitively derived and informal in nature, they comprise the best currently available approach to text evaluation. The 20-item checklist that follows has been adapted from these sources, with some additional factors that are essential to text comprehension.

Text Evaluation Checklist

Directions: Enter the intended grade level of the text. Compute an estimate of text readability using the Raygor Readability Estimate. Complete the 20-item checklist to determine the acceptability of the text for your students.

Title of Textbook _____

Author(s) _____

Publisher _____

Copyright date _____

Cost _____

Evaluated by _____

A. Readability

_____ 1. Intended grade level of text: _____ . Readability estimate: _____ . Is the computed reading level realistic for the students who will be using the text?

B. Format

_____ 2. The book is recently copyrighted and the contents genuinely up-to-date.

_____ 3. The text is suitable for achieving the stated course objectives.

_____ 4. The text contains a table of contents, an index, and a glossary.

_____ 5. The table of contents indicates a logical development of the subject matter.

_____ 6. When the text refers to a graph, table, or diagram, that aid is on the same page as the textual reference.

_____ 7. Captions under graphs, tables, and diagrams are clearly written.

_____ 8. Pictures are in color and are contemporary, not dated by dress unless the author's intention is to portray a certain period.

_____ 9. Various ethnic groups and male and female characters are depicted authentically in the text.

_____ 10. The text suggests out-of-class readings and projects to stimulate additional student interest.

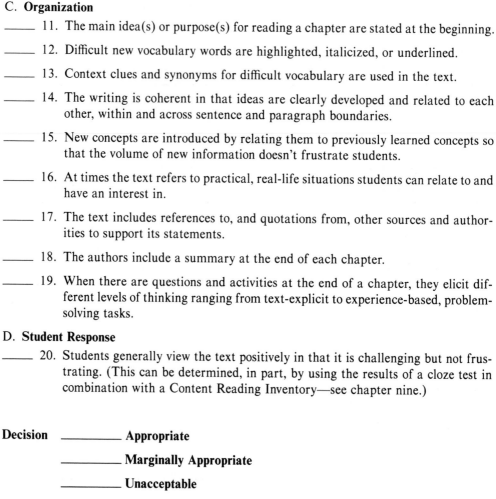

C. **Organization**

_____ 11. The main idea(s) or purpose(s) for reading a chapter are stated at the beginning.

_____ 12. Difficult new vocabulary words are highlighted, italicized, or underlined.

_____ 13. Context clues and synonyms for difficult vocabulary are used in the text.

_____ 14. The writing is coherent in that ideas are clearly developed and related to each other, within and across sentence and paragraph boundaries.

_____ 15. New concepts are introduced by relating them to previously learned concepts so that the volume of new information doesn't frustrate students.

_____ 16. At times the text refers to practical, real-life situations students can relate to and have an interest in.

_____ 17. The text includes references to, and quotations from, other sources and authorities to support its statements.

_____ 18. The authors include a summary at the end of each chapter.

_____ 19. When there are questions and activities at the end of a chapter, they elicit different levels of thinking ranging from text-explicit to experience-based, problem-solving tasks.

D. **Student Response**

_____ 20. Students generally view the text positively in that it is challenging but not frustrating. (This can be determined, in part, by using the results of a cloze test in combination with a Content Reading Inventory—see chapter nine.)

Decision _____ **Appropriate**

_____ **Marginally Appropriate**

_____ **Unacceptable**

The preceding text evaluation checklist and decision guide are based on the typical layout of most non-fiction text material. Hence, you may need to adjust the criteria somewhat if you are evaluating fictional material presented in literary anthology or workbook format. The checklist should not be interpreted as a rigid device for categorically accepting or rejecting text material. Rather, the more ways the textbook meets the given criteria, the better and more useful the book will be for your students. Additionally, the criteria are broad enough to allow for the exclusion of some items that are simply not present in a particular text. For example, item number eight would not be included in an evaluation of the text you are reading right now since pictures are not needed to understand the content. Simply code such items as "not-applicable" (N/A) and continue on. The following activity is designed to give you some practice in using the text evaluation checklist on the present text.

Activity

Directions: Using the Text Evaluation Checklist, rate this text as to its acceptability for a college-level classroom.

Introducing the Text

It is unlikely that any single content area text will be the most appropriate for all students in a course. The wide range in students' prior knowledge and subject interests practically insures that your text will be frustrating for some students and too easy for others. Assuming that your particular content area text survives the evaluation checklist and your own informed observations, there is something you can do to help students perceive the text as a familiar learning aid rather than as a threatening obstacle. You can conduct a *preview* of the text to acquaint students with the text they will be using. This simple procedure should be introduced early in the term. It will go a long way toward making students feel they can use the text effectively. Undoubtedly, many of us have had the experience of "discovering" by sheer chance, often half-way through the term, that our text contained a glossary of difficult vocabulary. The preview is designed to guide students to this and other text aids early in the term.

Conducting a Preview of the Text

The following activity should be conducted as a group task. The teacher reads each item on the preview and indicates its location. This procedure can also be used to collect information for item 20 on the text evaluation checklist (student response). The following guide will help you conduct a preview of the text in your content area.

Previewing Your Text

Name of subject _____

Title of textbook _____

_____

Author(s) _____

Author(s) qualifications (e.g., job experience, university degrees) _____

_____

Copyright date _____

Has the book been revised (brought up to date)? _____

1. *Prefaces, Forewords,* and *Introductions* contain essentially the same information. These lead-in comments give the author(s) a chance to talk about why the book was written and how it is organized. Often, a suggestion about how to read the book is provided.

   Read the *Preface (Foreword* or *Introduction).* In the space below, use your own words to explain what the *Preface* told you about your text.

   _____

   _____

   _____

   _____

2. The *Table of Contents* provides an early "road map" of the whole text. It gives a good indication of the learning aids which are provided in the text. Answer the following questions in your own words by referring to the *Table of Contents.*

   (1) Does the organization of topics in the book appear to be logical and easy to follow?

   _____

   _____

   (2) How many total pages are there in your text?

   _____

   (3) How complete do you think the treatment of the subject is in your book (i.e., very complete or only deals with a few aspects of the subject)?

   _____

   _____

   (4) Using the *Table of Contents,* see if your text contains each of the following learning aids. Answer *yes* if you find it, *no* if you don't.

   Glossary _____   Appendix _____   Bibliography _____   Index _____

3. The *Glossary* gives definitions of difficult technical terms used in the text. It is a valuable aid to understanding the vocabulary of a difficult subject. If your text has a *Glossary,* locate at least one difficult word supplied by your teacher and write the definition here.)

   _____

   _____

   _____

   _____

4. The *Appendix* provides additional information about a topic. An *Appendix* is located in the back of the book and contains information that supports and expands a chapter topic. If your text has an *Appendix* (or *Appendices*), write a list of some of the items you find there.

_____

_____

_____

_____

_____

_____

5. A *Bibliography* gives specific information about authors and books that were consulted during the writing of the text. Some of these books may be recommended as additional reading. The *Bibliography* is usually located at the end of the book (see the *Table of Contents* for its exact location), but it may follow each chapter. Locate the *Bibliography* in your text and write down three books you might want to read in addition to your text.

_____

_____

_____

_____

_____

_____

_____

6. The *Index* provides the fastest means for locating topic information and names of people referred to in the text. Locate the *Index* in your book. Study the *Index* and list two or three kinds of information you see there.

_____

_____

_____

_____

7. Many other textual aids, in addition to the *Preface, Table of Contents, Glossary, Appendix, Bibliography,* and *Index* are included in most texts. See if you can locate each of the following text aids (write YES if it's there; NO if it's not) and indicate in writing how each of these aids might help you understand the subject.

   (1) Questions at the beginning of the chapters

   _____

   _____

   (2) Objectives at the beginning of the chapters

   _____

   _____

   (3) Pictures

   _____

   _____

   (4) Illustrations or diagrams

   _____

   _____

   (5) Graphs

   _____

   _____

   (6) Maps

   _____

   _____

   (7) Words in italics, bold-faced words, large guide words

   _____

   (8) Pronunciation guide [e.g., paradigm (para dime)]

   _____

   (9) Footnotes

   _____

   (10) Headings

   _____

   (11) Marginal notes

   _____

   (12) Questions at the ends of chapters

   _____

(13) Summaries at the ends of chapters

_____

(14) Practice exercises

_____

(15) *Other*

_____

_____

Activity

Directions: Using this text as an example, conduct a preview. Did you find out anything that you were not aware of before?

In some cases, a teacher may feel it necessary to determine the extent of the students' knowledge about basic textbook elements before conducting a preview. The following exercise can also reinforce students' understanding of textbook learning aids. It can be used as a model to develop a similar activity in your own content area.

Directions: In column B you will find a brief description of the information contained in a particular textbook learning aid (listed in column A). See if you can match each textbook aid (column A) with its description (column B). Place the letter of the description on the line in front of the textbook aid to which it refers.

A.	B.
_____ 1. Index	A. Author discusses why the book was written and how to read it.
_____ 2. Table of Contents	B. The easiest place to locate topic information quickly.
_____ 3. Bibliography	C. Provides additional information about a topic.
_____ 4. Appendix	D. A "road map" of how the text is organized.
_____ 5. Preface	E. Provides definitions of difficult technical terms.
_____ 6. Copyright Date	F. Indicates when the book was published.
_____ 7. Glossary	G. A listing of what books were consulted in writing the text.

If your text should prove to be unacceptable for some of the students in your content class, there are a number of alternative approaches you can employ. For example, you might consider adopting multiple texts at varying levels of difficulty. Or you can use newspapers, resource speakers, demonstrations, simulations, and discussion groups. Finally, increasing the amount of guidance you provide students before, during, and after reading assignments should go a long way toward making the core text more understandable. Future chapters advance a variety of methods for helping students cope with difficult text material. Such methods range from individualizing assignments for some students to providing additional guidance in vocabulary development and comprehension.

Answers for Raygor Readability Formula

evaluation	1. The 100-word passage ends with this word.
5.1	2. The 100-word passage contains 5.1 sentences.
44	3. There are 44 words containing six or more letters in this sample.
PROF.	4. The dot on the graph that follows indicates that the text you are now reading is intended for college and professional audiences.

THE RAYGOR READABILITY ESTIMATE
Alton L. Raygor—University of Minnesota

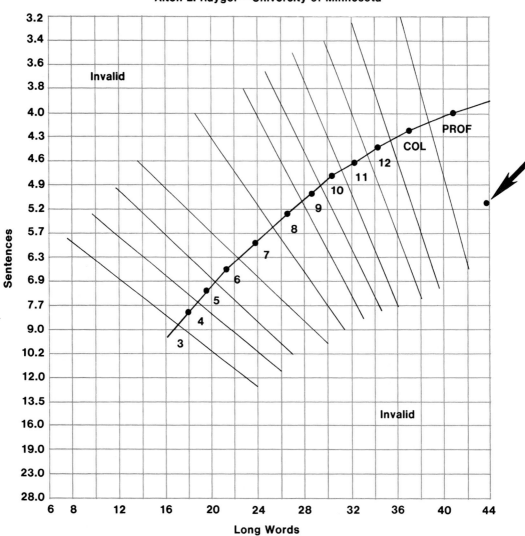

Summary

The present chapter has focused on quantitative and qualitative factors that combine to influence students' comprehension of text material. Quantitative factors are typically measured by readability formulas. An easily computed readability formula, the Raygor Readability Estimate, was described for classroom use. The inherent advantages and limitations of readability estimates were enumerated. More importantly, a number of qualitative factors that play a prominent role in students' comprehension of text material were described. Included among these factors are the text's organization and writing, and the students' prior knowledge and interest. A text evaluation checklist was introduced that encompasses both quantitative and qualitative factors. Finally, a procedure for introducing a text to students early in the term was described.

Now go back to the anticipation guide at the beginning of this chapter. React again to the statements as you did before, but this time record your answers in the column entitled "Reaction." Compare your responses with the ones you made earlier.

Miniprojects

1. Apply the Raygor Readability Estimate to a commonly used text in your content area.
2. Complete the text evaluation checklist for the same text you used in mini-project number one. Is the text appropriate for its intended grade level?

Additional Recommended Readings

Alvermann, D. E., & Dishner, E. K. (1986). The student connection: Content→students←materials. In E. K. Dishner, T. W. Bean, J. E. Readence, & D. W. Moore (Eds.), *Reading in the content areas: Improving classroom instruction* (2nd ed., pp. 104–112). Dubuque, IA: Kendall/Hunt Publishing Company.
   Discusses the match among content, students, and materials in promoting effective instruction in subject matter areas.

Klare, G. R. (1984). Readability. In P. D. Pearson (Ed.), *Handbook of reading research* (pp. 681–744). New York: Longman.
   Provides a comprehensive discussion and review of the literature on readability and readability formulas.

Singer, H. (1986). Friendly texts: Description and criteria. In E. K. Dishner, T. W. Bean, J. E. Readence, & D. W. Moore (Eds.), *Reading in the content areas: Improving classroom instruction* (2nd ed., pp. 112–128). Dubuque, IA: Kendall/Hunt Publishing Company.
   Describes text features that enhance or inhibit comprehension and provides an accompanying text evaluation checklist.

Zakaluk, B. L., & Samuels, S. J. (Eds.) (1988). *Readability: Its past, present, and future.* Newark, DE: International Reading Association.
   A series of readings on the role of readability in research and practice from its early years to predictions about its future.

References

Anderson, T. H., & Armbruster, B. B. (1984). Content area textbooks. In R. C. Anderson, J. Osborne, & R. J. Tierney (Eds.), *Learning to read in American schools: Basal readers and content texts* (pp. 193–226). Hillsdale, NJ: Erlbaum.

Baldwin, R. S., & Kaufman, R. K. (1979). A concurrent validity study of the Raygor readability graph. *Journal of Reading, 23,* 148–153.

Bean, T. W., Singer, H., Cowen, S., & Searles, D. (1987, December). *Acquiring concepts from biology text: A study of text-based learning aids and reader-based strategies.* Paper presented at the annual meeting of the National Reading Conference, St. Petersburg, FL.

Clewell, S. F., & Cliffton, A. M. (1983). Examining your textbook for comprehensibility. *Journal of Reading, 27,* 219–224.

Crismore, A. (1984). A message to authors about metadiscourse use in instructional texts. In J. A. Niles & L. A. Harris (Eds.), *Changing perspectives on research in reading/language processing and instruction* (pp. 66–74). Thirty-third Yearbook of the National Reading Conference. Rochester, NY: National Reading Conference.

Davison, A., & Kantor, R. N. (1982). On the failure of readability formulas to define readable texts: A case study from adaptations. *Reading Research Quarterly, 17,* 187–209.

Freebody, P., & Anderson, R. C. (1983). Effects of vocabulary difficulty, text cohesion, and schema availability on reading comprehension. *Reading Research Quarterly, 18,* 277–305.

Fry, E. (1977). Fry's readability graph: Clarification, validity, and extension to level 17. *Journal of Reading, 21,* 242–251.

Klare, G. R. (1974–1975). Assessing readability. *Reading Research Quarterly, 10,* 62–102.

Klare, G. R. (1984). Readability. In P. D. Pearson (Ed.), *Handbook of reading research* (pp. 681–744). New York: Longman.

Kretschmer, J. C. (1984). Computerizing and comparing the Rix readability index. *Journal of Reading, 27,* 490–499.

Marshall, N. (1979). Readability and comprehendability. *Journal of Reading, 22,* 542–544.

Nelson, J. (1978). Readability: Some cautions for the content teacher. *Journal of Reading, 21,* 620–625.

Palmatier, R. A., & Strader, S. S. (1977). Teacher performance in assessment of comparative reading difficulty of content materials. In P. D. Pearson (Ed.), *Reading: Theory, research, and practice* (pp. 60–62). Twenty-sixth Yearbook of the National Reading Conference. Clemson, SC: National Reading Conference.

Pearson, P. D. (1974–1975). The effects of grammatical complexity on children's comprehension, recall, and conception of certain semantic relations. *Reading Research Quarterly, 10,* 155–192.

Pearson, P. D., & Camperell, K. (1981). Comprehension of text structures. In J. T. Guthrie (Ed.), *Comprehension and teaching: Research reviews* (pp. 27–55). Newark, DE: International Reading Association.

Pepper, J. (1981). Following students' suggestions for rewriting a computer programming textbook. *American Educational Research Journal, 18,* 259–270.

Raygor, A. L. (1977). The Raygor readability estimate: A quick and easy way to determine difficulty. In P. D. Pearson (Ed.), *Reading: Theory, research, and practice* (pp. 259–263). Twenty-sixth Yearbook of the National Reading Conference. Clemson, SC: National Reading Conference.

Singer, H. (1986). Friendly texts: Description and criteria. In E. K. Dishner, T. W. Bean, J. E. Readence, & D. W. Moore (Eds.), *Reading in the content areas: Improving classroom instruction* (2nd ed., pp. 112–128). Dubuque, IA: Kendall/Hunt Publishing Company.

Teaching and Learning Strategies

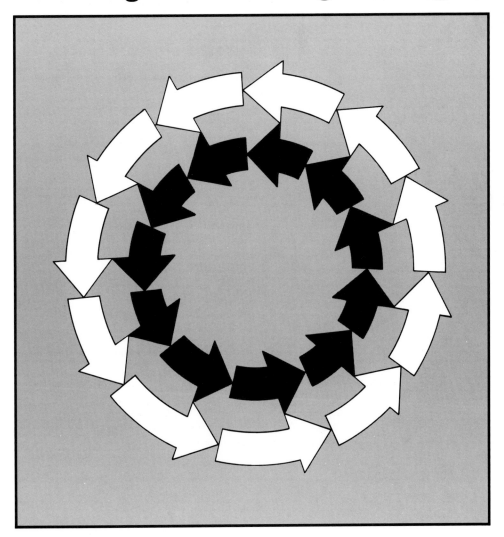

5

Anticipation   **Reaction**

_____ 1.   _____ 1. People either know a word or they don't.

_____ 2.   _____ 2. The meanings of words seldom change.

_____ 3.   _____ 3. The best way to teach vocabulary is to write words on the board and have students look up each word in the dictionary.

_____ 4.   _____ 4. Context clues are the most efficient method of unlocking the meanings of unfamiliar words.

_____ 5.   _____ 5. Content area vocabulary instruction should include virtually every new word which is introduced in a student's textbook.

Vocabulary Strategies

Rationale

Sometimes a mob might "grift" all day without "turning them over," but this is unlikely except in the case of a "jug mob" which takes a limited number of "pokes." Any pick-pocket who has on his person more than one wallet is something of a hazard both to himself and to the mob, for each wallet can count as a separate offense if he should be caught. Therefore, it is safer to have cash only. "Class mobs" usually count the money each time they "skin the pokes," one stall commonly is responsible for all of it, and an accounting in full is made at the end of the day. (Maurer, 1955, p. 194)

All groups of people, whether they be pickpockets, bridgeplayers, or educators, share special idioms and technical terminology which characterize the group. "Insiders" use this vocabulary freely and through it gain access to the collective knowledge of the group. Likewise, "outsiders" are identified as such and are restricted in their social and intellectual intercourse with the group due, in part, to their ignorance of its specialized vocabulary.

The task of the content teacher is to help students become "insiders" whose minds move with facility in the fields of science, English, social studies, or mathematics. To a large extent, this is accomplished by teaching them the technical terminology of each discipline. The following example, in which one student is explaining a math problem to another student, suggests the gravity of vocabulary acquisition in content areas.

"I don't remember what you call it, but it's like if you have three numbers—5,9, and 6—and you want to multiply them. It doesn't matter what order you do it in. You always get the same answer, 270."

This student apparently understands the concept of the commutative principle, the process of combining elements in such a manner that the order of multiplication is unimportant. Unfortunately, not knowing the word for this concept limits the student's capacity to utilize it. For instance, one might expect the student's reading or listening comprehension to be seriously impaired given the following textbook statement, ". . . The commutative principle applies to the preceding series of algebraic equations."

In all content areas, new concepts are sequentially introduced and defined in terms of concepts presented earlier. As students progress through texts, reading comprehension can diminish to the point of extinction if students have failed to master the words that symbolize important concepts, even when they have mastered the concepts themselves! In addition, research clearly indicates that teaching vocabulary can have a powerful and positive impact on reading comprehension (Stahl & Fairbanks, 1986). For this reason, considerable attention to vocabulary is fundamental to the purposes of every classroom teacher.

Chapter Objectives

After reading this chapter, you should be able to:

1. Discuss the pros and cons of various decoding strategies.
2. Justify direct vocabulary instruction as an essential component in your own content area.
3. Understand the general principles of vocabulary instruction.
4. Implement a variety of instructional strategies for introducing and reinforcing new vocabulary.

Graphic Organizer

The following graphic organizer is provided to give you some advance structure for new vocabulary and concepts that will be presented in this chapter.

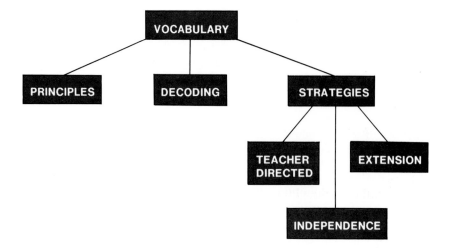

Words

For a variety of technical reasons, the concept of "word" is extremely difficult to define as a unit of language (Chomsky & Halle, 1968). Curiously, adult language users have little difficulty agreeing whether or not a particular sequence of sounds or symbols is a word. Bolinger (1968) accounts for this common sensitivity to the concept of "word" by defining words as prefabricated units which speakers know are not to be interrupted with fillers such as "um" or "uh" during speech. For instance, it would be quite natural for a speaker to say "The-workman-um-will-finish-um-Saturday," but not to say, "The-work-um-man-will-fin-um-ish Saturday."

Words may also be described in terms of semantic relationships; and, since the focus of this chapter is on the meanings of words rather than the sounds of words, the following definition is offered:

> A *word,* sometimes referred to as a lexical item, is a pattern of auditory or visual symbols which represent schemata (concepts).

The most important characteristic of this definition is the inclusion of *schemata,* because it suggests that word meanings—for individual persons—are in an endless state of flux. The concepts which words represent are constantly being modified by daily experiences during which: (1) new information is fitted into existing schemata, or (2) radically new or discordant information is accommodated through the modification of schemata. For instance, most people have internalized the concept of cat, but do they know all breeds by name? Could they correctly identify the habitats and mating customs of each? Could they name a type of cat which does not have retractable claws? If not, then there is a clear potential for the modification of their cat schemata.

The point is that the question of knowing the meaning of a word is not subject to a simple yes or no. There is always a need for qualification because a word is known or unknown, strange or unfamilar, to some "degree" which is determined by the richness of its known associations.

> The fact that children know the name of something does not mean they have an adequate concept of it. For example, a group of kindergarten children with whom one of the writers worked identified by name an anchor appearing on a ship in a picture. When questioned about the function of an anchor, individual children said it was used to catch big fish, drag things out of the ocean, clean the bay, stop the ships, start the ship, catch crabs. (Robinson, Strickland, & Cullinan, 1977, pp. 18–19)

Learning a new word (concept) requires more than a simple explanation because individual words are not simple isolated bits of information. Words are defined by the ways and the extent to which they are related to all other words. For instance, it would be possible to define the concept "anchor" as a device used on a boat or ship to keep the vessel stationary. However, such a definition does little to build an anchor schema that will allow a child to comprehend and use the word at will. A more effective strategy, one that builds a richer schema, might entail the following: (1) demonstrating the variation in sizes and shapes of anchors; (2) letting children touch or try to lift an anchor; (3) explaining how sailors get an anchor in and out of the water; (4) describing how an anchor keeps a ship from drifting; and (5) explaining why it is a good idea to keep boats from drifting.

On a more abstract level, knowing a word requires understanding its *connotations* as well as its *denotations,* sometimes referred to as *contextual* versus *definitional* knowledge. The denotation of a word is its broad meaning; in this sense, old/aged, end/finale, and surface/superficial are synonymous pairs of words. A word's connotations are its subtle shades of meaning and the specific contextual conditions in which it can occur. Connotations are meanings that differentiate among words which would otherwise be considered synonyms. Connotatively, "old" and "aged" are not synonyms because they cannot be used in the same contexts. For example, you can talk about "an old rock" but not "an aged rock" because "aged" connotes "living" as in "an aged woman." In this sense, there are probably few, if any, exact synonyms in English.

The following four sentences were written by students in a ninth grade English class. The sentences were constructed as part of an assignment in which the students were to write sentences and then make word substitutions based on an inspection of the classroom thesaurus. The italic words are those selected from the thesaurus.

1. The dirty old man went to church to ask God for *immunity.*
2. The car had a *putrefaction.*
3. It was clear from her actions that Susan was a fine *madam.*
4. It pays to be a *chivalrous* driver.

Aside from the amusing pictures which some of these sentences paint, what precisely is wrong with them? Denotatively, the words selected from the thesaurus are quite reasonable since pairs like immunity/forgiveness and breakdown/putrefaction are synonymous, or at least closely related in meaning. However, the members of each pair have different connotations that make them unacceptable substitutes in most contexts. For instance, putrefaction connotes a breakdown of a biological nature, and it is anomalous to use the word in reference to something made of such things as steel and rubber.

What we are suggesting is that the acquisition of new lexical items is sufficiently complex that vocabulary instruction should not be consigned to a mindless list of strange words followed by one-line definitions. If it is, the lack of examples and supporting contexts will doom students' understanding of new words to be both superficial and tentative.

Vocabularies

A *vocabulary* is a corpus of many thousands of words and their associated meanings. An individual's vocabulary may be analyzed in several ways. For instance, every person has a *receptive* vocabulary and an *expressive* vocabulary. The former refers to words that can be read and comprehended in print or heard and understood in spoken context. The latter refers to lexical items which a person can use properly when speaking or writing. In a sense, people have four vocabularies: *listening, reading, speaking,* and *writing;* and these categories are not mutually inclusive. Children usually begin school with respectable listening and speaking vocabularies but considerably less reading and writing vocabulary. On the other hand, the listening and reading vocabularies of literate adults—and secondary students— far outstrip their speaking and writing vocabularies. This is true because the schemata necessary to place words in proper contexts must be more fully developed than those required for recognizing word meanings when context has already been provided.

Finally, vocabularies may be classified as *technical* or *general*. Technical vocabulary refers to words such as "denouement," "secant," "Bull Market," "secede," etc., which are uniquely or usually related to individual academic disciplines. General vocabulary refers to words that are not specifically associated with any one teaching area, e.g., "germane," "astute," and "ubiquitous."

A second distinction between technical and general vocabulary involves "assimilation" and "accommodation," concepts introduced in chapter 2. Assimilation is a process in which new information is incorporated into existing schemata. Accommodation occurs when old schemata are modified or new schemata are created so that information can be assimilated (Wadsworth, 1971).

For the most part the acquisition of general vocabulary may be described as an assimilation process, whereas the learning of technical vocabulary more often requires some accommodation. By the time students are intellectually prepared to learn words such as "germane" or "astute," they already possess the concepts which those words symbolize, i.e., significant/relevant and alert/perceptive. Consequently, germane and astute are new, perhaps more efficient, labels for previously acquired concepts. Learning them does not demand a radical modification of existing schemata. In contrast, technical vocabulary present labels for unfamiliar concepts that must be accommodated by modifying extant schemata.

Content area teachers are primarily concerned with transmitting novel information and helping students develop new concepts, e.g., "Bull Market" or "secant." For this reason, the focus of the present chapter will be on the teaching of technical vocabulary and a general strategy for independently decoding unfamiliar words.

Decoding Unfamiliar Vocabulary

There are three basic coding processes: encoding, recoding, and decoding. *Encoding* is a process whereby thought or meaning is converted into a code. For example, if you ask a chef to prepare a medium rare steak, your thought (desire) is changed into a language code. You have encoded your gustatory craving for a nice hot pink fillet.

Recoding is a process in which one code is changed into another code. For instance, if your waiter writes down your message to the chef, he has recoded the oral language code into a written code.

Decoding is a process whereby a coded message is converted back into thought. In our continuing example, the chef reads the waiter's written message and decodes it, that is, comprehends how you want your steak prepared.

The process is similar in content area textbook communication. Authors encode their thoughts in a written form that their readers then decode. When the decoding process breaks down, comprehension suffers. In our opinion the major stumbling block to efficient decoding of text is students' inability to cope with words and concepts that are unfamiliar to them. There are four basic strategies for unlocking the meanings of unfamiliar words in text: phonics, morphemic analysis, context clues, and external references.

Phonics

Phonics refers to the rules that describe how sounds are represented by the letters in words. For example, in one syllable words with two internal vowels the first vowel is usually long (says its name) and the second vowel is usually silent: "fl*oa*t," "m*ea*t," "m*ai*l." Utilizing, such rules, which relate language sounds to graphic symbols, enables the reader to blend the sounds of letters together in order to identify words that are unfamiliar in print but that are familiar as part of the reader's natural language. What this means is that phonics is a useful strategy for teaching vocabulary only when the meaning of the word is already known to the reader. For this reason other decoding strategies are more useful in content area textbooks in which unfamiliar words are most often words that are not part of the students' expressive or receptive vocabularies.

Morphemic Analysis

When students encounter long words in print, it is valuable to break such words into more manageable parts. It is well known that a word part may have a meaning of its own. Such a word part is called a *morpheme*. A morpheme is the smallest unit of language which has an associated meaning; i.e., it possesses a definite meaning and cannot be subdivided into smaller units which have meaning. There are two types of morphemes, free and bound. A *free morpheme* can function alone as a word, e.g., "some" or "thing." *Bound morphemes* are those meaningful language units that occur only as attachments to words or other morphemes, e.g., "tele-," "-er," or "-cide." In essence, they are prefixes, suffixes, or roots. Just as a word may be a symbol that represents a schema in our knowledge structure, so may a word part or morpheme. Additionally, two or more morphemes may combine to give a combination of ideas, thus modifying a schema. For instance, "black" and "berry," two separate morphemes, may be combined to form a new or modified schema conveying a combination of meanings. Thus, *morphemic analysis* is a process by which readers can determine the meaning of an unfamiliar word by analyzing its component parts.

Attention to word parts to reveal the meanings of unfamilar words is a process that goes on all the time. For instance, if a reader encounters a word such as "patricide" in a contextual setting, the reader is likely to focus on the morphemes of the word, "partri-" and "-cide" to determine its meaning, particularly if the context is anomalous, or provides no clear interpretation. Such an anomalous context would be:

Robert has committed patricide.

Of course, the reader cannot perform such an analysis if the reader does not have prior knowledge of the two morphemes in "patricide." Yet because morphemic analysis focuses on meaning, it provides a more sensible approach to analyzing unfamiliar words than does phonics. Additionally, approximately 80 percent of the words listed in an English dictionary contain words which are composed of Latin or Greek morphemes. Consequently, a knowledge of these roots and affixes can be valuable in analyzing and then remembering the meanings of unfamiliar polysyllabic words.

Activity

Use your knowledge of morphemes to analyze the following unfamiliar polysyllabic word. Try to derive the meaning of it.

PNEUMONOULTRAMICROSCOPICSILICOVOLCANOCONIOSIS

Were you able to arrive at a definition without consulting a dictionary or did you "panic" because the word appears ominous? What you have encountered in this word is one of the longest words in the English language, yet one that readily lends itself to morphemic analysis. Perhaps the following context will help you come up with the definition:

Because of his proximity to Mount St. Helens, he contracted pneumonoultramicroscopicsilicovolcanoconiosis.

Using the context clues present in the sentence, in combination with your knowledge of morphemes, probably gave you the definition. The following word parts are present in the word:

Pneumono—related to the lungs
Ultra—transcending; super
Micro—small
Scopic—related to a viewing instrument
Silico—the mineral, silicon
Volcano—eruption in the earth from which molten rock, steam, and dust issue
Coni (konis)—dust
Osis—referring to a diseased condition

Thus, pneumonoultramicroscopicsilicovolcanoconiosis is a disease of the lungs caused by habitual inhalation of very fine silicon dust particles.

The authors are certainly not arguing that content teachers should have their students master lists of affixes and roots. This procedure is restrictive in that students memorize without meaningful context. Inserting information into long-term memory is best accomplished by making the information interesting and relevant—descriptors that hardly apply to lengthy lists of strange-looking morphemes.

In summary, what we are suggesting is that knowledge of morphemes has the potential for transfer to unfamiliar words that possess the same morphemes. Students should be taught to apply their knowledge of word parts to unfamiliar words they encounter. In this way they are encouraged to discover their own generalizations by intelligent inference or informed guessing. For instance, in the word you were asked to analyze in the beginning of this section, you may not have extracted the morpheme, "pneumon" and attached meaning to it directly. Rather, you may have associated the morpheme with the word "pneumonia" to arrive at a meaning for it. It is this type of learning process that the authors advocate.

Context Clues

All human experience is context dependent. Indeed, human behavior can hardly be interpreted without context. As an example, consider the question, "Is it OK for me to take my clothes off?" The answer obviously depends upon the context—at a nudist colony, yes; in church, no! Context is, therefore, a necessary and "natural" part of human functioning. Such is also the case in reading. For instance, if given the sentence, "Jo Ann loves her new, red _____ ," you would be able to supply a word in the blank even though no graphophonic information is present. Additionally, many investigators in reading education have also stressed the importance of readers' use of context in interpreting and verifying the meaning of words and sentences to be comprehended. Allington and McGill-Franzen (1980) suggest that the appropriate use of context leads to more effective processing and overall accuracy in recognizing unfamiliar words. It is in combination with readers' experiential background that the analysis of context provides meaning to the semantic subtleties of print.

To assess the value of context clues in decoding new vocabulary, we need to examine how context can supply meaning. There are three main types of *context clues:*

A. "Definition": The word is defined, usually in the same sentence. For example:

1. *Linguistics* is the scientific study of language.
2. *Uxoricide,* which means to murder one's wife, is the ultimate form of marital abuse.

B. "Description": The word is described by the context in such a way that the reader can take a good guess at its meaning. For example:

3. Because his approach to teaching seemed so *atavistic,* the students were always joking that their teacher must have been trained in a dungeon during the middle ages.
4. Their *vociferous* chatter made me wish I had ear plugs.

C. "Contrast": The word is compared with some other word or concept, often an opposite. For example:

5. Mike was *loquacious* while Susan said very little.
6. The popular girl was *comely* while the unpopular girl was homely.

Most textbooks rely on context clues when introducing new concepts. Generally, these new words are *italicized,* underlined, or written in **bold print** to call attention to the fact that a new word is being introduced. Typically, the context clue is some form of definition.

It is fairly obvious that context clues work in the sentences above, and researchers such as Quealy (1969) have found that students are capable of using such clues when they are presented. The real issue is whether or not sentences such as those in (B) and (C) above occur with sufficient frequency to make context clues a valid strategy for decoding unfamiliar words. Recent research based on the naturally occurring prose of novels, magazines, and textbooks strongly suggests that context clues are not nearly as useful for decoding unfamiliar words as has traditionally been assumed (Schatz & Baldwin, 1986). In three different experiments with high school students, subjects who were provided with contexts were no more successful in choosing or generating correct definitions than subjects who were given difficult words with no context at all. Moreover, in 24 percent of the items, such as (7) below, subjects without context performed better than subjects with context.

7. The wind cried and whisked in the brush, and the family went on monotonously, hour after hour. They passed no one and saw no one. At last, to their right, the *waning* moon arose, and when it came up the wind died down, and the land was still.

WANING
a. picturesque
b. brilliant
c. conspicuous
d. diminishing
e. everlasting

To illustrate this point, it is helpful to examine how words add meaning to sentences. In the diagrams below are two overlapping sets. Set A represents the meaning of an entire passage. Set B represents the meaning of a single word in the passage. Area 1 is the word's unique contribution of meaning to the passage. Area 2 is the overlap between the meaning of the total context and the meaning of the individual word; that is, area 2 represents the extent to which the meaning of the word is redundant with the meaning of the rest of the context. If the overlap is small, the word is contributing much information to the passage.

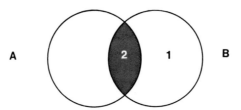

In other words, take the word out and the passage loses meaning, as in sentence (8) below. In contrast, if the overlap is great, then the meaning of the word is largely redundant and it contributes little information to the passage. Take the word out and the meaning of the passage is largely unaffected, as below, in sentence (9).

8. Rasputin's *necromancy* allowed him to rule the kingdom.

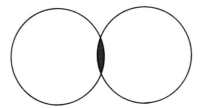

9. *Necromancy,* or sorcery, was once punishable by death.

The implication in this is that context clues only work well in the decoding process when the word in question is unimportant to the meaning of the passage (Finn, 1977–1978). Moreover, the Schatz and Baldwin (1986) study suggests that sentences such as (9) are relatively rare in comparison with the large numbers of unfamiliar words that students encounter in their texts. Since the major purpose of a decoding strategy is to promote comprehension during reading, we feel that context clues are less valuable than external references as an independent decoding strategy.

External References

An *external reference* is a source of information that falls outside the passage in which the unfamiliar word occurs. In this sense phonics, context clues, and morphemic analysis are internal sources of information, while textbook aids, dictionaries, encyclopedias, etc. are external.

Textbook aids are elements included in the text to help students with new vocabulary. When students come to an unfamiliar word, context clues and morphemic analysis usually will not be enough to decode its meaning. In most cases, references "outside" the passage must be used to find the meanings of the unknown words. The three most important references are the glossary, index, and dictionary.

A *glossary* is an alphabetized list of the technical words used in a textbook. With each word is the definition of the word as it is used in the book. For instance, the glossary in this textbook begins on page 281. Not all textbooks have glossaries, but those that do usually place the glossary at the back of the book. Sometimes authors put the glossary at the beginning or end of each chapter in the text.

When a textbook does not contain a glossary, the index is another good reference for finding word meanings. An *index* is an alphabetized list of important terms and topics included in the text. It is always located at the back of the text. Turn to page 289 and look at the index for this textbook. The index lists the page numbers in the text where information can be found on each topic. Frequently, the word for which a student is hunting will be defined in context on one of those pages. This is particular y true of technical vocabulary.

The Dictionary. When students need to find the meaning of a nontechnical word, they should use a dictionary. The standard word dictionary is undoubtedly the most commonly used of all reference tools. Unfortunately, it is also probably one of the most misunderstood and misused. Because the dictionary is used so widely, teachers have a tendency to assume that students know how to use a dictionary. This is a dangerous assumption. For example, one of the authors once asked a ninth grader in his English class to look up the word "embroil"." After a few minutes he returned to the student's desk only to find her moving her finger laboriously from entry to entry on page four of the *A's.* The student did not know that words in a dictionary are arranged alphabetically! This remarkable incident led the author to discover that half the class did not know what guide words were, and that over half did not know how to use the pronunciation key or choose from among the multiple definitions of a word.

If you want your students to use the dictionary, particularly as a means to verify the meanings of unfamiliar words in print, it might be well worth your time to diagnose their familiarity with this important book. The following guide words and entry are adapted from *Dictionary* (Halsey, 1977) and indicate the most common and important features of dictionaries.

Dictionary skills can be assessed informally by asking students to seek out and explain the various features of specific entries in the dictionary. This can easily be conducted as a group activity in which students must find an answer and then explain how they arrived at it. For example:

"Turn to page 253 of your dictionary and figure out how to pronounce the word '_____' (*daguerreotype* is written on the blackboard). Raise your hand when you have the answer, but be prepared to explain to the rest of the class how you got it."

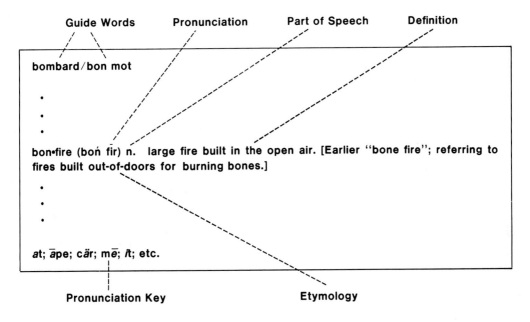

Once you have ascertained which dictionary features students need to practice, discuss them and then provide practice in identifying and interpreting those features. It is, of course, possible to create exercises on spirit masters. However, a simpler and more enjoyable activity entails having students compete with each other or with the clock to see how fast they can identify parts of speech, specific guide words, etymologies, and so on.

Activity

Directions: Create an activity for giving middle or secondary students practice in using one or more features of the dictionary.

A General Decoding Strategy for Textbooks

When students encounter an unfamiliar word as they are reading, they should first finish reading the sentence. If they determine the word is crucial for comprehension, we recommend that they rely heavily on external references, following these steps:

1. First decide whether the word is technical or general. When in doubt, assume the word is technical.
2. If the word is technical:
   a. Try the glossary first.
   b. Then try the index.
   c. Then try the dictionary.
3. If the word is general:
   a. Try the dictionary first.
   b. Then try the glossary.
   c. Then try the index.

4. After you have found a meaning for the word, check the meaning in the context of the sentence to make sure that the definition fits. This is particularly important when you use a dictionary. Context is critical as a verification procedure.

This strategy is recommended as a way for students to deal systematically and independently with unfamiliar words in print. The strategy concentrates on meaning since that is the task of students when they are reading textbook assignments. The strategy also avoids the pitfalls of haphazard or misleading guessing associated with context clues and morphemic analysis. Those who are knowledgeable in a subject area do not need to guess at the meanings of important words; those who are less knowledgeable should not.

Principles for Effective Vocabulary Instruction

If there is one thing which contributes most heavily to the burdens of learning technical vocabulary, it is the simple lack of direct instruction. Teachers frequently assume that students will automatically assimilate new words just because they are introduced in textbook assignments. This is a mistake. Consequently, almost any kind of direct instruction is better than none at all. The following principles should be considered in conjunction with the specific teaching strategies presented later in the chapter.

Be An Enthusiastic Model of Vocabulary Use

Reach out to your students and make them believe that you believe vocabulary development is something more than a dead paragraph from your teacher's syllabus. Let them see you using a dictionary once in awhile, and make an effort to use words you expect the students to learn. In addition to exemplifying new terms in appropriate verbal contexts, you will be demonstrating that they have some practical value. Nothing will facilitate the acquisition of vocabulary more than the enthusiasm which you convey to students.

Make Vocabulary Meaningful

Vocabulary instruction should have a long-term impact upon individual powers of communication and concept development. A vocabulary program that encourages students to squeeze the definitions for twenty words into a temporary memory store so that they can pass Friday's quiz is a waste of time. New words and their meanings must be stored in long-term memory if they are to add to the students' powers of perception and articulation. As we pointed out in chapter two, placing information in long-term memory is difficult unless the information is meaningful in terms of prior knowledge. Consequently, new words should be: (1) defined in multiple contexts; (2) drawn from reading or other experiences immediately pertinent to the student; and (3) defined in terms and with examples that clearly fall within the boundaries of the students' prior knowledge. In general, the greater the quantity of meaningful associations that teachers can tie to new words, the greater the likelihood that the students will remember and use them.

Reinforce Vocabulary

Give students an opportunity to use their new words as they read, write, speak, and listen. There is no substitute for meaningful practice. Research shows that drill, practice, and multiple exposures to a new word in various contexts will improve word knowledge and comprehension (Stahl & Fairbanks, 1986).

Be Eclectic

There are as many good ways to teach vocabulary as there are creative teachers, and probably no single one is best. However, any method can become boring if it is overused. A successful vocabulary program will employ a variety of methods. Moreover, research indicates that a balanced program emphasizing both contextual and definitional strategies works best (Stahl & Fairbanks, 1986).

Teaching new vocabulary prior to reading assignments is a direct application of the *readiness principle*. Readiness refers to the mental state in which an individual is prepared to derive maximum meaning from a learning situation, with a minimum of frustration. Pre-teaching content area vocabulary is a readiness aid that gives students direction and purpose for reading.

Introducing vocabulary facilitates reading comprehension by reducing the number of unfamiliar words in textbook reading assignments. If new terms are introduced in a meaningful and interesting manner, this will reinforce vocabulary, generate enthusiasm for the reading task, and provide background information that will help students relate what they know to the content of the text. The following strategies for introducing vocabulary are adaptable to reading assignments in most content areas.

Troubleshoot reading assignments for the students by identifying important words that are likely to engender confusion as they read. Then introduce those words before they begin their reading assignments. By introducing difficult terminology, the teacher will facilitate the retention of pivotal vocabulary, provide students with critical prior knowledge of the content they are being asked to assimilate, and improve reading comprehension by reducing the number of alien words in the text.

In most subject areas, reading assignments introduce so many unfamiliar words that it is impossible to teach all of them. Use the following criteria to select the words that seem most critical:

1. Restrict your selections to words that are critical to comprehending the selection.
2. Choose words that define key concepts.
3. Choose terms that you might include on a test.
4. Choose words that have a new technical meaning in addition to a general, familiar meaning, e.g., "complementary" angles as opposed to "complimentary" actions in social situations.
5. Ignore terms that will be of little or no use once a student has passed the test.
6. Don't spend time reinforcing the meanings of words just because they appear in italics. Words should also meet the criteria in 1–4 above.

Teacher-Directed Strategies

In addition to pre-teaching strategies, it is also good teaching to reinforce new vocabulary after reading. Reinforcing new vocabulary allows students to review the words that you introduced before reading and that they encountered during reading. In essence, reinforcement makes the words more meaningful to students. The following teacher-directed strategies for introducing and reinforcing vocabulary are adaptable to reading assignments in most content areas.

Contextual Redefinition

The authors recommend a strategy developed by Cunningham, Cunningham, and Arthur (1981) for its simplicity and ease for content teachers. To illustrate contextual redefinition, define each of the following words using only your own prior knowledge.

1. Carapace _____

2. Nonsectarian _____

3. Insipid _____

Were you able to write a definition without going to a dictionary? If not, read the following sentences and see if they help you with the definition of the words. After you write a definition, check the dictionary for your definition.

1. Without its *carapace,* the turtle would be subject to certain death from its enemies or the elements.
2. Although he was a believer in God, he had a *nonsectarian* attitude toward religion.
3. His teaching lacked spirit. He had presented his lesson in a dull manner, failing to challenge or stimulate the students. The teacher knew he had made an *insipid* presentation.

Did the sentences help you with the meaning of the unknown words? If they did, you were utilizing the surrounding context as clues to the meaning of the words. *Contextual redefinition* is a strategy that introduces new vocabulary in rich contexts that help to define words and facilitate memory by giving the words meaningful associations. The process is composed of the following five steps:

1. **Select Unfamiliar Words.** Identify those words that may present trouble to your students and that may be central to understanding the important concepts they will encounter in their reading.
2. **Write a Sentence.** An appropriate context for each word should be written with clues to its meaning. The categories of clues discussed earlier should be utilized in the writing of these sentences. In the sample sentences provided, carapace could be identified by previous experience, nonsectarian by comparison and contrast, and insipid by description or mood. If such a context already exists in the text material the students are about to read, it is appropriate to use that in lieu of creating a new context for it.
3. **Present the Words in Isolation.** Using the chalkboard or a transparency, ask students to provide you with a meaning for the unfamiliar word. Some guesses may be "off-base" or even humorous, but students should be asked to come to a concensus about the best meaning.
4. **Present the Words in a Sentence.** Using the sentence you developed previously, now present the word in context. Again, ask the students to provide a meaning for the unfamiliar word. It is important that students who volunteer definitions defend their guess by providing the rationale for it. In this way poor readers will be able to experience the thinking processes of other students and how they arrive at meaning. In essence, students can act as models for each other.
5. **Dictionary Verification.** A volunteer or volunteers can look up the word in the dictionary to verify the guesses offered by the class.

The students will gain several benefits from this strategy. First, they will realize that trying to identify an unfamiliar word by simply focusing on the word as an isolated element is frustrating, that it makes for haphazard guessing, and that it probably is not very accurate. They will be prompted to develop more reliable methods for determining meaning. Second, students will become actively involved in a more profitable process of discovering new words rather than in the rote memorization of them. Finally, the dictionary is cast in its most appropriate role—that of a tool used to verify the meanings of unfamiliar words by selecting the definition that is syntactically and semantically acceptable in a particular context.

Morphemic Analysis Strategy

The following strategy is recommended because it capitalizes on what students already know, i.e., it proceeds from the known to the unknown. Basically, the strategy is an analytical approach in which known, meaningful parts of familiar words are used to transfer their meanings to parts of unfamiliar words. The following steps should be used in teaching this strategy:

1. **Select Unfamiliar Words.** From the students' reading, identify those words that may be troublesome or central to conceptual understanding and that lend themselves to morphemic analysis. Utilize the author's context or one you construct when presenting the words.
2. **Identify Words with Identical Morphemes.** Similarly constructed words must be identified so the student may associate the new to the known. For example, with the word "matricide," you should identify words such as "maternal," "matriarch," "homicide," and "suicide." The same procedure may be used with affixes.
3. **Present the Unknown Words.** Morphemes can best be taught if they are presented in an interesting format and if real words are used that, when analyzed, reinforce the meaning of the root or affix in question. Consider the following sample lesson:

Teacher: On the board, I have written some words which are associated with the word "matricide." Let's see what we already know about these words.

Matricide seemed to pervade this ancient culture.

Maternal	Homicide
Maternity	Suicide
Matriarch	Insecticide

Student A: The words on the left begin like matricide and the ones on the right end like it.

Teacher: Very good! The words do have some parts in common. What else do we know about these common word parts?

Student B: All the words on the right have to do with killing—bugs or people.

Student C: Homicide means to kill people and suicide means to kill yourself.

Teacher: Good! So what part means to kill?

Students: The last part—cide!

Teacher OK! So what about the words on the left?

Student D: I think maternal has something to do with babies.

Student E: It does! Women have babies in the maternity ward in the hospital.

Teacher: Does matriarch have something to do with babies?

Student F: No, that's a woman who heads the family. You know, the mother.

Student G: And maternity is about mothers, too!

Teacher: OK, so what part means mother?

Students: The first part—matri-!

Teacher: So what does matricide mean in this sentence?

Students: Killing your mother! Those people killed their mothers.

Teacher: Good! Let's check the dictionary to see if we're right.

4. **Dictionary Verification.** A volunteer or volunteers can look up the word in the dictionary to verify the guesses offered by the class.

The Graphic Organizer

A *graphic organizer* (Earle & Barron, 1973) is a visual aid which defines hierarchical relationships among concepts. It lends itself particularly well to the teaching of technical vocabulary (Moore & Readence, 1984).

The graphic organizer may be used in a variety of ways. It may be used as an introductory strategy, as exemplified by the organizers at the beginning of each chapter in this text. Such usage is designed to provide relational guides to the prose that follows them. Graphic organizers may also be used as a post-reading technique to reinforce and summarize. Additionally, the graphic organizer is one strategy that can be used in the same lesson to enhance both readiness and recall of material (Readence & Moore, 1979). In all cases, the graphic organizer can be an excellent mechanism for defining related concepts. The following steps are recommended for generating graphic organizers.

1. **Concept Identification.** An analysis of the content is undertaken to identify all new terms and concepts that will be introduced in the reading assignment. Since there will often be a large number of these terms and concepts, it will save time simply to mark them in your own text. The following list was derived from chapter two, "The Behavior of Matter," in *Modern Science: Man, Matter, and Energy* (Blanc, Fischler, & Gardner, 1967):

Structure of matter	Natural elements	Electrons
Elements	Positive electrical charge	Protons
Compounds	Negative electrical charge	Neutrons
Metals	Nucleus	Electron shell
Nonmetals	Orbits	Energy levels
Atomic theory of matter	Law of definite or constant	Molecule
Atoms	proportions	Electrolysis
Mixtures	Chemical combinations	Inert gases
Physical combination	Particles	

2. **Concept Selection.** In order to prevent the organizer from being overly complex, it is critical to prune the initial list until it consists only of superordinate concepts, i.e., those that are most important or most essential to the integrity of the reading selection. The organizer is supposed to supplement the reading assignment, not replace it. Once the list has been reduced, subclassify the remaining terms in an informal outline.

    Structure of matter
        Chemical combinations
            Compounds
            Molecules
            Elements
        Natural elements
            Metals
            Nonmetals
        Physical combinations
            Mixtures
                Compounds
                Elements

3. **Diagram Construction.** Arrange the terms in a tree diagram which reflects the structure established in Step 2.

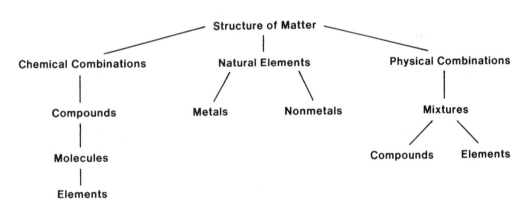

4. **Initial Evaluation.** Once you have created the organizer, step back and evaluate it. Does the organizer accurately convey the concepts you wish to teach? If not, "massage" the diagram until you are satisfied. One of the advantages of the graphic organizer is that it helps teachers to organize and clarify their own purposes.

    In addition to accuracy, consider the complexity of the diagram. Students can be overwhelmed if the visual display is too complicated. Under such conditions it may be desirable to present the organizer piece-by-piece.

5. **Organizer Presentation.** The physical presentation of the organizer is unimportant. Dittoed handouts, a permanent poster, overhead transparency, or chalkboard may be used as the teacher's resources dictate. The time required for the presentation will vary depending upon the complexity of the organizer and the extent to which the concepts in

question are unfamiliar to students. Begin the presentation with a general explanation of the purpose of the organizer and an explanation of how a tree diagram works. Talk students through the organizer, explaining each term, encouraging student questions and discussion, and indicating the ways in which terms are related to each other. In so doing you will be developing vocabulary, improving reading comprehension, and enriching schemata in ways which will make subject matter more meaningful to students.

Activity

Directions: Using the following words, create a graphic organizer. Be prepared to justify your arrangement:

Vertebrate	Mammal	Invertebrate
Snake	Grasshopper	Reptile
Cockroach	Crustacean	Aardvark
Animal	Whale	Insect
Lobster	Shrimp	Crocodile

Preview in Context

The *preview in context* is an informal discovery procedure for teaching new vocabulary, and it draws its strength from students' prior knowledge and the analysis of the immediate contexts in which words occur. The method is simple, requires minimal teacher preparation, deals with words that are relevant to current reading assignments, and is helpful in teaching students to resolve and remember the meanings of new words. The present procedure is similar to the context strategy presented earlier, except that the preview in context strategy utilizes a question and answer sequence. The preview in context is a four-step procedure.

1. **Preparation.** Select vocabulary from a passage or chapter that students will soon read. Choose words that are both important and likely to engender confusion as students read. Present only a few words at one time to prevent the lesson from becoming tedious.

2. **Establishing context.** Direct students to each word and its surrounding context. Read the passage aloud to the students as they follow along in their own texts. Then, have students read the passage silently.

3. **Specifying Word Meaning.** Use the questioning procedure which will help students identify the probable meaning of the word in its existing context, as in the following example:

   1. The "culpable" actions of the driver resulted in a short jail sentence and the loss of his license.

   Teacher: What does the sentence tell you about the word "culpable?"
   Student A: I guess the driver did something bad.
   Teacher: What do you suppose he did?
   Student B: He probably got drunk and ran over someone.
   Teacher: How should he be treated?
   Student C: He should be punished.
   Teacher: Then what might a culpable action be?
   Student D: Something you should get punished for.

4. **Expanding Word Meanings.** After students understand the meaning of the word in its given context, extend their understanding by briefly discussing antonyms, synonyms, or alternative contexts for the word. Such discussions will develop schemata for words and insure that students will recognize their meanings when they appear in other contexts. For example:

Teacher: Can you name other actions which we would consider culpable?
Students: Hitting a teacher, robbing a bank, not doing your homework, cheating on your income tax, smoking in school.
Teacher: Look at how "culpable" is used in your book. Are there any words we could substitute that would make the sentence mean about the same thing?
Students: Criminal, punishable, illegal.

Word Origins (Etymologies)

Introductory strategies for vocabulary will be successful to the extent that they are interesting and build meaningful schemata. Etymologies offer a colorful means of helping students remember word meanings. This is especially true for social studies and English where large numbers of relevant words have interesting etymologies.

The *etymology* of a word is its history, where it originated, and how it came to be a part of the language. Language is not a static feature of human behavior, all languages are in a constant state of change. Grammar mutates from one form to another; lexical items become popular and then fall into disuse, e.g., "groovy,"; and the meanings of words change, too. Every word that is now a part of the English language has a past, a present, and a future. Many word histories are quite interesting and can add flavor to an otherwise banal vocabulary lesson.

The etymological portion of a dictionary entry follows the pronunciation guide and part of speech and is enclosed in bold face brackets, although some dictionaries don't include any etymological information at all. The following example is the more colorful portion of the etymology for the word "chauvinism" taken from *Webster's New Collegiate Dictionary:*

[F "chauvinisme," fr. Nicolas "Chauvin" fl 1815 F soldier of excessive patriotism and devotion to Napoleon]

The *F* is an abbreviation for "French," *fr.* stands for "from," and *fl* is an abbreviation of a Latin word which means "flourished about." In addition to its interesting origin, chauvinism provides an example of how word meanings change over time. Originally, chauvinism referred to excessive patriotism or loyalty to a cause or creed. However, in recent years the meaning of the word has narrowed so that it refers primarily to men who are so loyal to their sex that they have condescending or disparaging attitudes toward women, i.e., "male chauvinist pig."

Other sources of word histories are books that provide more complete story lines. The following etymology of the word "berserk" is quoted from *Thereby Hangs a Tale: Stories of Curious Word Origins* (Funk, 1950).

In Norse mythology there was a famous furious fighter who scorned the use of heavy mail, entering battle without armor. His only protection was the skin of a bear fastened over one shoulder. From this he became known as "berserk," or "bear shirt." It was said of him that he could assume the form of a wild beast, and that neither iron nor fire could harm him, for he fought with the fury of a beast of the forest and his foes were unable to touch him. Each of his twelve sons, in turn, also carried the name "berserk," and each was as furious a fighter as the father. From these Norse heroes, it came to be that any person so inflamed with the fury of fighting as to be equally dangerous to friend and foe, as was that legendary family when engaged in battle, was called "berserk" or "berserker." (p. 48)

We submit that few students could forget the word "berserk" if it were introduced in conjunction with the story of Bear Shirt! This is a clear example of how rich and meaningful association can facilitate the learning of new words.

With advanced students it may be useful to have them check the etymologies of words in a dictionary. However, the numerous abbreviations, references to classical languages, and clipped versions of the histories may rob interest from otherwise interesting stories. For this reason, dictionary etymologies may be more useful as sources of information that teachers may incidentally insert into vocabulary presentations.

Not all words have flashy histories, and we are not recommending that the etymology of every new word be explored with students. Nevertheless, tossing one or two into a lesson is an excellent means of building interest and promoting recall. Collections of word histories are standard volumes in most secondary school libraries and can be found in the card catalogue under the headings *English Language* or *Etymologies*.

Activity

Directions: The following words, listed by content area, have interesting word origins. Select one of the lists and use an unabridged dictionary, an etymological dictionary, or a book on interesting word origins to determine their histories. Describe how you might work one or more of these words into a lesson in your own content area.

Science	**Social Studies**	**English**
alkali	assassin	anecdote
barnacle	ballot	dumbbell
cobalt	boycott	enthrall
crayfish	filibuster	fib
hurricane	indenture	gossip
larva	lynch	quixotic
nicotine	senate	sarcasm
parasite	sinecure	tragedy

List-Group-Label Lesson

The *list-group-label lesson* (Taba, 1967) is a classification technique similar to the graphic organizer in that it emphasizes word relationships. This type of lesson enables teachers to activate students' prior knowledge about a topic before they read about it. It can also actively engage students in the review process and allow them to see how other students associate and organize content area terminology (Bean, Inabinette, & Ryan, 1983). The following example illustrates the use of list-group-label as a postreading activity.

1. **Topic Selection.** After students have read a chapter or unit, select a topic that is comprised of multiple sets of related terms from the chapter. If the topic is a good one, you should be able to visualize the kinds of subgroupings and labels which students will create. As an example, we have chosen the topic "People and Places During the Civil War." The topic is based on "Brothers in Conflict" from *The Free and the Brave* (Graff, 1972). Following a unit on the Civil War, one would expect this particular topic to elicit the names of famous battles, generals, political leaders, etc.

2. **List Procedure.** Deriving the list is an enjoyable group activity. Begin by writing the topic on the blackboard and telling students that they will be reviewing important terminology. Have students volunteer any terms they can think of that fall under the topic heading. As each term is identified, write it on the board. Continue this procedure until students run out of observations or until you are satisfied that you have elicited as many terms as students can reasonably be expected to subclassify. Then, have students examine the list silently. If you feel that your students will have difficulty recalling important terms, you may ask leading questions or you may even eliminate step two by preparing the list in advance on the blackboard or on a ditto. The following list represents one possibility for the topic "People and Places During the Civil War."

People and Places During the Civil War

Georgia	Antietam	Texas
Grant	Pickett	Kansas
Maine	Gettysburg	Iowa
Pennsylvania	Vermont	Goodyear
Lee	Alabama	Burnside
Davis	North Carolina	Howe
Shiloh	South Carolina	Meade
Virginia	Borden	New York
Mississippi	Vicksburg	McCormick
Ohio	Sherman	McClellan

3. **Group and Label.** Have students reorganize the list into smaller lists of items which have something in common. Each of these sublists should then be given a label. Students may work individually or in small groups to reorganize and label the words. The lists below represent some possible groups and labels (but not all possible groups) from the present example.

Union Generals	**Battles**	**Inventors**
Grant	Shiloh .	Borden
Sherman	Antietam	Goodyear
Burnside	Gettysburg	Howe
Meade	Vicksburg	McCormick
McClellan		

Northern States	Southern States	Things Related to Gettysburg
Pennsylvania	Georgia	Pennsylvania
Ohio	Virginia	Lee
Vermont	Mississippi	Pickett
Kansas	Alabama	Meade
Iowa	North Carolina	
New York	South Carolina	
	Texas	

4. **Discussion.** It is worth the time it takes to have students explain their classifications; they may have some interesting observations. For instance, in contrast to the obvious groupings above, students might choose to list Civil War personalities on the basis of how "successful" they were.

Let students place their labeled subgroups on the board until they have exhausted all unique combinations. Students should have the opportunity to explain the rationales behind their lists, and the class should be able to comment on the accuracy and the completeness of each list. The teacher can, of course, footnote student comments, ask leading questions, and suggest alternative classifications.

Activity

Directions: Imagine that you have just finished teaching a series of units on human physiology, e.g., parts of the body. Describe how you would conduct an appropriate list-group-label lesson with your class. Be sure to include the following:

1. 20–30 terms likely to be elicited from students;
2. Probable groups and labels for those terms.

Semantic Mapping

A *semantic map* (Heimlich & Pittelman, 1986; Johnson & Pearson, 1984) is a diagram that groups related concepts; it combines the grouping activity of the list-group-label lesson with the structure of the graphic organizer. Semantic maps may be used as pre- or post-reading exercises that reinforce new vocabulary and help students relate their prior knowledge to new experiences and concepts. You and your students can construct a semantic map using the following steps:

1. Select an important word or topic from the lecture or reading assignment. This example is based on *Disastrous Volcanoes* (Berger, 1981). The word in this case will be "volcano."
2. Write the word (volcano) on the chalkboard or overhead projector.

3. Assign students to write down as many related words as they can think of, from their own experiences or from their reading of the text. In this case we will assume that students have read the text.

Vesuvius	Vulcanian	Pompeii
Mount St. Helens	cataclysm	lava
ash	magma	plate tectonics
earthquake	ring of fire	vent
conduit	volcanic bombs	gas
blocks	tsunami	explosions
shield volcano	plug	Krakatoa
pressure	hell	terrifying

4. Organize the words into an octopus-like diagram as in this semantic map.

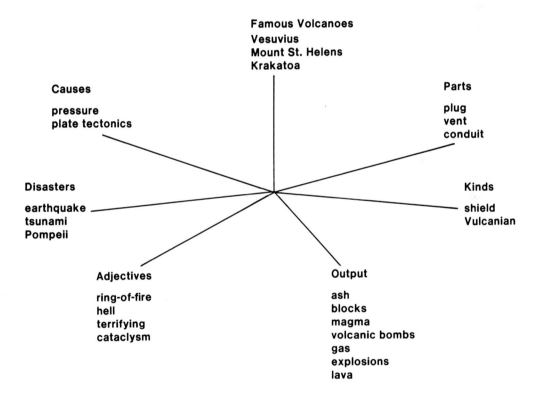

5. Students share words while you write them on the board. As new categories emerge, give the map new arms or add categories of your own. The diagram itself can be as simple or as complex as you desire.

6. Have students give names to the various categories or break categories into subcategories.

> Famous Volcanoes
> Parts of Volcanoes
> Adjectives That Describe Volcanoes
> Causes of Volcanoes
> Volcanic Output
> Related Disasters
> Kinds of Volcanoes

7. Johnson and Pearson emphasized that the most important step in this activity is the discussion and questioning activities that accompany the diagram. For example:
   a. Why are volcanoes considered disastrous?
   b. Which do you think was the all-time most disastrous volcano?
   c. Why is "ring of fire" a good name?
   d. In what ways are Mauna Loa and Vesuvius different? How are they the same?
   e. Tell what it would have been like to be on the island of Krakatoa in 1883.
   f. "Mark, imagine that you are Krakatoa. Susan, imagine that you are Mt. St. Helens. Now, each of you try to convince the other that you are the world's greatest volcano."

Feature Analysis

Feature analysis (Anders & Bos, 1986; Baldwin, Readence, & Ford, 1981; Johnson & Pearson, 1984) is a procedure that can help students make fine discriminations among concepts. With respect to general vocabulary the procedure works well for teaching word connotations. With respect to the technical vocabulary of the sciences, feature analysis can summarize distinctive ways in which related concepts are similar and different. We recommend the following steps:

1. **Category Selection.** The category should be one which consists of two or more items that are similar. Such categories could be things like kinds of animals, elements, foods, famous historical characters, or words that have the same denotation but different connotations.
2. **List Category Terms.** Place the terms along the left hand side of the blackboard or overhead transparency. Try not to use a large number of items the first time you use the procedure. In this case we will illustrate some of the similarities and differences among the planets in our solar system.

Mercury
Venus
Earth
Mars
Jupiter
Saturn
Uranus
Neptune
Pluto

3. **List Features.** Place the features that will be used to describe the terms (planets) across the top of the blackboard. Students may select the features or you may do it yourself. If you ask the students to provide the features, be prepared to give them plenty of hints and directions.

Category: Planets

	Hot	Cold	Big	Small	Rings	Life	Moons
Mercury							
Venus							
Earth							
Mars							
Jupiter							
Saturn							
Uranus							
Neptune							
Pluto							

4. **Complete Feature Chart.** Students should be guided through the matrix as they indicate whether or not each category item possesses a given feature. This can be done individually, in a group, or category item by item. A plus ($+$) shows that the category item has a feature. A minus ($-$) indicates that the category item does not have the feature. Every category item must have a plus or a minus for every feature; there should be no blank spots. Students will sometimes argue over a feature. This is good as long as the debate is well organized. In general, a plus sign indicates that a category item "usually" or "mostly" has the feature. The presence of two minuses can indicate a third category. For example, if a planet is neither large nor small, then it is probably medium sized.

Category: Planets

	Hot	Cold	Big	Small	Rings	Life	Moons
Mercury	$+$	$-$	$-$	$+$	$-$	$-$	$-$
Venus	$+$	$-$	$-$	$-$	$-$	$-$	$-$
Earth	$-$	$-$	$-$	$-$	$-$	$+$	$+$
Mars	$-$	$-$	$-$	$+$	$-$	$-$	$+$
Jupiter	$-$	$+$	$+$	$-$	$+$	$-$	$+$
Saturn	$-$	$+$	$+$	$-$	$+$	$-$	$+$
Uranus	$-$	$+$	$+$	$-$	$+$	$-$	$+$
Neptune	$-$	$+$	$+$	$-$	$+$	$-$	$+$
Pluto	$-$	$+$	$-$	$+$	$-$	$-$	$+$

5. **Explore The Matrix.** The final step is to have the students make observations about the category items. Give students an opportunity to make generalizations on their own. However, questions and hints may be necessary. For example, here are some questions that can be answered based on the information in the feature matrix. The questions are ordered from simple to complex:
   a. Which planets are the hottest?
   b. Which planets have rings?

c. In what way is Neptune different from Uranus?

d. What makes Earth unique among the planets?

e. Which planet is most like Earth? Why?

An enterprising student might argue that Mercury, because it has no atmosphere and doesn't rotate in its orbit around the sun, is half cold and half hot, in which case Mercury should be marked "+ hot" and "+ cold." This sort of reasoning should be welcomed, along with divergent comments, changes in categories, and other student interactions. When conducted in a thoughtful and flexible manner, feature analysis is a good way to build schemata and reinforce vocabulary.

Clues and Questions

This procedure is designed to help students review technical vocabulary (Bean, 1978). What makes *Clues and Questions* interesting is the fact that students provide the questions as well as the answers.

The teacher begins by collecting content area vocabulary that students should review. Each is typed on a notecard and placed in a shoebox or card file. Students randomly select several of these cards. Their task is to write questions whose answers are the words on each card.

The teacher encourages the students to use the textbook index to find where their vocabulary words are introduced and used. In addition, the teacher provides examples of different kinds of questions and clues, e.g., definition, analogy, comparison-contrast, context (see example below). As students finish writing questions, the teacher checks them for clarity and accuracy and then has the student print them on the vocabulary card directly below the word.

Molecule

1. _____ is to "compound" as "atom" is to "element."

2. What is the smallest unit of a compound which retains all the characteristics of that compound?

3. Two hydrogen atoms and one oxygen atom make one _____ of water.

When the vocabulary cards have been completed, the class is subdivided into small groups with each group having a portion of the vocabulary cards. One student shows a card to the others in the group, but does not look at the card. Each of the other students asks a question or supplies a clue until the word is identified. The activity proceeds in "round robin" fashion until the cards have been exhausted, at which point exchange cards and the clue sessions begin anew.

As a vocabulary builder, the clues and questions procedure has a number of strengths. First, allowing students to create their own questions for a game gives them a novel purpose for using the text. Second, students will benefit from trying to write clear and meaningful questions. And third, participating in the vocabulary review itself will enlarge and reinforce students' technical vocabularies.

Strategies for Vocabulary Independence

It is essential that students develop strategies that will continue to serve them when they do not have teachers to guide them whenever they encounter a new vocabulary word. In other words, students need to have their own repertoire of strategies to help them learn new words independently. In this section we describe four strategies that are relatively easy for students to learn and use across various content areas. However, as with any learning strategy, students will need to be shown how to apply them when reading and learning from text.

Keyword Method

The *keyword method* is a mnemonic strategy, i.e., a systematic procedure designed to aid memory, that is perhaps the best documented strategy for helping students remember new vocabulary (e.g., Pressley, Levin, & McDaniel, 1987; Roberts & Kelly, 1985). The technique is relatively simple and involves translating an unfamiliar word into a familiar word or phrase that (1) sounds like part of the unfamiliar word and (2) has an interesting visual image that is somehow related to the meaning of the new word. For example, for the word "licentious," the keyword could be "license-to-touch." In this case one might picture a dirty old man standing in line waiting to purchase a license that would allow him to translate all of his lecherous thoughts into deeds.

The keyword method can be a lively group activity as well as a technique that students can use independently to remember the meanings of new and difficult vocabulary. The steps for teaching the keyword technique are simple and straightforward:

1. Give students examples of keywords that you have created:

New Word	Keyword	Visual Image
potable	pot	Think of a *pot* of cool spring water sitting in front of you after you have crossed the desert.
masochist	mast	Think of a smiling person tied to a ship's *mast* and being beaten with whips and chains.

2. As a class activity have students generate keywords for familiar vocabulary.
3. Again as a class activity, have students create keywords for unfamiliar words that you have selected for them.
4. Finally, assign new words for students to work on independently. Then have them compare their keywords.

Activity

Devise keywords for the following:

extrasensory
ominous
naive
rustic
bombastic

A Verbal and Visual Word Association Strategy

Students can use this strategy on their own to learn and retain both general and technical vocabulary. Research by Eeds and Cockrum (1985) showed that students using this strategy to study vocabulary in a literary selection outperformed students using more traditional methods such as looking up a word in the dictionary and writing its definition. Moreover, the *verbal and visual word association strategy* we describe here was especially effective for low ability students. In our own work we have also found that this strategy can be learned and used effectively by second language learners in content area classes.

Suppose you are reading along in a novel and you encounter the following passage:

"Joan had recently taken up jogging. She used to live life in the fast lane—staying out all night dancing and partying till dawn. Now that she was middle-aged, Joan strived for a more *salubrious* lifestyle."

The word "salubrious" is a general vocabulary term not well known by most people. Let's assume you need to learn and remember this word. The following steps of the verbal and visual word association strategy will help you associate the word "salubrious" with personal experiences.

1. Draw a square with four boxes in it, as in the example that follows.

Salubrious	**Surfing**
Promoting Health	**Smoking**

Write the word "salubrious" in the top left hand square and its definition in the bottom left hand square. Salubrious, as you may have guessed by now, means healthful. Hence, Joan's jogging suggests she is now leading a salubrious lifestyle.

2. Now in the top right hand square you need to write a personal association for the word salubrious—something you do in your own life that is salubrious. For example, surfing is a healthful activity so you might put that in the upper right hand square.

3. In the bottom right hand square you need to include a word that describes something you do or something you experience that is not salubrious. Thus, smoking, an unhealthful habit, might go here. This verbal association for the word salubrious can then be used to study and retain a personally meaningful conception of the word. In speaking and writing activities, the word salubrious is one you might feel comfortable using.

A student in social studies trying to learn the word diplomatic formed the following verbal association:

Diplomatic	**Jesse Jackson**
Skilled in International Relations	**Omar Khadafy**

His association for someone who is diplomatic was Jesse Jackson, who has been successful in the past interceding on behalf of people taken hostage. This student's non-example—someone who is clearly not a diplomatic person—was Omar Khadafy.

We have found that second language students benefit from a modification of the original verbal association strategy. By including a visual association with the verbal symbol and omitting the non-example, second language students can quickly grasp and learn unfamiliar general and technical vocabulary using this strategy. For example, the word "nocturnal" can be associated with the drawing of a half moon and stars against a black background. Then, in the lower right hand corner, this student's personal association "owl" is written to reinforce the idea of a creature that hunts at night.

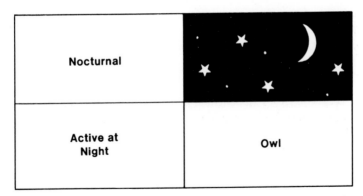

Nocturnal	
Active at Night	**Owl**

The visual and verbal association strategy can be introduced to students easily and, given some guided practice, it should quickly become part of their repertoire of independent strategies for learning new vocabulary. It works best for nouns and descriptive adjectives. Highly technical terms such as "photosynthesis" require the more elaborate conceptual networks that may be formed using a graphic organizer, mapping, or the vocabulary self-collection strategy that follows.

Vocabulary Self-Collection Strategy (VSS)

Given the enormous numbers of new words that students encounter in reading assignments, it is not surprising that most students have a difficult time deciding which unfamiliar words to learn. *The vocabulary self-collection strategy* (Haggard, 1986a) is a vocabulary acquisition technique that is designed to teach students how to select the most important vocabulary from reading assignments. VSS should first be introduced as a post-reading group activity, following guidelines adapted from Haggard (1986b, p. 637):

1. Student teams identify a word or term important for learning content information. The teacher identifies one word or term.
2. The teacher writes the words on the chalkboard as teams give definitions from context.
3. Class members add any information they can to each definition.
4. The teacher and students consult external references, e.g., glossary, index, and dictionary, for definitions that are incomplete or unclear.
5. Students and teacher discuss and then narrow the list to a predetermined number of words for a final class list.
6. Students record the class list with agreed-upon definitions in notebooks, vocabulary journals, or on notecards.
7. Class list words are used in extension activities and class tests.

Word Map

Once students are proficient at categorizing technical vocabulary through the list-group-label strategy, they can learn to use word maps to develop ownership of important terminology. Word maps provide students with a procedure for independently studying content area vocabulary (Schwartz & Raphael, 1985; Tierney, Readence, & Dishner, 1985). A *word map* is a visual representation of a definition, displaying three categories of semantic knowledge: (a) the general class or category to which the concept belongs; (b) the primary properties of the concept and how these properties distinguish it from other members of the class; and, (c) examples of the concept.

The following example demonstrates a student's effort to develop a word map in science class for the word "reptile."

The following steps help make students independent users of word maps:

1. Discuss the word map with students emphasizing its value as a study technique.
2. Walk through the incomplete word map, modeling the process with familiar words like "skateboard," "ice cream," "computer," and "sandwich." You can start by simply having students brainstorm associations for these words as you would in list-group-label, and then align the associations with category labels.
3. Give students independent guided practice with technical words in a rich sentence context. Then progress to words in less rich contexts that require students to consult other sources of information such as a dictionary, glossary, or encyclopedia.

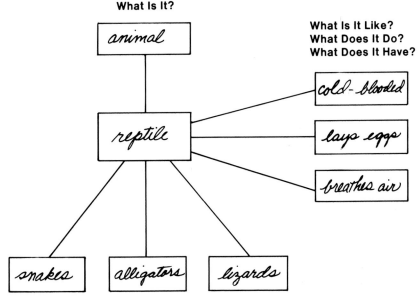

What Is It?

animal

What Is It Like?
What Does It Do?
What Does It Have?

reptile

cold-blooded

lays eggs

breathes air

snakes   alligators   lizards

What Are Some Examples?

Finally, once students have constructed a word map, you may want to add the requirement that they then create a sentence using the word to see if they have, in fact, internalized its meaning and truly "own" the word in writing and speaking. For example, the student studying "reptile" wrote: "Snakes are a reptile most people fear." This sentence demonstrates that the student knows specific examples of reptiles.

Extension Activities

Extension activities are pencil and paper exercises designed to reinforce and expand the schemata of newly acquired content area vocabulary. These activities allow students to explore word relationships and, in general, to manipulate and practice new terminology in a variety of ways. Recall and memorization are certainly a part of extension activities; however, these activities should also force students to think about the terms they are learning. The following extension activities are merely examples of exercises that teachers can use to enhance the acquisition of vocabulary in their own content area classrooms.

1. *Vocabulary Cloze*

   This activity requires students to make decisions regarding the appropriate use of vocabulary in some existing context. The example below was used with a group of students following a lesson on morphemes derived from Latin.

Directions: At the bottom of the page are four words. Pick the **best** word for each blank in the passage and write it in. Think about why you made the choices you did because we will talk about them later. Use each word one time.

To the small animals in the dark forest the _____ beast with drooling fangs appeared to be _____ because he could leap upon them from any tree at any time. The evil monster seemed to be _____ because he was bigger and stronger than they were. And it seemed _____ since it always knew where to find the helpless creatures.

*Omni*scient   —*All* knowing
*Omni*potent   —*All* powerful
*Omni*vorous   —Eats *all* things
*Omni*present   —Always there *all* the time

2. *Analogies*

Word analogies are useful thinking exercises. They require students to draw inferences, and they are an attractive method of exposing subtle word associations. In addition, analogies lend themselves to creative and divergent thinking. A word of caution—analogies can be extremely difficult, especially for students who have never worked with them. Be prepared to provide students with simple analogies which can be used as models for verbalizing relationships. For instance,

Night is to *day* as *big* is to _____
Large, black, little, simple

Verbalization: Night is the opposite of day, so big must be the opposite of something.

What is the opposite of big? Little.

Analogies are easier to complete if answers are provided; however, that leaves only one correct answer for each analogy. If no answers are provided, the analogies are more difficult but they allow for divergent answers and interesting discussion. The decision should be based on the capabilities of the class.

Directions: The following analogies are about science vocabulary that we have just studied. Pick the answer you feel makes the most sense.

1. *Gas* is to *liquid* as *liquid* is to _____

2. *Proton* is to *positive* as *electron* is to _____

3. *Atom* is to *element* as _____ is to *compound*

4. *Physical* is to *mixture* as _____ is to *compound*

5. *Hg* is to *mercury* as _____ is to *silver*

Solid	Atomic	Water	Energy	Molecule	Negative
K	S	Chemical	Ag	Salt	

3. *Matching Definitions to Scrambled Words*

This exercise provides straightforward reinforcement for meanings of basic vocabulary. Scrambling the spellings adds an extra challenge and makes the activity more interesting.

Directions: Below are two lists. The numbered list on the left is composed of some basic math terms that we have studied. (Notice that the spellings are mixed-up.) The lettered list on the right is composed of definitions for the math terms. Place the letter of each definition on the line next to the appropriate math term.

1. rcleci ‗‗‗‗‗‗

2. ip ‗‗‗‗‗‗

3. ets ‗‗‗‗‗‗

4. toinp ‗‗‗‗‗‗

5. recpiorclas ‗‗‗‗‗‗

6. nogatnep ‗‗‗‗‗‗

7. hcord ‗‗‗‗‗‗

8. irccumfreence ‗‗‗‗‗‗

9. daiemtre ‗‗‗‗‗‗

10. miepr ‗‗‗‗‗‗

A. A number that has only two whole number factors

B. A line segment with endpoints on a circle

C. A closed curved figure on which every point is an equal distance from a fixed point within the curve

D. 3.14159265

E. Two of these are necessary to determine a line

F. A polygon that has five sides

G. A collection of mathematical elements that have something in common

H. A chord running through the center of a circle

I. Two fractions whose product is 1

J. The perimeter of a circle

4. *Puzzles*

Word puzzles are activities that almost all students will respond to positively. Consequently they make good motivational devices for vocabulary review.

Hidden word puzzles are easy to make. Simply prepare the answers in any array; and then type in random letters to complete the rectangle. Triple-space between letters in each row and double-space between rows. A word of caution—always give clues that define the hidden words in some way. If the clues are eliminated, the hidden word puzzle simply becomes an exercise in word recognition rather than an extension activity for vocabulary development.

Initial Array

```
              G   R   A   N   T
                          L                           S
                  B   O   O   T   H               T
                          C                           U
      S   H   E   R   M   A   N   S   P           A   D
      T                       I       I           R
      A                   V   L       C       A   T
      N               A           E   K   W
      T           D               E
      O                       S   T
      N
```

Hidden Word Puzzle: Social Studies Civil War Personalities

Directions: What follows is a hidden word puzzle involving famous personalities of the Civil War era. Listed below are brief descriptions of these people. As you figure them out, circle their last names. These names may appear diagonally, horizontally, or vertically; and they may be printed from top to bottom or from bottom to top. Answers may be found in your text on the page indicated in parentheses.

1. Lee surrendered to him at Appomattox Courthouse. (246)
2. President of U.S. during the war. (221)
3. President of the Confederacy. (234)
4. He made a famous charge at Gettysburg. (240)
5. The Union's Secretary of State. (232)
6. He burned Atlanta on his march to the sea. (242)
7. Commanded the army of Virginia. (236)
8. A famous Confederate cavalry officer. (235)
9. Secretary of War for the Union. (232)
10. He assassinated the President. (249)

R	A	M	G	R	A	N	T	A	D	O	D	Q
E	B	E	T	O	T	L	W	M	O	S	S	C
A	F	O	B	B	O	O	T	H	M	Q	T	N
P	H	I	U	E	N	C	J	E	O	B	U	X
S	H	E	R	M	A	N	S	P	S	V	A	D
T	M	U	N	O	T	I	B	I	B	L	R	C
A	J	D	S	B	V	L	C	C	Y	A	T	G
N	U	Z	I	A	O	O	E	K	W	H	P	M
T	O	X	D	M	R	V	I	E	N	F	W	T
O	N	L	E	C	A	E	S	T	R	O	P	E
N	E	W	T	O	N	S	F	I	G	L	S	P

Crossword puzzles are somewhat more difficult to make because of the need to plan crossovers and draw the boxes. The following steps will simplify the procedure:

1. Select vocabulary and plan crossovers;
2. Place the answers, triple-spacing between letters in rows and double-spacing between letters in columns;
3. Type in the answers, triple-spacing between letters in rows and double-spacing between letters in columns;
4. Take the ditto out of the typewriter and remove the protective paper;
5. Using a ruler, draw boxes around the words.
6. Draw in numbers by hand or reinsert the ditto and type them in the upper left corner of appropriate boxes;
7. If you overextend lines for boxes, just cover them with correction fluid.

Crossword Puzzle: Geometry Terms

					¹S							²B			
					Q							B			
³R	A	⁴D	I	U	S				⁵L	I	N	E			
		I		A						S					
		A		R						E					
⁶C	I	R	C	U	M	F	E	R	E	N	C	E			
		E								T					
⁷H	Y	⁸P	O	T	E	N	U	S	E						
		O		E											
	⁹P	I		¹⁰R	I	G	H	T							
		N													
		T													

Across:

3. A line running from the center of a circle to the curve
5. An infinite number of points
6. The distance around a circle
7. The longest side of a right triangle
9. 3.14
10. A triangle with two sides perpendicular to each other

Down:

1. A figure with four equal sides and four right angles
2. To divide into two equal parts
4. Twice the radius of a circle
8. Two of these are enough to determine a line

Computer Software Extension Activities

While it is of course possible to create your own extension activities by hand, there are hundreds of PC computer software programs available that will accomplish the same tasks much more efficiently. One software publisher, Mindscape, offers interactive software (*Word Magic*, 1984; and *Vocabulary Challenge*, 1986) as well as programs that create reproducibles for the classroom (*Crossword Magic*, 1984; *Puzzle Disk*, 1987; and *Wordmaze*, 1987). There are many other software publishers with similar product lines, and they will be accessible through local software retailers and stores that sell educational supplies.

Summary

In this chapter we have attempted to provide a rationale for the direct teaching of vocabulary in content area classes. General principles have been introduced with emphasis on the need to develop both receptive and expressive vocabularies. The primary focus of the chapter has been on pre- and post-reading strategies for introducing, reinforcing, and extending the meanings of content area terminology.

Now go back to the anticipation guide at the beginning of the chapter. React again to the statements as you did before, this time recording your answers in the column entitled "Reaction." Compare your answers with those you made in the Anticipation column.

Miniprojects

1. Choose a chapter from a textbook in your content area and develop an appropriate graphic organizer.
2. Select a set of related terms from your own content area and conduct a List-Group-Label lesson with members of your class.
3. Based on a chapter in your content area, develop an extension activity to foster creative and divergent thinking about key vocabulary in the chapter.

Additional Recommended Readings

Dishner, E. K., Bean, T. W., Readence, J. W., & Moore, D. W. (1986). *Reading in the content areas: Improving classroom instruction* (2nd ed.). Dubuque, IA: Kendall/Hunt. Chapter five contains a series of useful articles on vocabulary instruction.

Ernst, M. S., & Thurber, J. (1960). *In a word*. Great Neck, NY: Channel Press. An interesting collection of words with colorful etymologies. Humorous cartoons by Thurber accompany many of the entries.

Funk, C. E. (1948). *A hog on ice and other curious expressions.* New York: Harper.
Provides explanations for common expressions such as "straight from the horse's mouth" and "spill the beans."

Funk, C. E. (1950). *Thereby hangs a tale: Stories of curious word origins.* New York: Harper & Brothers.
Contains hundreds of words with fascinating etymologies.

Journal of Reading (1986, April), *29* (8).
This special theme issue contains 13 articles on vocabulary instruction.

References

Allington, R. L., & McGill-Franzen, A. (1980). Word identification errors in isolation and in context: Apples vs. oranges. *The Reading Teacher, 33,* 795–800.

Anders, P. L., & Bos, C. S. (1986). Semantic feature analysis: An interactive strategy for vocabulary development and text comprehension. *Journal of Reading, 29,* 610–616.

Baldwin, R. S., Ford, J. C., & Readence, J. E. (1981). Teaching word connotations: An alternative strategy. *Reading World, 21,* 103–108.

Bean, T. W. (1978). Developing content area vocabulary. *Journal of Reading, 22,* 102–103.

Bean, T. W., Inabinette, N. B., & Ryan, R. (1983). The effect of a categorization strategy on secondary students' retention of literary vocabulary. *Reading Psychology, 4,* 247–252.

Berger, M. (1981). *Disastrous volcanoes.* New York: Franklin Watts.

Blanc, S. S., Fisher, A. S., & Gardner, O. (1967). *Modern science: Man, matter, and energy.* New York: Holt, Rinehart and Winston.

Bolinger, D. (1968). *Aspects of language.* New York: Harcourt, Brace and World.

Chomsky, N., & Halle, M. (1968). *The sound pattern of English.* New York: Harper and Row.

Crossword Magic (1984). Chicago, IL: Mindscape.

Cunningham, J. W., Cunningham, P. M., & Arthur, S. V. (1981). *Middle and secondary school reading.* New York: Longman.

Earle, R. A., & Barron, R. F. (1973). An approach for teaching vocabulary in content subjects. In H. L. Herber & R. F. Barron (Eds.), *Research in reading in the content areas: Second year report* (pp. 84–110). Syracuse, NY: Reading and Language Arts Center, Syracuse University.

Eeds, M., & Cockrum, W. A. (1985). Teaching word meanings by expanding schemata vs. dictionary work vs. reading in context. *Journal of Reading, 28,* 492–497.

Finn, P. (1977–1978). Word frequency, information theory, and cloze performance: A transfer feature theory of processing in reading. *Reading Research Quarterly, 13,* 508–537.

Funk, C. E. (1950). *Thereby hangs a tale: Stories of curious word origins.* New York: Harper & Brothers.

Graff, H. F. (1972). *The free and the brave* (2nd ed.). Chicago: Rand McNally.

Haggard, M. R. (1986a). The vocabulary self-collection strategy: An active approach to word learning. In E. K. Dishner, T. W. Bean, J. E. Readence, & Moore, D. W. (Eds.), *Reading in the content areas: Improving classroom instruction* (2nd ed., pp. 179–183). Dubuque, IA: Kendall/Hunt.

Haggard, M. R. (1986b). The vocabulary self-collection strategy: Using student interest and world knowledge to enhance vocabulary growth. *Journal of Reading, 29,* 634–642.

Halsey, W. D. (1977). *Dictionary.* New York: Macmillan.

Heimlich, J. E., & Pittelman, S. D. (1986). *Semantic mapping: Classroom applications.* Newark, DE: International Reading Association.

Johnson, D. D., & Pearson, P. D. (1984). *Teaching reading vocabulary* (2nd ed.). New York: Holt, Rinehart, & Winston.

Maurer, D. W. (1955). Whiz mob. *Publication of the American Dialect Society,* No. 24.

Moore, D. W., & Readence, J. E. (1984). A quantitative and qualitative review of graphic organizer research. *Journal of Educational Research, 78,* 11–17.

Pressley, M., Levin, J. R., & McDaniel, M. A. (1987). Remembering versus inferring what a word means: Mnemonic and contextual approaches. In M. G. McKeown & M. E. Curtis (Eds.), *The nature of vocabulary acquisition* (pp. 107–127). Hillsdale, NJ: Erlbaum.

Puzzle disk (1987). Chicago: Mindscape.

Quealy, R. J. (1969). Senior high school students' use of contextual aids in reading. *Reading Research Quarterly, 4,* 512–523.

Readence, J. E., & Moore, D. W. (1979). Strategies for enhancing readiness and recall in content areas: The encoding specificity problem. *Reading Psychology, 1,* 47–54.

Roberts, J., & Kelly, N. (1985). The keyword method: An alternative vocabulary strategy for developmental college readers. *Reading World, 24,* 34–39.

Robinson, V. B., Strickland, D. S., & Cullinan, B. (1977). The child: Ready or not? In L. O. Ollila (Ed.), *The kindergarten child and reading* (pp. 13–39). Newark, DE: International Reading Association.

Schatz, E. K., & Baldwin, R. S. (1986). Context clues are unreliable predictors of word meanings. *Reading Research Quarterly, 21,* 439–453.

Schwartz, R. M., & Raphael, T. E. (1985). Concept of definition: A key to improving students' vocabulary. *The Reading Teacher, 39,* 198–204.

Stahl, S. A., & Fairbanks, M. M. (1986). The effects of vocabulary instruction: A model-based meta-analysis. *Review of Educational Research, 56,* 72–110.

Taba, H. (1967). *Teacher's handbook for elementary social studies.* Reading, MA: Addison-Wesley.

Tierney, R. J., Readence, J. E., & Dishner, E. K. (1985). *Reading strategies and practices: A compendium* (2nd ed.). Boston: Allyn & Bacon.

Vocabulary challenge (1986). Chicago: Mindscape.

Wadsworth, B. J. (1971). *Piaget's theory of cognitive development.* New York: Longman.

Word magic (1984). Chicago: Mindscape.

Wordmaze (1987). Chicago: Mindscape.

CHAPTER

6

Anticipation Guide/Reaction Guide

Directions: Before you begin reading this chapter, take a moment to put a check
mark next to any of the following statements with which you agree. Use
the column entitled "Anticipation."

Anticipation   **Reaction**

_____ 1.   _____ 1. The knowledge students possess before
                               reading a subject area text is essential for
                               their understanding of the author's ideas.

_____ 2.   _____ 2. Students naturally approach text reading in
                               an active, questioning frame of mind.

_____ 3.   _____ 3. Students consciously look for an author's text
                               structure.

_____ 4.   _____ 4. Most teacher questioning causes students
                               to relate subject concepts to their own lives
                               and experiences.

_____ 5.   _____ 5. Small group discussion should be heavily
                               monitored by the teacher.

Comprehension Strategies

Rationale

Comprehension of challenging ideas in a content area is rarely easy for students. No collection of textbook aids will substitute for the careful guidance you can provide. In order to guide students' comprehension of ideas in your content area you must have a good working knowledge of comprehension strategies. The aim of this chapter is to introduce and demonstrate an array of strategies you can integrate with your current approach to content teaching.

Chapter Objectives

After reading this chapter, you should:

1. Understand the principles of guiding comprehension in a content area.
2. Be familiar with a wide array of teaching strategies for guiding students' comprehension of content area concepts.
3. Be able to apply specific teaching strategies in your content area in order to guide students' understanding of your course content.

Graphic Organizer

The following graphic organizer is provided to give you some advance structure for new vocabulary and concepts that will be presented in this chapter.

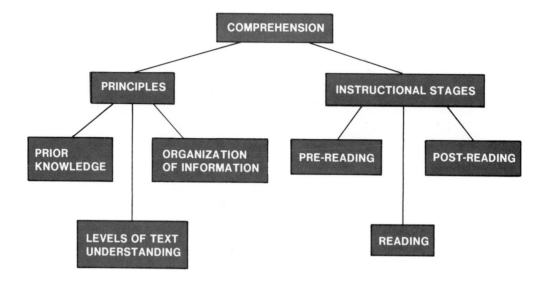

A Review of Instructional Recommendations

In chapter one we made five important instructional recommendations that are worth reiterating at this point. Try to keep these in mind as you attempt the various strategies.

1. *Present content and processes concurrently.* The particular comprehension strategy you select for an assignment should grow out of a careful content analysis of the material. What is the purpose of the assignment? What text structure does the author use to portray ideas? This analysis should suggest which comprehension strategies are likely to be most helpful.

2. *Provide guidance in all aspects of the instructional lesson—before, during, and after reading.* This requires an awareness that many students need you to explicitly *model* the content reading process at various stages. They need *feedback* on their attempts to comprehend, and they need to have instructional guidance removed once they have a grasp of the material.

3. *Use all language processes to help students learn from text.* Efforts to guide students' comprehension should help them to be effective communicators in speaking, listening, reading, and writing. The strategies in this chapter rely on this integrated view of learning content material.

4. *Use small groups to enhance learning.* In order for students to become effective at communicating in a content area they need ample opportunities to risk expressing their ideas. Small group activities encourage risk-taking and expression. Many of the strategies in this chapter are enhanced by small group discussion and cooperative learning.

5. *Be patient in strategy implementation.* It takes teachers and students time to become comfortable with a new teaching strategy. Give the strategies you decide to try enough trial runs with modifications if needed so you can fully judge their effectiveness.

Principles of Comprehension

A comprehensive content area lesson displays an awareness of three psychological principles in the comprehension process. These principles include: (1) the importance of students' prior knowledge in the acquisition of new information; (2) the level of text understanding to be achieved in the lesson; and (3) the organization of information to aid long-term retention. Let's examine each of these principles and their respective instructional stages in more detail.

Prior Knowledge. The first principle of comprehending unfamiliar content area material is embodied by students' applying what they already know to what they are learning. Fortunately, teachers exert some degree of control over this aspect. Through guided instruction we can appraise and, if need be, increase students' knowledge of a topic before they begin text and course assignments. A teacher can accomplish this task by using a variety of pre-reading strategies. Thus, the principle of prior knowledge corresponds to the pre-reading stage of a content lesson.

Levels of Text Understanding. The second principle of comprehension emphasizes the fact that content material frequently demands in-depth study beyond the factual, literal level for adequate understanding and application in future lessons. Thus, students must be encouraged to think deeply about what they are learning. Memory researchers Craik and Lockhart (1972) emphasized that depth of processing is a key factor in the retention of information. A content teacher can guide this process during the reading stage by insuring that students adopt an active, questioning approach to the text, based on their prior knowledge and experiences. In order to construct lessons that guide students in the assimilation of factual text concepts with their own experiences, it is helpful to have a procedure for characterizing different levels of understanding. Those levels are text-explicit, text-implicit, and experience-based; and students should be given every opportunity to reason across this full range of understanding. The specific teaching strategies suggested in this chapter can become the means to move students' thinking beyond the text-explicit level toward critical thinking.

Organization of Information. The third principle of understanding, organizing for long-term retention of information, is the most often neglected aspect of comprehension instruction. In the post-reading phase, ideas are refined and extended. Additionally, this final instructional stage relates directly to how well new information will be understood in a subsequent lesson. The post-reading stage of a lesson must involve activities that encourage students to synthesize and organize information.

Since all three principles and their related instructional stages are simply useful constructs for talking about the comprehension process, they overlap when translated to practice. For example, the post-reading stage in one content unit may well contribute, or provide the foundation for, a reader's prior knowledge in an upcoming unit. Therefore, as we introduce each of the three instructional stages and their related strategies, they should be viewed in an integrated fashion. It should also be mentioned that before you begin to utilize strategies for guiding the comprehension process, you must have already identified the important concepts and vocabulary terms in the material to be read by students. (See chapter five for a discussion of this procedure.) By doing this you will be prepared to construct and apply strategies that focus on the introduction and reinforcement of those concepts and vocabulary terms.

Levels of Text Understanding

We have chosen to adopt a view of comprehension consisting of three categories: 1) text-explicit, 2) text-implicit, and 3) experience-based. The categories have been modified from those suggested by Pearson and Johnson (1978) and, in our opinion, offer the best description of the processes involved in comprehending text at various levels of understanding. As such, this simple framework captures the essence of comprehension—the interaction of printed information with prior experience.

In order to gain a more concrete understanding of the three categories, try the following activity.

Activity

Read the paragraph below and answer the questions that follow.

Failing to remember things is a problem that plagues most of us. We forget to perform routine tasks like stopping at a grocery store on the way home or picking up the dry cleaning. Worse still, we may forget important information such as a new student's name. Fortunately, there are some reasonable solutions to our forgetfulness. (Bean, Haehl, & Bishop, 1983, p. 29)

Q: 1. What is a problem that plagues most of us?
A:

Q: 2. What specific group or audience is the paragraph addressing?
A:

Q: 3. What are your solutions to the problem posed in the paragraph?
A:

In answering question one from the previous activity, "What is a problem that plagues most of us?", your response "forgetfulness" was taken directly from the text. In fact, you were able to "point" to the answer in the paragraph because it was literally stated by the author. Such comprehension is called *text-explicit*.

In question two, "What specific group or audience is the paragraph addressing?", you had to engage in a different type of comprehension from question one. Your response did not come explicitly from the text; rather, it had to be inferred from a hint in the passage. The phrase "new *student's* name" implies that teachers are the audience being addressed. When you must infer from the text to derive an answer to a question, you are engaging in *text-implicit* comprehension.

Finally, answering question three, "What are your solutions to the problem posed in the paragraph?", requires still another form of comprehension. Your response this time was drawn from your previous experience. You had to search your schema for strategies you might use to remember a new student's name. In doing so, you may have responded in a number of different ways including "bizarre associations," "where the student sits," and so on. Your inference, was not derived from the text, but from your existing schema or knowledge structure. This is called *experience-based* comprehension. This type of thinking is at the heart of curiosity, invention, and problem-solving. It is also one of the most neglected forms of questioning in many classrooms (Bean, Sorter, Singer, & Frazee, 1986; Durkin, 1978–1979; Goodlad, 1983).

Explicating Levels of Comprehension

Let's examine each of the three levels of comprehension in depth. Following Pearson and Johnson's (1978) recommendation, we will be examining question and answer relationships, rather than classifying questions in isolation. *Text-explicit comprehension* involves getting the facts of a passage, as stated by the author. The question asked is based directly on the text, and the answer is explicitly cued by the language of the text. Raphael (1984), in an effort to use language familiar to students, uses the phrase "right there on the page" to describe text-explicit comprehension. Answers are literally found on the page and readers can actually point to the answer. In essence, you are reading the lines. Text-explicit comprehension requires you to tell what the author said, and there is usually only one answer. Therefore, answers to such questions have no middle ground—they are either right or wrong.

Text-implicit and experience-based comprehension, on the other hand, require you to think about your answers—they are not explicitly stated by the author and answers may vary depending on each respondent's experiential background. In fact, the less the text is involved and the more experiential background comes into play, the larger the number of possible answers.

Text-implicit comprehension involves answering a question derived directly from the language of the text, but also requires the reader to derive an answer when no obvious clues to it are visible in the passage. You are asked to infer what the author meant. Thus, the relationship between the question and the answer is implicit; it necessarily requires some logic to get from the question to the answer. Raphael (1984) calls this "think and search." As such, questions that require paraphrases of text information result in text-implicit comprehension. In essence, you take the facts presented by the author and add knowledge from your experiential background to derive a reasonable implicit relationship. In other words, you are asked to read between the lines.

Finally, *experience-based comprehension* results when a question is asked and the plausible answer is derived almost exclusively from previous knowledge. Thus, the answer cannot be derived directly from the text. In Raphael's (1984) words, you are "on your own." Students draw inferences from previous knowledge; hence they are involved in reading beyond the lines.

Summarized below are the distinctions between the three levels of comprehension:

Levels of Comprehension

Level	Information Source			# of Possible Answers	Alternate Definition
	Question	Inference	Answer		
Text-Explicit	Text	No	Text	One	Reading the Lines
Text-Implicit	Text	Yes	Text	One Plus	Reading Between the Lines
Experience-Based	Text	Yes	Reader	Many	Reading Beyond the Lines

Implications Concerning Questions

Questions are one of the most prominent forms of comprehension instruction used. Questions are used to activate students' memory processes of text, focus their attention on significant aspects of text material, and aid them in synthesizing seemingly different parts of text into a coherent whole. It may be fairly safe to say that those teachers who are good questioners promote the process of comprehension. However, there are certain considerations you should be aware of when you attempt to use questions effectively.

First, and foremost, it takes time and thought to compose good questions. Good questions do not flow like water from a fountain. You need to examine carefully the material you have covered in order to ascertain the best kinds of questions to ask. You possess a wealth of information concerning your subject matter area; students do not. Asking questions that come from your knowledge base, rather than from the text, will do nothing more than confuse and befuddle your students.

Second, in asking good questions, be sure not to ask too many text-explicit questions. Answers to such questions, though they form the basis for questions at higher levels of comprehension, require little or no thought, do not challenge the student, and do not enhance your role as a facilitator of learning.

Third, asking questions at higher levels of comprehension requires that you give students the freedom to respond. Without this, you may inhibit divergent reponses.

Fourth, be aware that sometimes you may not get the type of comprehension you expect. For example, consider the following sentence: "Tom rode through the park at a slow gait, thinking about the day's activities. As Tom daydreamed, she searched the afternoon shadows for a few blades of grass." Your intended text-explicit question to students might be: What kind of animal is Tom riding? Although most students are likely to respond with "horse," a few may say "mare." Thus, at times you may be pleasantly surprised at divergent, high-level responses to a seemingly straightforward question. The student has just processed your question differently to draw the above mentioned inference. The point is that you should be prepared for divergent responses to your expectations.

Fifth, the levels of comprehension model has implications for textbook questions, also. Take care to avoid relying entirely on questions provided by text authors. Such questions are written by experts in their field, and as good as these authors may be, they can't possibly understand your students' special needs. Only you, their teacher, can tailor questions that will involve your particular students in comprehension at varying levels. Questions so intended by text authors may not accomplish that task.

Sixth, students can be taught to generate their own questions. If you truly want your students to become active, critical readers of text, you need to become familiar with strategies designed to help them develop a questioning approach to reading (Yopp-Nolte & Singer, 1985). Helping students adopt this inquisitive stance can boost students' interest in pursuing a topic that may otherwise seem distant from their own personal lives.

Last, though questions are a major means to teach students, the value of statements should not be neglected (Bean, 1985; Herber & Nelson, 1986). They have suggested using statements as a prelude to using questions. This involves using statements at first that will help students to **recognize** information before they are required to **produce** it through the use of questions. Such statements will simulate comprehension at higher levels of thinking and familiarize students with that process. Once familiarity has been achieved, questions again become an appropriate and valuable way to help students comprehend text material. In this chapter we will introduce the Anticipation-Reaction Guide, a strategy which exemplifies the value of statements as a means of enhancing students' comprehension.

Text Structure

The third principle of understanding, organization of information, relates to the ability to perceive an author's *text structure* or organizational pattern, since this influences how well students comprehend and retain information. When you alert students to the structure of an author's thoughts, you provide students with a powerful strategy for organizing information in a memorable fashion. Moreover, as you develop strategies to guide students' comprehension, your analysis of a text passage should reveal the author's pattern of organization. With adequate guidance, students can eventually become adept at detecting an author's structure independently.

The following activity will give you an idea of your well-developed, largely unconscious use of patterns in your own reading.

Activity

Read the following sentences. Place them in the proper order of occurrence.

He was well thought of by his peers.

John volunteered for extracurricular activities.

His principal gave him an excellent recommendation for the university doctoral program.

He never missed school unless very ill.

John was a conscientious teacher.

Recognizing the structure of prose is a great aid for students in comprehending and recalling text material. Students who can perceive the structure that binds the ideas in text will understand and remember ideas much better than if they are viewed only as separate entities (McGee & Richgels, 1986; van Dijk & Kintsch, 1983). In the above example, your recognition of the *cause-effect* pattern should have enabled you to organize the text in its proper sequence. Because John was such a good teacher and did fine things for his school, his principal was only happy to fulfill his desire. Additionally, with your knowledge of the apparent organizational pattern, you, more than likely, started the sequence with "John was a conscientious teacher," because the other attributes concerning his abilities logically follow that topic sentence. This same knowledge allowed you to place this sentence last: "His principal give him an excellent recommendation for the university doctoral program." In essence, your knowledge about the world and the organization of text allowed you to make logical predictions about the arrangement and sequence of the above sentences. It is this same knowledge that students use, or should be taught to use, with their context textbooks.

Text structure influences students' reading in many ways. Niles (1965) has stated that attention to the relationships of text affect readers in three ways: 1) initial comprehension; 2) efficiency in recall; and, 3) critical analysis of text. Structural patterns used in comprehending text are so pervasive, in fact, that Guthrie (1979) found that readers activate such plans in understanding even simple newspaper articles. He also found that readers have a variety of schemata to use in comprehending written material having different organizational plans.

Helping your students perceive an author's text structure gives them a valuable independent strategy they can use to comprehend text efficiently. For example, Bartlett (1978) taught ninth graders to identify and use four text structures as aids to comprehension and recall of information. These students significantly outperformed an untrained control group on recall of important ideas. Similarly, Meyer, Brandt, and Bluth (1980) found that ninth grade students' ability to identify and use an author's text structure accurately predicted passage recall scores.

Recently, Taylor and Samuels (1983) found that intermediate grade students possessing an intuitive awareness of text structure patterns recalled significantly more important passage information than students unaware of these structures. They cautioned that only a small percentage of students acquire this ability without direct modeling and guided instruction by a teacher. Your efforts to help students use text structure in comprehension and recall will reap benefits in their reading and writing.

Text structure serves a dual purpose in print: 1) to help writers communicate their thoughts; and 2) to help readers comprehend what authors are attempting to communicate. Since reading is an interaction between the thoughts and language of both writers and readers, text structure serves as a convenient vehicle to facilitate this communication. Meyer and Freedle (1984) have emphasized the importance of the text (the writer's) organization in comprehending connected discourse. Other researchers, such as Rumelhart (1975), have emphasized the importance of text structure that readers impose on text.

While both of these emphases are valid it makes sense to consider a third position, one to which the authors adhere. Schallert and Vaughan (1979) and Tierney and LaZansky (1980) have described the obvious connection in communication between authors and readers. It certainly cannot be denied that authors attempt to communicate their thoughts to readers through structural patterns in text. These patterns are real and they are visible on the printed page. On the other hand, one also cannot deny that readers attempt to use their logic in thought and reasoning to understand the printed page. The continuous process that readers employ in imposing their own organizational structure to communicate with authors, though not visible, is also very real, as previously discussed in this text. Meaning construction entails active interchange between writers and readers. This principle is succinctly stated as follows:

Rules Which Guide the Writer-Reader Interaction

1. *Guidance Principle:* A writer should guide the reader through the task of reconstructing the intended meaning.
2. *Writer's Specific Rules:*
   a. *Purpose:* The writer should have a purpose in writing a text, such as to interest, amuse, or instruct a reader.
   b. *Message Organization:* A writer should construct a coherent plan for the ideas to be presented.

    c. *Text Organization:* A writer should adhere to a plan for the presentation of ideas which reflects orderliness, connectivity, and good structure.

    d. *Economy:* A writer should present only as much as is essential, mentioning significant details to serve a purposeful function and reflecting importance in length of exposition.

    e. *Discrepancy:* A writer should mention only those departures from the typical that are important to the message.

  3. *Reader's Specific Rules:*

    a. A reader should assume that the writer is observing the implicit contract of the guidance principle.

    b. A reader should work at using the clues provided by the writer to reconstruct the message (Olson, 1978, as referenced in Schallert & Vaughan, 1979, p. 52).

In summary, patterns of organization in text and memory serve as a means of enhancing comprehension. By recognizing structural patterns, students will begin to understand ideas as authors intend. Content teachers should acquaint students with such patterns and not assume they have knowledge of text organization. The acquisition of such structures is crucial in effectively learning from text.

Explicating Text Structure

Knowledge of text structure helps to guide students' comprehension of text. While there are many types of patterns of organization in written materials, Niles and Memory (1977) recommend the following as most prominent:

1. *Cause/Effect:* This pattern links reasons with results. It is characterized by an interaction between at least two ideas or events, one taking an action and another resulting from that action.

   Example: Because it snowed so heavily, the city traffic came to a standstill.

2. *Comparison/Contrast:* Comparison/contrast patterns of organization demonstrate apparent likenesses and differences between two or more things.

   Example: While a lion and a giraffe are both mammals and bear live young, the lion is a carnivore and the giraffe is a herbivore.

3. *Time Order:* Time order is exemplified by a sequential relationship between ideas or events considered in presence of the passage of time.

   Example: In December Scott took a job with a new company. Things went so well with the new job that he soon became a supervisor. Now, because of continued successes, he is vice-president of the firm.

4. *Problem/Solution:* Similar to the cause/effect pattern, this pattern is exemplified by an interaction between at least two factors, one citing a problem and another providing a potential answer to that problem.

   Example: Certain plants need an environment with a constant, moderate temperature and high humidity or they will die. Consequently, a greenhouse is ideal for those plants.

To further help students in recognizing such patterns, Vacca (1973) provided a useful list of key words or phrases that signal, or cue, a particular text type. Such *signal words* provide mind sets that enhance the perception of text structure and learning from text. On the following page is a list of suggested signal words:

1. **Cause/Effect:** because, since, therefore, consequently, as a result, this led to, so that, nevertheless, accordingly, if . . . then.
2. **Comparison/Contrast:** however, but, as well as, on the other hand, not only . . . but also, either . . . or, while, although, unless, similarly, yet.
3. **Time Order:** on (date), not long after, now, as, before, after, when.
4. **Simple Listing:** to begin with, first, secondly, next, then, finally. (Vacca, 1973, p. 78)

It should be noted that cue words signaling the problem/solution pattern will be similar to those signaling the cause/effect pattern.

Recent studies suggest that teaching students to be on the lookout for signal words assists their awareness of an author's text structure and improves their recall. Meyer, Brandt, and Bluth (1980) found that text in which signal words were underlined facilitated ninth graders' recall of important ideas. Geva (1983) had positive results from teaching community college students to use signal words as an aid to paragraph comprehension. In the section that follows we outline an instructional procedure for developing your students' ability to use text structure to their advantage.

Suggestions for Helping Students Perceive Text Structure

Perhaps the key factor in teaching students to actively use the organizational structure of text is you, the content teacher. It is erroneous to assume students will recognize and utilize organizational patterns. Direct teaching in the recognition of patterns is essential, and all patterns should be pointed out continually to students. The time you spend in stimulating the perception of organizational patterns will take little away from your instructional time and will facilitate comprehension. Below is a suggested sequence for teaching students to perceive patterns of text organization.

1. **Modeling.** You should demonstrate the use of text structure first before expecting students to utilize it. Passages drawn from their reading should be used to illustrate your demonstration because they are most relevant to the students. Showing students a particular organizational pattern and pointing out *why* it is a certain type and *how* that pattern type is organized is essential. Any signal words that clue the reader to the organization of the material should also be pointed out and discussed.
2. **Recognition.** Next, you should "walk" students through a particular passage type by asking judicious questions that focus their attention on the text structure. For students experiencing difficulty, you may wish to read the material to them first rather than having them read it. In this way your students can concentrate entirely on perceiving the pattern. You may also wish to start with sentences only and then move to paragraphs and longer passages. Essential to this recognition step is students' verbalization of the *how* and *why* of the text structure.
3. **Production.** Producing a communication is a logical extension of receiving one. Writing, therefore, becomes a valuable means to reinforce text structure. From time to time all content teachers require students to write. Requiring logical organization in students' own writing can become a vital extension of perceiving text organization. As part of a writing assignment, you should ask students to frame a logical response by utilizing a particular pattern of organization and the signal words associated with it. Skeletal outlines or a graphic organizer may also be provided to facilitate production of an organized writing sample. We demonstrate how to teach structure awareness through writing in chapter seven.

Strategies for Guiding Comprehension

The Pre-Reading Stage

Anticipation Guides. Throughout this text we have been using a number of pre-reading strategies to introduce each chapter. One of them, the *anticipation guide,* introduces each chapter and is an attractive way to activate your thoughts and opinions about a topic. As you are well aware by now, many of the guide statements are "loaded" in the sense that we want to challenge commonly held beliefs about content area reading. Indeed, one of the major features of an anticipation guide is that it brings misconceptions about a topic to the surface. Then we can begin to modify these misconceptions through a well-formulated instructional sequence.

In a paper outlining instructional approaches designed to stimulate curiosity and motivation to learn, Shablak and Castallo (1977) emphasized the key role conceptual conflict plays in the process. Since anticipation guide statements operate at the experience-based level of understanding, they elicit a response based on one's current belief system. Therefore, at the pre-reading stage a student may adamantly defend a response to a guide statement with little fear of failure. As the learning sequence progresses into the reading and post-reading stages, a mismatch between the students' preconceptions about a topic and the information being introduced should result in a subsequent modification of their initial knowledge base.

An additional feature of the anticipation guide is the way in which it functions as an informal, diagnostic tool. A teacher can appraise prior knowledge at the pre-reading stage and evaluate the acquisition of content based on post-reading responses to the guide statements. Since anticipation guides encourage a personal, experience-based response, they serve as ideal springboards for large and small group discussion. Furthermore, they seem to work equally well with print and non-print media including films, lectures, and field-trips.

The following guide was designed to accompany a poem by Richard Brautigan (1968, p. 114) and illustrates an approach that combines pre- and post-reading stages (Bean & Peterson, 1981).

Anticipation Guide/Reaction Guide

Directions: Before reading the poem, check those statements with which you agree. Then, after reading the poem, check the statements with which you think the poet would agree. Be prepared to give reasons to support your choices.

You	**Poet**	
_____	_____	1. Technology frees us to enjoy the wonders of nature.
_____	_____	2. Life in the city is crazy—life in the country is the way to go.
_____	_____	3. The advantages of technological growth far outweigh the disadvantages.
_____	_____	4. There is already abundant evidence that computers will someday control our lives.

All Watched Over by Machines of Loving Grace*

I like to think (and
The sooner the better!)
Of a cybernetic meadow
Where mammals and computers
Live together in mutually
Programming harmony
Like pure water
Touching clear sky.

I like to think
   (right now, please!)
Of a cybernetic forest
Filled with pines and electronics
Where deer stroll peacefully
Past computers
As if they were flowers
With spinning blossoms.

I like to think
   (It has to be!)
Of a cybernetic ecology
Where we are free of our labors
And joined back to nature.
Returned to our mammal
Brothers and sisters,
And all watched over
By machines of loving grace.

Richard Brautigan

Although the preceding example comes from the content area of English, anticipation guides should not be viewed as an exclusively literary strategy. Rather, they lend themselves to application in diverse subject areas such as science, art, physical education, and history. The following steps apply to the construction of an anticipation guide in any content area.

Step One

Identify the major concepts and supporting details in a text selection, lecture, or film. This step is analogous to the content analysis step in the development of a pre-reading graphic organizer (see Chapter Five).

Step Two

Identify students' experiences and beliefs that will be challenged and, in some cases, supported by the material.

Step Three

Create statements reflecting your students' pre-reading beliefs concerning a course topic that may challenge and modify those beliefs. Include some statements that are consistent

---

*"All Watched Over By Machines of Loving Grace" excerpted from the book *The Pill Versus the Springhill Mine Disaster* by Richard Brautigan. Copyright © 1968 by Richard Brautigan. Reprinted by permission of DELA-CORTE PRESS/SEYMOUR LAWRENCE.

with both your students' experiential background and the concepts presented in the material or lesson. Three to five statements are usually adequate.

Step Four

Arrange the statements on a sheet of paper, overhead transparency, or the chalkboard. Have students respond positively or negatively to each statement on an individual basis. Have them record their justification for each response in writing, so they will have a reference point for discussion.

Step Five

Engage students in a pre-reading discussion highlighting their current justification for responding positively or negatively to each statement.

With a little practice you will discover that anticipation guides serve to clarify your content objectives and to motivate students to approach a learning task in an active fashion. Used in conjunction with a film, they can reduce the kind of haphazard, passive processing of film concepts that often characterizes the use of media in a classroom. The following physical education Anticipation-Reaction Guide was developed to accompany a fitness film (Rayl, 1984).

Anticipation-Reaction Guide: Stretching

Directions: Before watching the fitness film, put a (+) by those statements with which you agree and a (−) by those with which you disagree. Jot down some notes that will help you defend your point of view in a class discussion. After watching the film, reconsider each statement using the "Reaction" column.

Anticipation	**Reaction**	
_____	_____	1. Most doctors prescribe stretching for relief of tension and stress.
_____	_____	2. A gymnast and a football player should stretch about the same length of time.
_____	_____	3. Stretching is neglected because it is painful and boring.
_____	_____	4. Stretching with the aid of a partner can bring about greater flexibility.

Guide statements such as these can serve as a focal point for review of important concepts during the post-reading stage of a lesson.

In a social studies class, Anticipation-Reaction Guides help students to appraise ideas critically in a text (Ericson, Hubler, Bean, Smith, & McKenzie, 1987). For example, the following guide was designed to accompany junior high students' reading of a United States history chapter on the Constitution in *American Spirit* (Ver Steeg, 1982). One student's pre-reading ideas are included.

Anticipation-Reaction Guide: The Constitution

Directions: Before reading pages 186 to 193, read each statement and place a (yes) by those statements with which you agree and a (no) by those statements with which you disagree under the section labeled Anticipation. Write your reasons for agreeing or disagreeing so you can be part of a class discussion. When you have read the text, return to the column called Reaction and look at each statement again. Do you want to change your mind on any of them?

Anticipation	**Reaction**	
yes	*yes*	1. Writers of the Constitution were everyday working class people. *Because they had to work for a living and they were not royalty.*
no	*no*	2. The President, like a king, has complete power to rule the country. *Because he can be kicked out of office by the process of impeachment.*
yes	*yes*	3. A Ford mechanic cannot become President. *Because it doesn't matter as long as he is the right age and is elected.*
no	*yes*	4. People who are rich and people who are poor have equal protection under the law. *Because the rich people have more influence over the law because they can bribe the law.*
yes	*no*	5. Students should have the right to decide what classes they take. *After the 10th grade they should be able to, because by that time they will know what they want from life and they would take courses to prepare for their career.*
no	*no*	6. People in all countries have a Bill of Rights. *Just look at U.S.S.R. and South Africa.*

Even factual texts in United States history can serve as rich sources for critical thinking when they are supplemented with an Anticipation-Reaction Guide like this one. Students begin to see some link between their lives and the often distant concepts in a text. Moreover, they must adopt a critical stance toward a topic, weighing their preconceptions against the author's ideas. Indeed, philosophers regard the development and evaluation of arguments as the essence of critical thinking (Facione, 1984).

Anticipation-Reaction Guides are best used in small group or cooperative learning pairs (Ericson et. al., 1987). Students can then discuss their perceptions of the topic, which helps them see that these statements are not a test. At first, you may need to make it clear to students that these statements are designed to jog their thinking, not to serve as another true-false test of Trivial Pursuit facts to be memorized. In our experience, students at various levels enjoy reacting to well constructed guide statements to narrative and expository material as well as lectures and films.

Text Previews

Text previews are another pre-reading strategy you can use to introduce students to complex narratives or expository texts (Grave, Cooke, & LaBerge, 1983). A text preview is a teacher-devised introductory passage that provides a detailed framework for comprehending a reading selection. Text previews consist of three sections: (1) an interest-building section; (2) a synopsis of the selection; and, (3) a review of characters in a story or important points in an expository selection, along with definitions of key words and questions to guide students' reading.

The first text preview we will examine was developed to accompany a well known short story often introduced in junior high. The story, "The Lady or the Tiger" was written by Frank R. Stockton in 1884. Although its plot is fairly simple, the story contains many archaic words students are likely to find troublesome. The story describes a "semi-barbaric" princess who falls in love with a commoner. Her father, the king, discovers this and has the commoner placed in an arena before the people of the village where he is confronted with two doors. Behind one door is a beautiful woman, behind the other, a tiger. Tension in the story hinges on whether or not the princess, who knows which door is safe, will save her lover or have him killed out of jealousy. Indeed, the final outcome is never revealed and the reader must infer the princess's decision.

The text preview that follows is one we have used successfully with junior high English classes to introduce and discuss "The Lady or the Tiger" (Ericson, Hubler, Bean, Smith, & McKenzie, 1987).

Text Preview: The Lady or the Tiger

Build Interest

Many adults read fairy tales to their children. Did any adult ever read fairy tales to you? Which ones do you remember?

Many fairy tales have a princess who falls in love. The young man she falls in love with must often prove himself worthy to her father, the king. Perhaps he must slay a dragon or survive other dangerous experiences. In some fairy tales, the young man even saves the princess from some horrible beast.

Stories like this are not only for children, however. Stories for teenagers and adults may have many similarities with fairy tales. For example, there are many stories in which modern day parents disapprove of the boy their daughter loves, but they change their minds about him when he does something wonderful, and everything ends happily. Can you think of examples from television or the movies which are modern day fairy tales?

Based on "The Lady or the Tiger," by Frank R. Stockton.

Sometimes in a story or television program something happens that you don't expect. Maybe there is a sad ending instead of a happy ending, or the thief turns out to be a king in disguise. Another unexpected ending might involve having the ugly woman turn out to be a beautiful fashion model working under cover for the police. Can you think of other examples?

Synopsis

In "The Lady or the Tiger," a king has an unusual way of deciding if a man accused of a crime is guilty or innocent. The accused man is forced to walk into an arena and must open one of two doors. Behind one door is a ferocious tiger who immediately tears the man to pieces as punishment for being guilty. Behind the other door is a beautiful woman who immediately marries him as a reward for his innocence. All the people of the kingdom are required to attend this trial.

Review of characters, vocabulary, and guiding questions

Now it happens that a common man falls in love with the king's daughter. She loves him in return. But the king finds out about their love and the young man's fate is to be decided in the arena. The princess knows which door hides the tiger and will be able to give her lover a signal. But she is very jealous of the beautiful young woman behind the other door.

What signal does she give her lover? You will have to read to find out.

Before you read the story, we want to tell you again the three most important people in it. They are the king, the princess, and the young man.

There are also some words we would like to define:

The king is "semibarbaric" and "authoritarian." "Semibarbaric" means that he is only half civilized. The other half of the king enjoys bloody shows in the arena. "Authoritarian" means that he demands that everything be done his way.

The princess is "fervent" and "imperious." "Fervent" means that she openly shows her feelings. "Imperious" means that she demands her own way, just as her father does.

As you read, be thinking of these questions:

(1) What signal does the princess give her lover?
(2) What does the young man find behind the door he opens?
(3) Why did the princess choose that door?
(4) If you were writing this story, how would you have ended it?

Text previews like this one draw on readers' background knowledge and increase their interest in reading a selection. We have found that junior high students enthusiastically participate in the pre-reading discussion stage of a text preview, and the exercise makes them feel they have some power over complex material before they begin reading. One study of below average readers in junior high who were introduced to text previews showed that these pre-reading aids contributed significantly to students' comprehension of difficult short stories (Graves et al., 1983).

The following steps should guide your development of text previews.

Step One

Create an interest-building section consisting of several statements and questions that connect the major topics and issues with experiences familiar to students. Think about real life, day-to-day events that are analogous to the critical target concepts in a text.

Step Two

Write a synopsis that may, in the case of a story, describe setting, characters, provide definitions of important vocabulary, and include several questions for guiding students' reading. In the case of expository text, we have found that it is effective to use focusing questions in this section, ones that move students from text-explicit to higher implicit and experience-based thinking.

Step Three

Introduce the text preview to students by having them read the first interest-building section, followed by a discussion. Use this same approach for the synopsis and last section. Much like an anticipation-reaction guide, a pre-reading discussion will give you a chance to determine students' background knowledge as they approach a challenging selection.

Since it takes a great deal of effort to develop and introduce text previews, we recommend that you create them only for particularly challenging selections. In addition, you may find that having students write text previews for students in other classes is another powerful way to use this strategy (Ericson et al., 1987).

When you develop a text preview for an expository selection in science or social studies, the interest-building section is critical. Unfortunately, textbooks rarely include the sort of author intrusions found in diet books and other tradebooks sold in most bookstores. Author intrusions generally offer familiar analogies, use personal pronouns, and seek to guide the reader's pursuit of meaning (Bean, Singer, Cowen, & Searles, 1987). Your text previews fill this gap by speaking directly to students.

The following text preview was developed and used in a junior high United States history class where students were reading a chapter on the "Politics of Protest" (Smith, 1987; Ver Steeg, 1982). During the late 1800s farmers protested unfair business practices that overcharged them for the transportation of their goods. The plight of farmers in the 1800s can be related to the desire of any group for fair treatment. We tried to make this connection in our text preview. The last part of the preview asks seven study guide questions designed to help students grapple with these issues in a contemporary context. One student's responses to these questions are featured.

Text Preview: The Politics of Protest

Suppose that you like to ride a skateboard around your neighborhood. Then, one day, older people in the neighborhood band together and say that there can be no more skateboarding where you live. If you are caught skateboarding, they will take away your board and charge you a $50 fine. How do you feel about this situation? What would you do about it?

The chapter you are about to read shows how groups of people such as small business people, workers, and farmers in the 1890s protested what they felt were unfair practices by big business. Like the people that banned skateboarding, big business had a lot of power in the 1890s. Big business could make life miserable for the little guy. For example, the farmers felt they were paying too much interest on equipment loans from big business banks. Farmers band together to protest this unfair treatment. They looked for help from the federal government, especially Congress. As you read pages 537 to 539, see if you can answer the following questions:

Right There on the Page

1. How did farmers solve their problems with big business? (pg. 538, paragraph 2 & 3)

    Patrons of Husbandry talked about political "junk."

2. What good did the Interstate Commerce Act of 1887 do? (p. 539, paragraph 1)

    It helped lower the rates of railroads.

3. What was the purpose of the Sherman Antitrust Act? (p. 539, paragraph 3)

    To break-up large groups or combinations of big businesses that had become trusts.

Think and Search

4. Why didn't the Sherman Antitrust Act work the way it was supposed to in 1890?

    Because the wording was not very clear. And, the people who were supposed to make it work didn't believe in it.

On Your Own

5. Do you think the Sherman Antitrust Act is working today?

    Yes, they still try to break up large groups.

6. If you were a small farmer in Idaho, do you think your business would be doing well today? *No, because farms are now owned mostly by big groups. I couldn't keep up with them.*

7. Do you think big business monopolies are as much of a problem today as they were in 1890? Why? Why not?

    Yes, but now we break some of them up--like A.T.&T.

This text preview and its guide questions helped students' comprehension of a potentially dull and distant topic—the farmers efforts to gain fair treatment in the late 1800s. Having students work on the guide questions in cooperative learning pairs also helps those students who may be unaccustomed to grappling with experience-based, on-your-own issues. Text previews can be created for particularly problematic text reading assignments in science and other content areas. They help students approach text reading with a schema for a topic based on prior knowledge.

Graphic Organizers and the Organization of Texts. In this section we will expand on the graphic organizer strategy described in chapter five. By now, you are probably well-aware that graphic organizers not only introduce new, technical vocabulary, but that they also provide a simultaneous introduction to text concepts and their interrelationships. Hence, graphic organizers provide a comprehension framework that should promote both the initial reading and long-term retention of content information. With careful guidance, students can become adept at using graphic organizers as an independent study strategy and a pre-writing aid to organize a paper (Bean, Singer, Sorter, & Frazee, 1986).

Readers tend to remember information from texts in a hierarchical fashion. Fortunately, text authors typically introduce concepts in this same, "building block" framework. Thus, a graphic organizer that reflects the structural pattern of the text and is presented to students before they read will function as a road map of important concepts. Indeed, Bartlett (1978) demonstrated that teaching ninth-grade students to identify organizational patterns improved the quality and structure of their memory for this information.

Earlier we introduced some of the most dominant organizational patterns of nonfiction. It is now time to review these and see how they can be reflected in a pre-reading graphic organizer. Four of these patterns and a brief, illustrative organizer follow.

1. **Cause/Effect:** The interrelationship of two or more events, objects, or ideas.

    Example: When Sally arrived home from work last night she forgot to shut the garage door. Now, in the bone-chilling air of early morning, she struggles to start her car. It is clear that she will be late for work again. Moreover, she might even lose her job.

    Organizer:

In this example, it is explicitly stated that Sally will be late for work as a result of her car trouble (effect) resulting from the flow of cold air through the open garage door (cause). Yet, there is also the implication that she may lose her job since this is not the first time she has been late for work. Thus, the levels of understanding required for comprehending cause/effect structures may encompass text-explicit, text-implicit, and experience-based levels of thinking. A pre-reading graphic organizer may facilitate comprehension at each of these levels by alerting students to the author's important ideas and their relationships.

2. **Comparison/Contrast:** The similarities and differences among two or more events, objects, or ideas.

Example: Few would argue that large cities offer more job opportunities and cultural activities than rural areas. But cities are plagued by some very unattractive side effects of economic and cultural abundance. The two most noticeable side effects are overcrowding and pollution. Indeed, rural folk frequently argue that their uncrowded vistas and clean air far surpass any urban advantages. Yet rural areas have few jobs, which makes cities the more popular dwelling places, despite their discomforts.

Organizer:

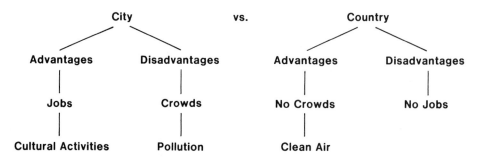

3. **Time Order:** The chronological ordering of two or more events, objects, or ideas.

Example: John decided to buy a new motorcycle in the coming spring. That winter he began to read all the consumer reports on different makes and models. In the early spring he went to a number of different motorcycle dealerships and did some test riding. Finally, he settled on an 850 with the features he wanted. He got a loan from the credit union and picked up the bike in April. Then he was ready for a trip to California in the summer.

Organizer:

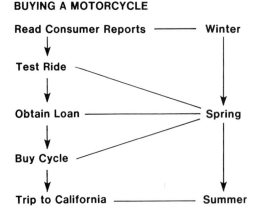

4. **Problem-Solution:** The interaction of two or more factors, one citing a problem and another providing a potential answer to that problem.

Example: Crime is increasing in the city. It is not safe to be on the streets at night. The mayor and city council should pass the gun control law and hire more police.

Organizer:

It should be noted that in text material these patterns frequently overlap. For example, in history, time order, cause/effect, and comparison/contrast are all prevalent patterns. A pre-reading graphic organizer can aid students as they try to perceive the author's structure and its relationship to their current knowledge base. Ideally, we would like students to be able to generate these organizers independently as they develop some familiarity with a subject area.

It takes students some time before they can effectively develop their own graphic organizers. One effective way to teach this process is to gradually increase the amount of student participation in construction of the organizer. To do this, we have found this sequence useful. At first, the teacher provides partially completed graphic organizers that accompany a reading assignment. For example, in physical education the following graphic organizer might be used to guide students reading of a chapter on running (Singer & Bean, 1988).

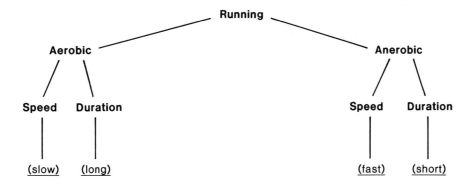

Students are advised to read in order to identify the differences between aerobic and anerobic running. (In this example, the differences are listed here in parentheses, which are blank in the actual guide). At times, we even include page numbers directing students to the essential information.

Once students grasp how the graphic organizer assists their comprehension, the next stage involves the teacher walking them through the construction of one. The material used for this activity should be familiar to students so they can devote their effort to following the steps of constructing the graphic organizer.

Next, have student teams read a section of text and develop graphic organizers. Since graphic organizers are based on the structure and vocabulary of the text, the resulting organizers should be quite similar. They should provide a good basis for extending students' text-explicit comprehension of the material through discussion and post-reading assignments.

Finally, students should construct their own graphic organizers of a reading assignment and should be given minimal guidance. For example, in biology, you may simply provide the top level category labels for a chapter such as "functions" and "properties" of carbohydrates. These should be collected so you can provide feedback to students. A simple ($\checkmark$, $\checkmark+$, or $\checkmark-$) and some comments of praise or helpful criticism usually help students become comfortable with the strategy.

Once you feel students are adept at constructing their own graphic organizers you can phase out the requirement. Some students will continue to use the technique, some will prefer outlining, and still others will use rereading. They will be much more aware of the text structure the author uses, regardless of the degree to which they employ graphic organizers.

It is important to note that in our experience, this teaching sequence may require a span of 10 or more weeks. You may need to develop many of the initial graphic organizers, despite students' previous experience in outlining. Yet graphic organizers have some distinct advantages over outlining. In a recent study, Bean, Singer, Sorter, & Frazee (1986) found that student-constructed graphic organizers were significantly more effective aids to long-term comprehension of difficult world history text than outlining. They also serve as good pre-writing structures for essays and longer papers. Your careful efforts to teach students to use graphic organizers will be beneficial to them years later.

Activity

Directions: Browse through a chapter in this text or in a content text of your choice. What patterns of organization have been used? How do you know? Can you organize one of those patterns you identified into a graphic organizer?

Pre-Reading Questions. Teacher-posed pre-reading questions constitute another traditionally popular approach to aiding students' comprehension. Pre-reading questions have been employed in the content area teaching and learning sequence for years. As a result, a large body of data has been collected on how pre-reading questions influence the comprehension process. Some of the findings from this research may come as a surprise to you. The answer to the simple query, "Do pre-reading questions increase comprehension?" turns out to be a bit more complex than one might suspect.

In a summation of pre-question studies, Faw and Waller (1976) noted that pre-questions tend to focus students' attention on the questioned information while simultaneously suppressing their overall comprehension of text concepts. This focusing effect is particularly pronounced for factual or text-explicit pre-questions and less true of experience-derived pre-questions. Thus, although pre-questions do facilitate comprehension of the questioned information, they may be one of the least attractive pre-reading methods unless they are combined with other strategies that encourage overall comprehension. You will need to evaluate your purpose in asking pre-reading questions before you use them in your class.

In a discussion that relates to the issue of focused versus overall comprehension, Tierney and Spiro (1979) emphasize that there needs to be a balance between what they termed text-based information and reader-based ideas. In the case of text-explicit, factual pre-questions (such as "How would you tune a carburetor on a motorcycle?"), the learner, devoid of knowledge about the topic, is being asked to operate in an exclusively text-based mode. In contrast, when the learner is called upon to form a mental image of a text selection, there is greater integration of experiential and textual information (e.g., "While reading 'How to Buy a Motorcycle,' think of a bike you might buy.")

The foregoing comments should not be taken as a suggestion that we completely abandon text-explicit pre-reading questions. In fact, Singer and Rhodes (1976) noted that pre-questions provided much needed guidance for students who lack the ability to select important information from texts. What we need to do is to strike a balance between text-explicit information and reader-based strategies for acquiring this information. For example, Yopp-Nolte and Singer (1985) found that having students formulate their own pre-reading questions was a promising approach. One of the most successful strategies for activating students' expectations about a topic involves a combination of teacher- and student-generated questions. In the next section we will explore this reciprocal questioning approach.

ReQuest. This unusual representation of the word "request" is actually a blend of "reciprocal" and "questioning." The *ReQuest* strategy was developed by Manzo (1969) to help students adopt an active, questioning approach to text reading. Students are guided in this process by the teacher, who models the question-asking procedure and attempts to elicit higher-level, text-implicit and experience-based questions.

In the ReQuest activity, both the teacher and students silently read specified portions of the text together and then take turns asking each other questions. Students ask the first series of questions. This order gives the teacher an opportunity to appraise the level of their analysis. If the students merely produce text-explicit questions (e.g., "What color was the main character's hair?"), then the teacher attempts to model higher-order questions on that same section of the text after students have fully exhausted their array of questions. The teacher models higher-order questions such as: "What is the significance of the main character's iron-grey hair?" (text-implicit); "How would you feel if you were in the main character's predicament?" (experience-based); "What do you think is going to happen next?" (prediction based on text-implicit and experience-based factors). Moreover, when students produce similar questions during their interrogative turn, the teacher should praise their efforts with such phrases as: "That's a good question! It really makes me think!"

Now that you have a general notion of what ReQuest is all about, we want to outline the preparatory steps for a ReQuest session and illustrate the procedure with a story we devised. The following preparatory steps are essential for a successful ReQuest session:

Step One

Analyze the text selection for major concepts and sections portraying these concepts. For example, a story can usually be divided into the following units: setting and characters; an event that introduces conflict; attempts to resolve the conflict or achieve a goal; resolution of the conflict; and finally, a reaction on the part of the protagonist.

Step Two

Determine prediction points in the story or text selection that allow the reader to form expectations about upcoming events. These prediction points can be labeled in your copy of the material as P_1, P_2, P_3, etc.

> *Example:*   She treaded water, trying to remain calm as the full moon illuminated the last features of her once majestic sloop, now sinking into oblivion. The tropical air was warm and the Pacific deceptively gentle, yet she knew, danger was lurking in the depths that surrounded her.

P_1----------

> Sharks are particularly bold at night. . . .

Step Three

Explain the general ReQuest procedure to your students.

Example:

Teacher: "We'll each read a portion of the text silently. I will close my book and you can ask me all the questions you can think of referring to your book as needed.
Teacher: "Let's read the first paragraph. . . ."

Step Four

When you reach the final prediction point in the story or text selection, have students generate all the predictions they can think of for the final outcome of the selection. List the predictions verbatim on the board and have students vote on the ones they feel are most plausible. This step is particularly exciting with story selections that have a surprise twist at the end.

The following story and ReQuest scenario illustrates one approach to the use of this procedure in an English class.

The Round Swing

The round swing stood in a little clearing behind the Robinson's cabin. It was nothing more than a tall pine tree with all its branches cut off and a long rope hanging from the top to within about three feet of the ground. A piece of cloth was tied to the end of the rope. The tree was set back about ten feet from the edge of a steep ravine, carpeted with pines at the bottom.

P_1----------

I looked down, far down into the valley below. And the same nervous sickness that overcame me on the thirty-foot diving tower at summer camp bounced into my stomach. But I had to go on the round swing. There wasn't anyone else to refuse with me. I was alone.

P₂----------

"I'll go first!" Terry said.

"Okay, I'll hold the rope while you get in," Mike Robinson offered.

Terry put his feet through the cloth seat and tested it with his weight.

"I'm no fat man like Mark Rogers. It won't give," he said.

And then he was running hard around the half-circle plateau. Seated and airborne. Yelling his lungs out in nervous excitement. A human puppet soaring over the valley. Stumbling back onto the other side of the plateau and he was off again. Till the rope had coiled itself tightly around the tree and Terry crashed into it panting.

"Wow! It's great, Mike! Hey, you gotta try it, Kev! It's so hairy!" "Go ahead, Mike. After all, it's your swing." I said.

"Okay. I'll just go around a few times, then you can try it."

He took off, hooting his way over the ravine like Terry. The third time around he skidded back onto the ledge.

"C'mon, Kev! You can try it now!" Terry said.

P₃---------

"No, I don't know. I'm not that hot on trying it," I said.

"What? You aren't afraid, are you?"

"No, I just don't care about it that much," I answered.

A car crunched over the dirt road, winding its way into the Robinson's front yard. Mike pulled himself out of the swing.

"Hey, that's probably my parents. Let's go inside. Don't say anything about the swing."

"That's okay. We have to go home now anyway. We'll just go through your backyard and work our way down to the river," Terry said.

"Do you know where the trail is?"

"Yeh, Mike. See you later."

"Too bad you didn't get to try the round swing, Kev," Mike said.

"Yeh, some other time," I answered.

Terry looked disgusted but didn't say anything all the way down the trail. When we reached the river I let myself flow along with it.

Three prediction points have been established for guiding students' collaborative discussion and comprehension of this story. The teacher and students would read the first paragraph (i.e., P₁) silently, then the students would ask the teacher questions based on just that section. It has been the authors' experience that even fairly sophisticated students will begin ReQuest by asking rather low-level, text-explicit questions. The following hypothetical scenario is representative of a typical ReQuest session:

Student(s): "What was the round swing?" (text explicit)
Teacher: "A rope tied to a pine tree. . . ."

Notice that this form of text-explicit question has a tendency to stifle further discussion. Also note that the teacher did not provide any positive comment on the quality of the question. At this point in the scenario, let us assume that students have exhausted their array of questions on this paragraph and it is now the teacher's turn.

Teacher: "What do you think is going to happen in this story?" (prediction via text-implicit and experience-based information)

Student A: "Someone's going to fall out of the round swing."

Student B: "We're going to find out how it feels to ride the round swing."

Student C: "It's too early to tell."

Teacher: "Okay, let's read the next paragraph and see what happens!"

As you can see, in contrast to text-explicit questions, the teacher's question, comprising a blend of implicit and experience-based elements, asked students to predict the next event in the story. This type of question generates discussion and provides a good model for students to emulate when it is their turn. In addition, it is impossible to produce a wrong answer on a prediction question. For the sake of illustration, let us assume that some of the students in this example have grasped the concept of asking higher-order questions as we move into the second paragraph (i.e., P_2).

Teacher: "Okay, you can ask me any questions you can think of from the first two paragraphs."

Student D: "What is below the round swing?"

Teacher: "A valley."

Student E: "What would you do if you were the speaker in the story?" (experience-based)

Teacher: "Ah, that's a good question—I'll have to think about that a minute. . . . If it looked sturdy enough I might try the round swing. I think I would test out the cloth seat first!"

Student F: "Where do you think this story takes place?" (text-implicit)

Teacher: "That's interesting to think about. Maybe in the high Sierras somewhere in California? It doesn't really say, so it could be in the hills of Georgia. . . . Probably not in Iowa!"

It should be readily apparent at this point that ReQuest is an attractive method for guiding students' comprehension of a story or text selection. At the final prediction point (i.e., P_3), the teacher would elicit all possible predictions pertaining to the outcome of the story. These would be listed on the board and their probability would be rank-ordered by way of a class vote. Students should be advised that the author's chosen ending is not necessarily preferable to the endings they have generated.

As you can see, ReQuest functions as an effective pre-reading strategy or, if extended as in the preceding example, it may be useful to guide the entire reading of a selection. Thus, ReQuest overlaps with the reading stage of a well-integrated content lesson.

The Directed-Reading-Thinking-Activity and Student-Generated Questions. Although ReQuest is an ideal means of guiding students toward asking their own questions of well-structured story material, the *Directed-Reading-Thinking-Activity* (DRTA) works well with expository texts, especially in social studies (Stauffer, 1969). The DRTA is a self-questioning process that encourages students to predict oncoming information in expository text and set purposes for reading that are personally interesting. Questions not answered by a text may call for supplemental reading, class discussion, consultation with an expert source, or further exploration of a topic.

The following steps should guide a DRTA lesson.

Step One

Before reading the text in detail, have students survey a chapter topic by considering the title, headings, illustrations, and diagrams. This survey will form the basis for pre-reading questions. Longer chapters can be broken-up into smaller increments if necessary, or students in small groups can each survey a section of the chapter and share their questions.

Step Two

Have students write questions called to mind in the chapter survey. If you have students keep a journal, they can enter the questions there.

Step Three

As a class, discuss various student-generated questions, emphasizing the value of personal purpose setting.

Step Four

Have students read the text to consider answers to their questions. They can then discuss their answers in small groups or as a class.

Step Five

Have students in small groups develop questions that the text does *not* answer about the topic. Through discussion, help them identify sources such as people and other texts able to supply answers to their questions. Provide time and credit for tracking down these answers.

The following DRTA was conducted in a multicultural junior high geography class. Students were reading a section of the text describing peasant life in China leading up to the peasant revolt. They had to consider two sub-headings: (a) "Peasants in China," and (b) "The Road to Revolt." Here are some of the representative questions they generated for steps one through four. Answers are in italics.

DRTA: China

Peasants in China

1. What kinds of jobs do peasants work on?

   Farming.

2. Where do most peasants live?

   In the country

3. Do they have enough food to eat and sell?

   Yes. But they have just a little to sell. To survive, peasants could rent or sell their land. They could sell their children.

The Road to Revolt

4. Why did the rulers dislike peasants?

*Because they thought of them
as servants.*

5. How did the rulers make life harder for the peasants?

*Peasants did not have enough land to support
their rapidly growing population.*

Students generated a wide array of interesting questions not answered by the text.

Student Questions Not Answered By the Text

1. What is life like out in China now?
2. Do teenagers go to school, come home, sometimes cook dinner, and do homework?
3. Do the Chinese listen to the same music we do?
4. Do their homes and houses look like ours?
5. Are the parents very strict to their children? Because we get away with a lot of things!
6. What do they do when they have free time?

In this instance, a visitor to the class had spent the previous summer traveling throughout mainland China visiting schools. She was able to provide answers to students' questions. When immediate answers to student-generated questions are not available, it is important to identify available resources that will shed light on the questions and allot adequate time and rewards for sharing this information with the class at a later date. In our experience, authors would do well to pay attention to the experience-based questions students ask in a DRTA lesson. Perhaps our textbooks could be more responsive to the active interest students display in topics that sometimes seem very distant from their lives. In any case, the DRTA increases students' interest in reading for purposes they set.

The Reading Stage

Sitting down with a textbook in the solitude of your own personal study corner is a lonely activity, devoid of the language interaction afforded by the classroom. You may well wonder what possible strategies exist to help students cope with this inherently solitary task.

Indeed, many text assignments are of the "sink-or-swim" variety. "Go home and read chapter 13 in your text" is an all too familiar edict for many students. Unfortunately, textbooks are rarely amenable to such independent reading assignments. Texts are instructional tools that require a good deal of guidance if students are to gain anything from them. In the section that follows we will describe some approaches that assist students in coping with their individual text reading assignments.

Study Guides. The term *study guide* has been used loosely for years to describe almost any form of supplementary material that accompanies a text. Often, study guides are nothing more than a series of text-explicit questions supplied by an author at the end of a text chapter. We subscribe to a very different view of the process involved in the development of a good, content area study guide. The mini-study guide that follows contains the basic ingredients necessary to extend students' thinking beyond a mere "parroting" of text-explicit concepts.

Mini-Study Guide

Directions: Use the information in Chapter 6 to answer the following questions. Compare your answers to those of a colleague.

 *1. What is the second principle of comprehension advanced in the introduction to Chapter 6? (page 123, paragraph 3)

 **2. Why is it important for students to be able to generate their own graphic organizer of text concepts?

 ***3. Of the comprehension strategies introduced so far in Chapter 6, which one(s) do you prefer for use in your context area? Why?

 * Text-explicit
 ** Text-implicit
 *** Experience-based

Notice that a study guide of this form asks students to react to text concepts at multiple levels of understanding. For example, the first question, which is text explicit, includes a detailed reference to assist students in locating the answer. For some students, this detailed form of guidance may be necessary. Indeed, some students may only be able to answer this form of question, particularly in the early stages of the course. In contrast to question one, question three asks the reader to build a bridge of text concepts and individual teaching needs. Both questions two and three offer the potential for discussion and expanded thinking. Although this study guide example has been presented "after the fact," in practice, study guides typically accompany a text assignment and the reader completes the guide while reading. Thus the guide provides a pathway to the major concepts in a content area and counters a more traditional, "sink-or-swim" reading assignment. A good study guide should mirror the thinking process by which a reader extracts information from text (Herber, 1978; Raphael, 1986). As such, a teacher-devised study guide should possess the following characteristics (Earle, 1969). The study guide:

1. Focuses students' attention on major concepts at three levels of understanding (i.e., text-explicit, text-implicit, experience-based).
2. Fosters student reaction to the text material at each student's own, individual level of understanding.
3. Directs students' thinking processes in extracting information from text material.
4. Serves as a basis for follow-up discussion in small groups to collaborate on the explication of text concepts and extend individual comprehension.

One might expect that students would regard study guides as an additional burden along with the text reading assignment. In a study designed to explore secondary students' opinions of study guides, Laffey and Steele (1979) found that study guides were well received. The majority of students evaluating study guides felt they understood text concepts better as a result of completing and discussing guide material.

The development of a study guide involves a process of content analysis similar to the construction of an anticipation guide. Indeed, developing these two comprehension aids simultaneously with a text chapter is a good idea. The following steps should be followed:

Step One

Determine the major concepts and important details in a text chapter or reading selection.

Step Two

Develop questions that reflect these major concepts and details at multiple levels of understanding. Use vocabulary terms students can understand and, in the first few guides you develop, provide page and paragraph indicators to demonstrate the process of locating and extracting information.

Step Three

Assign the study guide as an adjunct to independent text reading. Then, have students discuss and defend responses in small groups.

Since not all students will be able to answer the whole study guide, the discussion step gives everyone exposure to the complete array of information. This study group step is an integral part of the application of study guide material and is essential to its success as an aid to comprehension. Generally, about ten questions per study guide should be adequate for a text chapter. The guide should look attractive in that adequate space is allowed for student answers and information does not appear to be crowded on the page.

The following study guide was used to guide high school students' discussion in United States history. Text-explicit questions are labeled "right there on the page," text-implicit questions, "search and think," and experience-based questions, "on your own." Raphael (1986) found that using these phrases helps students focus on the source of information needed for answering questions. This study guide was developed to accompany reading in chapter seven, "The Confederation and the Constitution," of *The American Pageant* (Bailey & Kennedy, 1983). Students read the text and answered the study guide questions. Then, they engaged in small group discussions of their answers and a large group follow-up discussion focusing on the "on your own" items. One student's answers are included in italics.

Study Guide: The Confederation and the Constitution

Right There On the Page

1. What political changes occurred in the 13 colonies as a result of the American Revolution? (p. 119–120) *Colonial self-rule, the recognition of minorities, new constitution, an increase in voting, and the legislature was more responsive to people.*

2. What social changes took place in the 13 colonies as a result of the American Revolution? (p. 120–121) *The separation of church and state, department of Loyalists, uprooted the Anglican Church, loosening of morals, weakening of slavery, and the development of the feminist movement.*

3. What economic changes happened in the 13 colonies as a result of the American Revolution? (p. 122) *Inventive influences, the loss of commerce because of England, high inflation, great amounts of land available, freedom of trade, a distaste for government.*

Search and Think

4. Can you identify some political, social, and economic *disadvantages* that resulted from the American Revolution? *We did not have many great strong leaders that we had before. We really did not have much control. We were on our own so we needed to spend money to manufacture goods and find people to buy them.*

5. Why wasn't slavery abolished in the 1770's? *Political fighting over slavery was avoided to preserve national unity. Too many people needed workers to make money and get their lives going again.*

6. Why do you think the authors see the American Revolution as "accelerated evolution" rather than "outright revolution?" *Because the Revolution was unknown to many people living in small, isolated villages and, it wasn't as radical as other revolutions. It made future changes possible.*

On Your Own

7. Would you want to travel through time back to the 1770s during the drafting of the Constitution? If so, why? If not, why not? *Yes, so I could maybe put things in or take things out that may help the United States.*

8. If you decide to travel back in time to visit the drafting of the constitution you would be taking with you the powerful knowledge of the future! What advice could you give the writers of the Constitution? *Be clearer in what is written. Today, interpretations of the constitution are all different.*

Study guides are particularly important in the early part of a course as students are getting a grasp of an author's writing style and dominant text structures. We have used study guides effectively in the early grades and at the academic level. Study guide questions can form an effective model for student-generated questions. Indeed, study guides and the selective reading guides considered in the next section help model fluent, efficient text reading. Textbooks are not designed to be read word-for-word. Rather, they should be read selectively with an eye toward important ideas.

The following activity is designed to give you further practice with the process of constructing a study guide for a content area text.

Activity

Directions: The following three study guide questions pertain to the present section of chapter 6. See if you can generate three additional study guide questions on this same material.

***1. Based on your own academic experience, can you think of any courses you have taken where you would have appreciated study guides with the text? Which ones? Why?

  *2. What is the second step in constructing a study guide?

 **3. How does the study guide foster the psychological principle of in-depth processing of text material?

  *4.

 **5.

***6.

Selective Reading Guide. If you could unobtrusively observe students attempting a content chapter reading assignment in the solitude of their study corners, the following events might be fairly representative of what you would see. The students open the text to the assigned chapter and begin reading from the first page. By about the middle of the chapter our subjects are becoming fatigued, losing concentration, and are seen rapidly turning the pages to gauge how much of this task is left. Sound familiar? Obviously this sort of mindless plodding through a text chapter is the antithesis of an active, purposeful approach to comprehending text concepts. As an alternative to such an approach, Cunningham and Shablak (1975) proposed a procedure for guiding students' independent text reading called the "Selective Reading Guide-O-Rama," which we simply call a Selective Reading Guide. The *Selective Reading Guide,* much like a study guide, is a series of teacher-devised guide statements that accompany a text reading assignment. The guide statements are structured in such a way as to direct students' reading of a text chapter toward the most important information. In addition, a Selective Reading Guide provides students with a model of purposeful and selective text reading.

The steps that follow outline the construction of a Selective Reading Guide for any content area:

Step One

Determine the overall purpose for a particular reading assignment. For example, in chapter six the purpose might be to apply at least one of the comprehension strategies in your own content area.

Step Two

Select those sections of the text chapter that are necessary to achieve the overall purpose. Decide which sections of the chapter are tangential to the overall purpose.

Step Three

Based on close analysis of your own reading strategies for this chapter, decide what operations students must engage in to achieve the purpose of the reading assignment.

Step Four

Develop guide statements that direct students' reading of the text chapter.

Step Five

Provide students with the written guide specifying what to look for and what to do with the text information.

The following examples of guide statements should give you some idea of how they look in practice:

1. The rationale and graphic organizer on pages 121–122 provide a good indication of what to expect in this chapter. You should read this section thoroughly.
2. The section entitled "Principles of Comprehension" on page 123 is basically a capsule review of the concepts introduced in chapter two. If you feel comfortable with these ideas, skip this section.
3. Page 170, paragraph 5: This paragraph summarizes the entire reading selection. Read it slowly. If there is anything you do not understand in this paragraph, go back to the reading and check it over carefully. Ask me if anything still bothers you.

Selective Reading Guides are helpful across a wide variety of content areas. In the example that follows you can see how an art teacher used a Selective Reading Guide in a ceramics class at the crucial stage of firing and glazing pottery (Kasparek, 1983). This is the stage where the potential for disaster is greatest. The guide refers to pages 196–203 in Nelson's (1971) *Ceramics: A Potter's Handbook.*

Selective Reading Guide: Art

Directions: Use the following guide as you read the important portions of our book before you continue with your project. Be prepared to discuss this information.

Pages 196–197: Start with the section "Clay in the Bisque State." *Skip* engobe. *Read* and try 2 of the next 3 methods. *Record* the methods and results in your notebook.

Page 197: *Skip* the section on glazing in the raw clay state. This method will not be used in our ceramics class. We will discuss the reasons why at the end of the reading.

Page 197: *Skim* the section on glazing in the bisque state.

Page 198: In the "How to Glaze" section, *note* the two things you must do to your project after you have glazed it. Be sure you *do these two things* on your project or it will not be fired.

Pages 199–200: *Read* and *use* the methods of: dip glazing, pouring, and brushed glaze. *Skip* the section on sprayed glazes (we do not have the equipment).

Pages 201–203: *Refer* to this if you have a glaze defect.

Both the Selective Reading Guide and study guide are intended as models of proficient reading. Therefore, you may not want to develop guide material for every unit or chapter assignment. Guide material tends to be most helpful to students in the initial stages of a content class, when the text and its related concepts may be somewhat unfamiliar. You will find, however, that the teacher time it takes to construct these adjunct aids is well worth the effort.

Options Guides. An *options guide* is another form of study guide that, unlike the focused guidance provided in a traditional study guide, offers possibilities and predictions to be evaluated in subsequent reading (Bean, Sorter, Singer, & Frazee, 1986). It asks students to function in an active, decision-making role. Unlike a study guide, which is designed to accompany a reading assignment, an options guide is discussed prior to text reading. It then serves as a guide during reading. Options guides are ideal for reading assignments in social studies texts, where students often adopt a passive role, mindlessly turning pages or trying to memorize facts.

The following steps are used to develop and introduce the options guide.

Step One

Carefully analyze a text reading assignment for major concepts and key sub-headings that foreshadow upcoming events. You want to identify (1) key historical figures and the specific impact they had on other groups of people; and (2) the economy, the arts, religion, and other sociocultural aspects of life.

Step Two

Since up to the time you introduce the options guide students' previous text reading is all they have to go on in discussing the guide, you should construct a brief background statement that will remind students of the material they have read and studied up to this point.

Step Three

Develop one or two central questions that ask students to consider various options open to specific groups of people within the particular historical context the text is presenting.

Step Four

When students have completed a text reading assignment up to the sub-heading or section of text upon which your options guide is based, have them convene in small groups for about 10 to 15 minutes to discuss and complete the *before reading* section of the options guide. Then, when they finish reading the assignment, they should check their listed options against actual events in the text and complete the guide's *after reading* section. Engage students in a follow-up small group discussion to clarify any sections of the guide that need further explanation.

The options guide that follows is designed to precede a text reading assignment in chapter 17, "The Emergence of Japan," in *History and Life: The World and Its People* (Wallbank, Schrier, Maier, & Gutierrez-Smith, 1982), a high school world history text. Students have read the portion of the chapter up to section 3, on the developing samurai warrior-class. The first sub-heading of this section comprises the major heading for the guide. Subsequent sub-headings were used to list various groups affected by shogun society. Representative group answers before and after reading are listed in italics.

Options Guide: The Kamakura Shogunate (1192–1333) Began

Background:

In 1156, civil war broke out between two large landowning families. Each family had a band of loyal warriors called "samurai." In 1192, one samurai, named Minamoto Yoritomo, became the supreme general of all Japan. The emperor named him the "shogun."

During this period of military rule, what *options* for political influence do you think were available to the following groups?

1. Nobles?

    1.1 Before Reading: *They will be even more powerful with the strength of their loyal samurai warriors.*

    1.2 After Reading: *The emperor's power was less but the local "daimyos" (nobles) became supreme rulers of their lands. They fought with other daimyos. There was no effective central government in Japan during this time. Later, in the Tokugawa Era (1603–1868) central government was strong.*

2. Artists?

    2.1 Before Reading:
    In this military era, we feel there will be no time for the arts. Artists will be forced to fight or flee. It will be a very backward time.

    2.2 After Reading:
    It seems strange but the arts did flourish. Poetic "No" plays were created, landscape painting was prized, flower arranging, tea ceremonies, and artistic gardens were important in Japanese homes.

3. Farmers?

    3.1 Before Reading:
    With all the fighting, there will be no time for farming. Agriculture will suffer.

    3.2 After Reading:
    Farmers thrived since the daimyos ruled to maintain peace within their own communities. But gradually, cities grew and merchants became important. The landing of the Portuguese in 1543 made the people aware of European trade possibilities.

4. The Samurai?

4.1 Before Reading:

They are soldiers, so, like all soldiers, they will have little power. They must follow orders.

4.2 After Reading:

Samurai knights were very loyal to their shogun generals. They felt a total moral obligation to do well in battle. If they did not, they would commit suicide or "harakiri." As we suspected, they didn't have much power. The shoguns held the power.

5. If the Chinese try to invade Japan, how will they do?

5.1 Before Reading:

Since they are an older, more powerful people, they will win.

5.2 After Reading:

Kubla Khan invaded Japan but his Mongal warriors were swept into a big typhoon. The Japanese called this the Xamikaze or "divine wind." As we said before reading, without this typhoon, China's Mongol warriors might have defeated the samurai.

As you can see, in some instances students generated options that were borne out in the text. In other cases, their predictions proved far afield of what actually occurred. Options guides make potentially dull text reading assignments considerably more interesting. The guides' success hinges in large measure on the small group discussions that precede and follow their use as a reading guide. Consider using options guides for selected topics in social studies as a student-centered alternative to traditional study guides.

A recent study, which introduced students to the use of graphic organizers as an independent study strategy and combined their use with regular options guides, found that to read tenth-grade world history students became adept at seeing relationships among disparate revolutions in England, France, and Russia (Bean, et al., 1986). Indeed, they were able to make significantly better predictions about the stages of the Cuban revolution before reading about it than students who used traditional outlining to study their text and followed text reading with large group lecture and discussion.

You might consider using a fluid strategy, utilizing more teacher-directed study guides and selective reading guides in the early part of a course and shifting to greater use of options guides, DRTA, and student-directed strategies. A progression from careful guidance to increasing student responsibility helps students develop the independent reading strategies necessary for reading at advanced levels. You may want to begin with fairly detailed options guides, like the one on Japan, and slowly fade to skeletal options guides that place the responsibility on students to speculate about the impact of an event on sociocultural aspects of the economy, arts, agriculture, and so on. In our experience, your efforts to develop guide material will be richly rewarded in increased levels of student understanding and participation.

Analogical Study Guides. Another form of study guide has been developed for application in science classes. The *analogical study guide* is aimed at getting students to study new science concepts they are attempting to learn by thinking about the underlying properties of more familiar concepts and comparing these to new, unfamiliar concepts (Bean, Singer, & Cowan, 1985; Bean, Singer, Cowen, & Searles, 1987).

We use analogies spontaneously in our everyday speech and thinking. For example, if we plan a field trip to a marine biology laboratory and the trip is successful, we may say the job "went like clockwork." If our field trip plans failed, we may say they "collapsed like a house of cards."

It is not unusual for scientists to use analogies to explain complex processes or theories. For example, scientists use the analogy of a giant pinwheel or disk to understand the nature of the Milky Way. Texts in biology sometimes feature analogies, but students often do not know how they can use these analogies to comprehend and recall concepts. The analogical study guide is designed to make students aware of using analogies to understand concepts. In order to get a feel for just how useful analogies are, try the following activity.

Activity

Your last science class may have been quite some time ago, or you may be a science teacher. In any case, we would like you to try the following activity. See if you can correctly match the six cell structure parts on the left with their related functions on the right. Simply write the letter of the correct function on the line to the left of the cell part. Good luck.

Structure

1. _____ mitochondria
2. _____ cell membrane
3. _____ vacuoles
4. _____ nucleus
5. _____ endoplasmic reticulum
6. _____ ribosomes

Function

a. controls heredity
b. storage
c. boundary
d. intracellular transport
e. cellular respiration
f. protein synthesis

These cell structure-function relationships comprise just a small part of a basic chapter on the cell. This material constitutes an important foundation for subsequent chapters that explore more complex aspects of the cell, such as cell division. Most biology texts contain a chart of at least 14 cell parts and functions for students to study (e.g., *Living Systems* by Oram, Hummer, & Smoot, 1983). Many students simply memorize this chart without really understanding how the different cell parts function. In your case, we gave you a small number of cell parts to match to their functions. How did you do? Our guess is that you successfully matched nucleus and cell membrane, but (unless your field is science) you flubbed the other four items. Here are the correct answers: 1-e; 2-c; 3-b; 4-a; 5-d; 6-f. Now, consider students who have access to an analogical study guide that a teacher introduces and explains. Do you think your comprehension of these six cell structure–function relations would have been better with such a guide?

Analogical Study Guide: Cell Structure and Function

Directions: You will be studying the parts of a cell and their functions. In some ways a cell resembles a factory, because, like a factory, a cell uses raw materials to manufacture a product. You will find that comparing the different parts of the cell to the parts of a factory will help you remember the functions of the various cell parts. For example, in the guide, the cell "walls" are compared to factory walls because both provide "support and protection."

Structure	*Function*	*Analogy (Like A)*
cell wall	support and protection	factory walls
cell membrane	boundary, gatekeeper	security guards
cytoplasm	site of metabolism	the work area
chloroplasts	photosynthesis	snack bar
endoplasmic reticulum	intracellular transport	conveyor belts
golgi bodies	storage, secretion	packaging, storing, and
lysosomes	intracellular digestion	shipping
mitochondria	cellular respiration	clean-up crew
nucleus	controls heredity	energy generation plant
ribosomes	protein synthesis	boss's office and copy
vacuoles	storage	machine
		assembly line
		warehouses

The overall factory analogy provides a coherent structure for the whole guide. In a study of this guide's contribution to students' comprehension in high school biology, we found that students who were achieving low grades significantly outpaced peers in a control group when the guide was introduced as a means of studying the text (Bean et al., 1985). The control group simply used the cell structure-function chart provided in the text without any analogies.

Constructing an analogical study guide involves three important steps.

Step One

Analyze the reading task facing students by identifying those concepts you want them to acquire (e.g., a basic understanding of cell structure and function relationships).

Step Two

This is the most difficult and crucial step—creating appropriate analogies that will connect with students' diverse experiences. A good analogy is one that contains underlying properties similar to the target concept but it is usually dissimilar at the surface level. For example, comparing the cell membrane to a security guard provides a familiar analogy sharing underlying properties of entry and exit control, even though there are no surface-level similarities.

Step Three

You need to go over the analogical study guide with students, explaining how they can use the analogies on the right side of the guide to comprehend and recall the function of a particular cell structure. Some students may wish to generate their own analogies, so you can gradually transfer responsibility for this process to students.

Whenever we see a glazed look on students' faces during a classroom explanation, we spontaneously search for an appropriate analogy to provide a vivid image of the concept we are introducing. Analogical study guides make this process explicit for students by showing them how they can effectively use analogies to link new information with prior knowledge. We recommend that you use analogical study guides when appropriate for complex topics in science. Although such guides take some time to create, they help alleviate the sink-or-swim experience many students have as they try to fathom science texts. Their feelings are much the same as you experienced trying to complete the cell structure-function matching activity. Unguided reading of a complex text simply produces frustration and hostility rather than comprehension and a feeling of power over the material.

In the section that follows we explore the last stage of a content reading, listening, or viewing assignment, the post-reading stage.

The Post-Reading Stage

Despite the intuitive and proven value of review for long-term retention of content area concepts, this activity remains the most often neglected component of a lesson structure. In her year long investigation of comprehension instruction, Durkin (1978–79) found that important concepts were glossed-over far too rapidly in an effort to cover the book and get on to new material.

The review stage of a lesson is typically viewed as an independent activity that students perform on their own time. While the phrase "Now it's time to review the concepts we explored last week" may engender a chorus of yawns, review activities do not have to be a devastating bore. It is true, however, when they consist of nothing more than a teacher-centered lecture recounting previously learned concepts, the outcome is likely to be counterproductive. In fact, classroom observations suggest that small group, collaborative discussions are rare, occupying less than 20 percent of classroom time (Wood, 1987). Oddly enough, when we, as adults confront some thorny problem, we often collaborate with others in ad hoc groups or more formal committee structures to tackle and solve the problem. Overemphasizing independent review fails to provide experiences that will help students respond to real world challenges in a cooperative fashion.

In contrast to those who see review sessions as teacher-centered activities, we perceive the review process to be a natural outgrowth of the pre-reading and reading activities in a well-integrated lesson. Activities that acknowledge and, in some cases, refine students' prior knowledge of a topic also can be applied at the post-reading stage. For example, the reaction guide column of the anticipation guide you have been rechecking at the close of each chapter is essentially a modest review activity. The graphic organizer and the study guide also lend themselves to the review process. Indeed, we regard review as more than a solitary pondering of text concepts. Review activities should involve active manipulation and collaborative discussion of information. By definition, cooperative learning involves "an equal partnership in which paired students study together with the mutual goal of mastering academic information" (Larson & Dansereau, 1986, p. 516). Indeed, Wood (1987) pointed out that recent studies of cooperative learning groups suggest that such teams contribute to significant gains in achievement, self esteem, and sociocultural understanding. Additionally, she listed a number of advantages in using such groups in a class:

1. Students are more motivated to learn when they are cooperating rather than competing individually with their peers.
2. Students display a more positive attitude toward both the class and the instructor when there are opportunities for this less teacher-centered form of learning.
3. Students in the role of the tutor and the tutee both benefit. They have to know the material in order to effectively teach it to another student.
4. Students' self esteem is enhanced by helping one another learn content material.
5. Students display more positive perceptions of the intentions of other students. This is especially crucial in multilingual, multicultural classrooms. By working together in cooperative groups, students perceive their peers more positively than when they are isolated from each other. There is a decrease in prejudice and stereotyping.
6. There is a decrease in competitive goal structures. Students come to view other students' ideas as important to their individual learning.
7. Students become less dependent on the teacher as the only source of reliable information. They begin to take charge of problem solving in a cooperative fashion. (pp. 11–12)

We would expect that, given the compelling advantages of using small groups to review content material, teachers would place more emphasis on this mode of instruction. However, Conley's (1987) analysis of small group learning in content classrooms found that, understandably, many teachers are reluctant to break out of the more controlled teacher-centered role. Using small groups entails a different style of classroom management that is, unquestionably, more of an art than orchestrating instruction from the front of the room and acting as an authority figure. Since we recommend using small groups to discuss material in the various guides introduced in this chapter, and particularly at the post-reading review stage of a lesson, what are some of the features that seem to insure small groups work effectively?

General Guidelines for Using Small Groups. It is important to first consider the role you plan to play in guiding small group review. Alvermann, Dillon, & O'Brien (1987) described four possible teacher roles and commented on their characteristic limitations.

The first role they call "the instructor." The teacher retains the normal "fountain of truth" position and serves to clarify any confusion or difficulties that arise in the small groups. The disadvantage of adopting this role is that it may limit students' sense of their own responsibility for maintaining discussion and resolving problems.

A second possible role is that of "participant." The teacher becomes part of a small group discussion. Although this sounds attractive, you may inadvertently inhibit students from participating. After all, in your normal role you are perceived as the content expert.

A third, and more appropriate role, is that of a "consultant." In this way you are free to rove about the room, responding to request for help from various groups. It is important to restrain yourself from over-assisting a group. Rather, encourage students to exhaust all their efforts in resolving problems or clarifying information before you offer to step in.

A fourth, and most difficult role, is that of a "neutral" observer of small group discussion. In this case, you remain silent, offering neither opinion, clarification, or conflict resolution. Although this may be an ideal role to adopt, it requires a slow, methodical release of responsibility to students that may span many weeks. Indeed, Conley (1987) cautioned that it may take a full semester before students are comfortable and skilled at working in small groups.

An important and often overlooked facet of using small groups effectively is the furniture and layout of your room. If students are in desks arranged by rows, they can easily work in pairs, side-by-side. Or, if you have circular tables, these can be ideal for groups of four to five students. In general, as group size increases, the level of individual participation decreases (Alvermann et al., 1987).

Small groups should be composed of four to five student members of mixed-ability with a clear learning goal (Stevens, Madden, Slavin, & Farnish, 1987). This may range from a discussion of study guide questions or reaction guide statements to debating an issue. Stevens et al. (1987) recommended that students' learning be assessed individually, with the small group receiving recognition for the success of its members. This can be accomplished by adding up individual's scores to arrive at team scores for various assessments.

Conley (1987) also recommended developing clearly defined student roles within a group. One student may be chair for the week, guiding discussion of study guide questions. The group may need a recorder and a gatekeeper to maintain the flow of discussion. These roles can be exchanged periodically. In his analysis of small group learning in content classrooms, Conley found that low ability and high ability students both make important contributions to learning. When a small group is discussing a study guide, low ability students often function as excellent fact-finders, while high ability students may see connections from text-based ideas to more global issues. Both types of students offer opportunities for creative debate, and they learn effectively from each other. There is general agreement that it is very important to compose groups that include mixed-ability students, so they can balance each others' strengths and weaknesses.

Although these general guidelines for your role in guiding small group learning and review are based on recent synthesis of research in the area of cooperative learning, you must decide how to best use small groups in your own classroom. The next section offers some specific guidelines for developing and managing small groups effectively.

Specific Guidelines for Discussion Groups. A good way to demonstrate clearly how you want a small group to function is to model this process. Using guide material as a focal point for the discussion, compose a small group at the front of the room and act in the role of a group chair to demonstrate the process for about 10 minutes. Conley (1987) recommended keeping early efforts fairly simple and focused. Remember that students are often unaccustomed to working in this cooperative fashion.

If a group is going off course, straying far afield of the task, how should you respond? Unfortunately, this is not a simple issue. Conley (1987) used the terms "heavy" and "light" group monitoring to characterize this dilemma. As we pointed out earlier, if you adopt the role of the authoritarian instructor and monitor too heavily, you may interfere with the development of independent student problem-solving. On the other hand, total chaos in your classroom is equally undesirable. Fortunately, there are some solutions to this problem.

In conjunction with a study of content area guide material, Vacca (1977) found that small study groups functioned productively when the teacher set the stage for the review. To prepare students, the teacher would first explain the goals and advantages of collaborating in the study process via interdependent groups. The key idea here hinges on the phrase "interdependent groups." That is, the success of the group in solving a problem is evaluated collectively but it also depends on the contribution of the individual members. To achieve such interdependence, stress the following:

1. Explain the desired discussion behaviors that students should strive for (e.g., encouraging each other to respond; valuing each others' ideas; allowing an adequate amount of time for a group member to explain a point without dominating the discussion); and,
2. Explain the reward system by which you would rate group performance.

Reward systems utilized with discussion groups will vary according to the maturity and ability of the students involved. The reward system instituted by Vacca (1977) in his study is designed to foster an active small-group review session. Each group receives one of four colored disks representing the teacher's estimate of the groups performance according to the desired discussion behaviors. Each disk is worth points comprising part of the students' grades (e.g., red = 0; yellow = 1; green = 2; blue = 3). The group members, in consultation with the teacher, arrive at a group score after each session. This overall group score is also assigned to each member in the group. The scores can be tallied on a chart for the class if students are to be randomly reassigned to groups periodically. This step is probably unnecessary, since the key aspect of this strategy is the tangible evidence of success small groups have with the colored disks during the discussion. The following example illustrates how such an approach would work with three groups of four members engaged in a post-reading discussion of the reaction guide items for chapter six of this text.

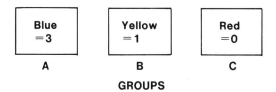

In this example, each of the members in group A would receive a score of three, indicating superior performance, on the discussion procedures with the reaction guide for chapter six. Conversely, the members of group C talked about their upcoming weekend plans with only minimal attention to the reaction items, and that accounts for their low scores(s) on the review session. As a result of this concrete indication of their performance, group C may decide to modify their discussion approach during subsequent review sessions.

Reaction Guides. A *reaction guide* provides a good prelude to a more intensive review when it serves as a focal point for small group discussion. When you complete a chapter in this text and then reassess your pre-reading responses to the anticipation guide, you are using a reaction guide to examine your beliefs about a topic. More than likely you alter at least some of your pre-reading beliefs and can defend this change by referencing explicit statements in the text.

A reaction guide is easy to construct since it is essentially another form of the anticipation guide, and the text analysis steps are the same for both comprehension strategies. You can simply add, as we have done, a second column to the anticipation guide for a post-reading reaction to the same statements. While the mechanics of the guide are simple, they should not be used as individual worksheets to be completed in silence. Rather, two or three of the most important statements should be considered and discussed by small groups. For example:

Anticipation	**Reaction**	
_____+_____	_____−_____	Rote memorization fosters long-term retention of information.

Notice that although many students might have agreed with this statement at the pre-reading stage, upon considering the psychological importance of deep processing and organization for retention, they would tend to disagree at the post-reading stage. More importantly, they would be able to defend this shift by referring to relevant portions of the text that lend support to the respective roles of deep processing and hierarchical organization in the memorial process.

Polar Opposites. When students have a concrete series of Reaction Guide statements to support or refute, they are more likely to engage in group discussion. *Polar Opposites* is a strategy that also provides a concrete basis for post-reading discussion (Bean & Bishop, 1986).

A Polar Opposites guide consists of descriptive adjectives such as "happy" versus "sad" that are supported or challenged by events in the text. Three steps are involved in developing a Polar Opposites guide and using it with students.

Step One

Develop four or five polar opposite statements and their accompanying adjectives. Place five blanks between the adjectives. For example:

Cairo's third city is . . .

new _____ _____ _____ _____ _____ old

Step Two

After students have read a selection or listened to a film, have them place a check mark (✓) closest to the adjective that they feel best describes the events or character. They can also score events and characters using a five point scale.

Step Three

Have students defend their rating in small group discussion or a writing activity by referring to specific examples or events in the selection.

The following example from world geography (Kleeman, 1983) should help you develop your own Polar Opposites guides. The passage is from the text, *New Exploring a Changing World* (Schwartz & O'Connor, 1975, pp. 364–365).

> On the roofs of Cairo there is a third city—a town of modern roof dwellers. Tens of thousands of people live on Cairo's rooftops. In the days when you could fly a small plane over Cairo, you could clearly see its two levels of life. One is on the ground and one is in the air. . . . I have seen on a roof opposite the Continental Hotel, someone cooking under a bamboo shelter, village women washing clothes, naked children, a goat or two, and a mangy dog. These rooftop slums are mostly servants' quarters but in the old city, they are the result of overcrowding.

Cairo's third city is . . .

	5	4	3	2	1	
new	____	____	____	____	____	old
spacious	____	____	____	____	____	crowded
healthful	____	____	____	____	____	unsanitary
safe	____	____	____	____	____	hazardous
rich	____	____	____	____	____	poor
friendly	____	____	____	____	____	hostile

In this particular guide, Cairo can be viewed either positively, with a rating of 30 (i.e., 5 points × 6 adjectives), negatively with a rating of 6 (i.e., 1 point per item), or somewhere between these "polar opposites." Indeed, some of the adjectives entail careful, critical reading to infer a response. For example, the last pair of adjectives, "friendly" versus "hostile," usually engenders heated discussion. If you are a member of Cairo's rooftop culture, then it is undoubtedly "friendly," or at least somewhat friendly. However, for the outsider unaccustomed to this overcrowded lifestyle, Cairo's rooftops may well be hostile. Thus, students can critically evaluate the author's perspective. If it seems to be overly ethnocentric, outside sources may be considered to confirm or deny information in the text. In this way, Polar Opposites can be used to guide students into independent projects involving library and database research.

Polar Opposites provides even the most reticent students with a basis for participating in discussion and writing activities. In order to defend or refute a particular rating, students must return to the text for support. Thus, it encourages critical reading in much the same way as the Reaction Guide.

Graphic Organizers. Although the graphic organizer was suggested as a pre-reading vocabulary and comprehension strategy, it is an equally good review guide. In the early stages of a unit, items from the graphic organizer developed by the teacher can be written on notecards. Students working in small groups can attempt to reconstruct the author's conceptual organization or pattern by arranging the notecards in a logical diagram. This review activity can be conducted as a game with points awarded for reconstructing successive portions of the unit organizer.

But students need not merely reconstruct information exactly as the teacher's schema portrayed it. Instead they can use the top-level skeletal structure of the teacher's organizer and add on information they have acquired in text reading. Barron (1979) emphasized that such student-constructed post-reading organizers seem to contribute more to comprehension than a teacher-devised organizer. The following activity illustrates the use of a skeletal graphic organizer as a review guide.

Activity

Directions: Before we go on, think about the comprehension strategies you have acquired so far in chapter six for each of the three stages of an integrated lesson (i.e., Pre-Reading, Reading, Post-Reading). In the organizer that follows, one strategy has been listed in each stage. See if you can supply at least two additional strategies per stage.

Instructional Stages

	Strategies
┌ — **Pre-Reading**	1. **Anticipation Guides**
	2.
	3.
Reading	1. **Study Guides**
	2.
	3.
└ — **Post-Reading**	1. **Reaction Guides**
	2.
	3.

Post-Reading Questions. Perhaps the most popular means to assess comprehension of text material is the use of post-reading questions. Much research has been conducted concerning the validity of post-reading questions, and the general finding has been that post-reading questions substantially enhance the learning of specific information from text. Post-reading questions also have a general facilitative effect for overall learning of non-questioned information. Such effectiveness contrasts with that of pre-reading questions, which only seem to facilitate students' learning of specific, questioned information.

Though it may seem that post-reading questions are more appropriate than pre-reading questions in helping students learn from text, the authors would like to emphasize that the issue really is not pre-reading vs. post-reading questions. Rather, the issue is the variety and level of question used to get at the desired learning teachers wish students to obtain as a result of reading text material. Pre-reading questions may serve as an excellent means to motivate, while post-reading questions will often enhance retention of new information. Care should be given, therefore, to utilize all three levels of understanding to enhance and refine new learning, whether using pre-reading or post-reading questions.

Cloze Concept Guides. Thomas (1979) proposed that teachers develop *cloze concept guides* designed to cue readers to an author's text structure or to review key concepts. To develop a concept guide for review, selectively delete technical vocabulary terms that portray key concepts. The following example of a concept guide for review comes from the early part of chapter six.

Principles of Comprehension

A comprehensive content area lesson displays an awareness of three psychological principles of the comprehension process. These principles include: (1) The importance of students' _____ _____ in the acquisition of new information; (2) The _____ _____ _____ _____ to be achieved in the lesson; and (3) the _____ _____ _____ for long-term retention.

You can include the missing items in random order at the bottom of the page if you feel these clues are helpful or necessary. In the above example the missing words are "prior knowledge," "levels of text understanding" and "organization of information." As with the graphic organizer and reaction guide, concept guides based on cloze can be used as a small-group or team review activity. Additionally, if your text has a fairly comprehensive summary at the end of each chapter, you can develop a concept cloze exercise very simply by deleting key words from the summary.

Projects. Throughout this text we have been introducing mini-projects at the close of each chapter to help you see, in a concrete way, how our ideas can be applied in your own subject area teaching. These projects undoubtedly constitute the most meaningful form of review since they move beyond the acquisition of text-explicit knowledge. Whenever feasible, you should try to build into your own teaching a wide array of applied projects that extend students' understanding beyond the domain of the text.

Integrated Approaches

By now you are undoubtedly aware that all of the teaching strategies we have introduced share some common ingredients. Specifically, they all involve language activities designed to supplement and develop understanding of text concepts. For example, the anticipation/reaction guides call for small-group discussion and verbal justification for a particular point of view. Similarly, the graphic organizer entails pre-reading and post-reading discussion. And the study guide encompasses the full range of language activities, since reading, writing, speaking, and listening are all integral to its success. The intent of all of these strategies is to increase students' interaction with an author's ideas so they will acquire and retain important content information. Put another way, all of the teaching strategies introduced thus far emphasize the importance of processing information deeply if it is to become a retrievable unit in long-term memory. The two integrated approaches that follow continue in this vein and should add to your developing repertoire of varied teaching strategies that share a common psychological base.

The Guided Reading Procedure. The *Guided Reading Procedure* (GRP) (Manzo, 1975) is an integrated lesson approach designed to insure that students understand and remember key information from their text. The GRP highlights the comprehension processes of collaborative brainstorming, rereading a selection to correct inconsistencies and fill-in incomplete information, and organizing information for long-term retention and retrieval. In short, the GRP provides a good model of the essential processes for independent growth in comprehension.

Manzo (1975) proposed the following steps in a well-integrated GRP lesson:

Step One

Have students read a text selection in class according to the following scenario:
a. Set a specific overall purpose for the assignment, e.g., in a health education unit on mystifying maladies, a section on "warts" might suggest the following purpose: "Determine whether or not there is an effective cure for warts."
b. Set a second more general purpose: "Be prepared to recall as many supporting details as you can without looking back at the text selection."

It is recommended that the approximate length of a reading assignment for the GRP should be 500 words (seven minutes) for junior high students and 2,000 words (ten minutes) for senior high students (Manzo, 1975). This may be adjusted according to students' differential abilities, interests, and attention span.

Step Two

After the initial text reading is completed, have students recall everything they remember and record this information on the board. You may want to have a volunteer or two help you write down the class's ideas, since brainstorming activity tends to produce a barrage of ideas. For example, ideas students acquired from the "warts" selection might look like the following:

come and go	Pliny the Elder	medical treatments
unpredictable	caustic painting	polyoma virus
no cures	electrocautery	autosuggestion
spunkwater	folk treatments	

Step Three

As students become aware of information not recalled or of inconsistencies requiring correction, have them go back and review the selection to fill in missing information. Include these additions and modifications with the other information on the board.

Step Four

Now have students organize the random, verbatim information recorded on the board into categories, or main ideas and subordinate details. This can be accomplished by voting on the importance of each idea with the teacher playing the role of a devil's advocate by arguing for the inclusion of minor details. The end result may be an outline or a graphic organizer. For example, the "warts" topic might result in the following graphic organizer:

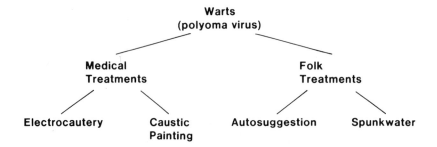

Step Five

Now give students a short-term memory/comprehension quiz on the GRP selection. About five to ten true-false, short answer, or multiple-choice questions that elicit thinking at the three levels of understanding (i.e., text-explicit, text-implicit, and experience-based) should be adequate. Have students keep a graph of the quiz results.

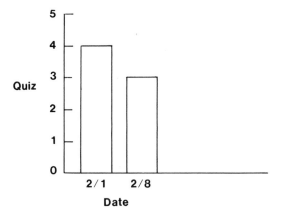

Step Six

This is a key step in the GRP. One week later give students a delayed-recall pop quiz on this same selection. Again, have students graph their delayed results. Chances are, some forgetting will have occurred. However, on subsequent GRP sessions, students will have a mind-set to organize and synthesize information for long-term retention.

In a study designed to field-test the GRP in a content classroom (Bean & Pardi, 1979), an additional pre-reading step was included in the strategy. Before reading a text selection in cultural geography, students conducted a five-minute survey of chapter headings, pictures, and tables and graphs. This survey step became the basis for a pre-reading brainstorming session that helped establish a cooperative, rather than teacher-dominated, purpose for reading. This modification, in conjunction with Manzo's (1975) six-step guided reading procedure, helped students retain the important concepts from the cultural geography lesson. You may find that supplementing the GRP with a five-minute survey make the whole procedure a bit less threatening. The survey step activates students' existing knowledge of the GRP topic and gives you a preliminary indication of their readiness to cope with it.

Another modification you may want to make to the GRP involves the short- and long-term quizzes. Since this strategy is designed to guide students' reading of text, as well as to provide a model of the comprehension process, there is no reason why the quizzes cannot be two- (or more) person team efforts. You can still institute a point system for scoring and graphing the GRP quizzes, and the team approach makes the whole activity more exciting.

Listen-Read-Discuss. Manzo & Casale (1985) developed the integrated strategy of *Listen-Read Discuss* to ensure that students genuinely grasp content information. Because students receive multiple exposure to concepts through listening, reading, and discussion, they are more likely to learn and retain information you feel is worthy of this intensive process.

There are three steps to a listen-read-discuss lesson.

Step One

The first part of the lesson entails presenting a well structured lecture on the material students are about to read in the text. Students need to have a good grasp of the content you are presenting if they are to participate actively in a listen-read-discuss lesson. Therefore, consider providing a clear lecture guide, perhaps in the form of a graphic organizer, that will serve to cue students to the text's structure. For example, the following graphic organizer might be used to assist high school students' comprehension of a lecture on Japan's rise to a world power. Reading in their text, *World history: Patterns of civilization* (Beers, 1983) would follow about a 15 minute lecture on the topic. Notice that the graphic organizer displays the cause-effect structure of the text. Items one and three would be provided by the teacher on the graphic organizer lecture guide passed out to students. Those items in italics would be filled in by students as the lecture progresses with clear cues from the teacher signalling each important point.

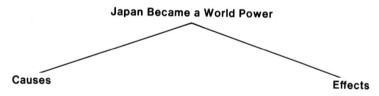

Japan Became a World Power

Causes

1. In 1603 Tokugawa clan rules
2. *Warriors went into debt—forced peasants to pay high rents*
3. In 1853 Perry opens Japan to American trade
4. *Japanese adopted some Western ways*
5. *Japan is the first industrialized country in Asia*
6. *In 1889 Japan creates a limited constitution*

Effects

1. *Unified Japan*
2. *Peasant uprisings*
3. *Large scale foreign influence in Japan*
4. *Antiforeign demonstrations (as now)*
5. *Achieve power at international levels*
6. *The emperor remains supreme ruler*

Once the lecture is completed and students have filled in their graphic organizer lecture guides, the teacher is ready to progress to step two, the reading portion of a listen-read-discuss lesson.

Step Two

The teacher directs students to read the text pages on which the lecture was based. Their purpose for reading should be to compare their understanding of the lecture with the information presented in the text. In addition, they can identify vocabulary and concepts that need clarification and pinpoint any inconsistencies between the text and the teacher's lecture. They are then ready to discuss the information on Japan's rise to international power.

Step Three

The discussion step can begin with small groups and progress to a summary discussion as a whole class. Three major questions should guide students' discussion of the lecture and text reading: (a) What did you understand best from what you heard and read? (b) What did you understand least from what you heard and read? and, (c) What questions or thoughts did the topic raise in your mind? Much like the final phase of the DRTA discussed earlier in the chapter, this last question is one that is often glossed over in our desire to cover the content. Yet it goes to the heart of students' personal interest in a topic. For example, Japan's influence on our economy has grown considerably over the years. It would be important to raise and consider contemporary issues like this, which have their roots in the mid-1800s.

Needless to say, both the GRP and the listen-read-discuss strategies require a good block of class time to complete. They should be reserved for topics you feel are important enough to warrant this extra time. Because of integrated, multiple exposures to concepts students receive in both the GRP and listen-read-discuss strategies, these strategies help those students who often need extra time to learn content material. Combining these strategies with the small group discussion process can go along way toward helping students experience success in your content classroom.

Once students acquire some independence with the material, other strategies such as study guides or the selective reading guide can be introduced. You may find that a blend of two strategies makes sense. For example, you might introduce the topic of irrational and rational numbers in a math class with a few anticipation guide statements and accompany the reading and problem solving part of the lesson with a study guide that moves students through successively more involved problems. Indeed, vocabulary strategies from chapter five can be combined with the comprehension strategies in this chapter or those in chapter seven on writing in the content areas. In short, don't be afraid to experiment with the strategies offered in this and other chapters. Modify them to fit your own teaching style and student needs. Field-testing the strategies will, more than likely, improve them. Certainly, you are in the best position to evaluate the success of these strategies in the classroom.

Summary

In this chapter we applied the psychological and sociocultural principles introduced in chapter two to the development of a three-stage, integrated lesson structure. Based on such a view of guiding students' understanding of content material at pre-reading, reading, and post-reading stages, a number of specific teaching strategies were introduced and illustrated. At the pre-reading stage, Anticipation Guides, Text Previews, Pre-reading Questions, ReQuest, and the Directed-Reading-Thinking-Activity were discussed. Study Guides, Options Guides, Analogical Study Guides, and the Selective Reading Guide were introduced as valuable adjuncts to the core text at the independent reading stage. Finally, comprehension strategies for the post-reading stage included Cooperative Small Group Discussion, Reaction Guides, Polar Opposites, Graphic Organizers, Post-Reading Questions, Cloze Concept Guides, and Projects. In reality, all of these strategies overlap; and the two integrated approaches, the Guided Reading Procedure and the Listen-Read-Discuss lesson, demonstrate a holistic view of comprehension. Although we have divided each of these strategies into stages largely for the sake of explanation, they need to become a well-integrated part of your own teaching.

Now go back to the anticipation guide at the beginning of this chapter. React again to the statements as you did before, but this time record your answers in the column entitled "Reaction." Compare your responses with the ones you made earlier.

Miniprojects

Project number five in this list is essentially a synthesis of projects one through four. Therefore, you should attempt to weave these individual projects together if at all possible.

1. Pick one of the pre-reading strategies advanced in this chapter. Using a text (or a film or activity if your classes do not use a text), develop this strategy and try it out with a small group of students or your peers. Evaluate the strategy in terms of its value as a means of preparing students for a content reading assignment.
2. Develop a Study Guide, Selective Reading Guide, Options Guide, Analogical Study Guide, or one of the other approaches to accompany a text reading assignment in your content area. Try out your guide with a small group of students or your peers. Use the follow-up discussion phase recommended in this chapter for guide material. Evaluate your guide as an independent learning aid.
3. Try out one of the post-reading strategies (use the project format described for projects one and two).
4. Develop a lesson based on either a Guided Reading Procedure or a Listen-Read-Discuss plan. Try out the lesson with a small group of students or your peers. Following the long-term quiz stage of the GRP or the discussion stage of the Listen-Read-Discuss plan, evaluate your lesson.
5. Develop an integrated mini-unit of instruction containing one strategy from each of the three stages proposed in this chapter.

Additional Recommended Readings

Alvermann, D. E., Dillon, D. R., & O'Brien, D. G. (1987). *Using discussion to promote reading comprehension.* Newark, DE: International Reading Association.
This monograph provides good classroom examples of teachers encouraging independent student interchange.
Alvermann, D. E., Moore, D. W., & Conley, M. W. (1987). *Research within reach: Secondary school reading.* Newark, DE: International Reading Association.
The editors provide research-based answers to common teacher questions about how to increase students' ability to learn from text.

Baumann, J. F. (Ed.). (1986). *Teaching main idea comprehension.* Newark, DE: International Reading Association.
This book discusses how best to help students' understand and retain important information in reading. Graphic Organizers, questioning strategies, and other approaches are considered.
Dishner, E. K., Bean, T. W., Readence, J. E., & Moore, D. W. (Eds.). (1986). *Content area reading: Improving classroom instruction* (2nd ed.). Dubuque, IA: Kendall/Hunt.
Chapter six in this book of readings contains additional comprehension strategies.
McNeil, J. D. (1987). *Reading comprehension: New directions for classroom practice* (2nd ed.). Glenview, IL: Scott, Foresman.
Provides a clear explanation and illustration of schema theory, along with an excellent chapter on asking questions.
Moore, D. W., Readence, J. E., & Rickelman, R. J. (1988). *Prereading activities for content area reading and learning* (2nd ed.). Newark, DE: International Reading Association.
A succinct and readable explanation of comprehension strategies.

References

Alvermann, D. E., Dillon, D. R., & O'Brien, D. G. (1987). *Using discussion to promote reading comprehension.* Newark, DE: International Reading Association.
Bailey, T. A., & Kennedy, D. M. (1983). *The American pageant* (7th ed.). Lexington, MA: D. C. Heath.
Barron, R. F. (1979). Research for the classroom teacher: Recent developments on the structured overview as an advance organizer. In H. L. Herber & J. D. Riley (Eds.), *Research in reading in the content areas: The fourth report* (pp. 171–173). Syracuse, NY: Syracuse University Reading and Language Arts Center.
Bartlett, B. J. (1978). *Top-level structure as an organizational strategy for recall of classroom text.* Unpublished doctoral dissertation, Arizona State University.
Bean, T. W. (1985). Classroom questioning strategies: Directions for applied research. In A. C. Graesser & J. B. Black (Eds.), *The psychology of questions* (pp. 335–358). Hillsdale, NJ: Erlbaum.
Bean, T. W., & Bishop, A. L. (1986). Polar opposites: A strategy for guiding students' critical reading and discussion. In E. K. Dishner, T. W. Bean, J. E. Readence, & D. W. Moore (Eds.), *Reading in the content areas: Improving classroom instruction* (2nd ed., pp. 246–250). Dubuque, IA: Kendall/Hunt.
Bean, T. W., Haehl, J. H., & Bishop, A. L. (1983). *Rapid reading for professional success.* Dubuque, IA: Kendall/Hunt.
Bean, T. W., & Pardi, R. (1979). A field-test of a guided reading strategy. *Journal of Reading, 23,* 144–147.
Bean, T. W., & Peterson, J. (1981). Reasoning guides: Fostering readiness in the content areas. *Reading Horizons, 21,* 196–199.
Bean, T. W., Singer, H., & Cowan, S. (1985). Analogical study guides: Improving comprehension in science. *Journal of Reading, 29,* 246–250.
Bean, T. W., Singer, H., Cowen, S., & Searles, D. (1987, December). *Acquiring concepts from biology text: A study of text-based learning aids and reader-based strategies.* Paper presented at the annual meeting of the National Reading Conference, St. Petersburg, FL.
Bean, T. W., Singer, H., Sorter, J., & Frazee, C. (1986). The effect of metacognitive instruction in outlining and graphic organizer construction on students' comprehension in a tenth-grade world history class. *Journal of Reading Behavior, 18,* 153–169.

Bean, T. W., Sorter, J., Singer, H., & Frazee, C. (1986). Teaching students how to make predictions about events in history with a graphic organizer plus options guide. *Journal of Reading, 29,* 739–745.

Beers, B. F. (1983). *World history: Patterns of civilization.* Englewood Cliffs, NJ: Prentice-Hall.

Brautigan, R. (1968). All watched over by machines of loving grace. *The pill versus the springhill mining disaster.* New York: Delacorte Press.

Conley, M. W. (1987). Grouping. In D. E. Alvermann, D. W. Moore, & M. W. Conley (Eds.), *Research within reach: Secondary school reading* (pp. 130–140). Newark, DE: International Reading Association.

Craik, F. I., & Lockhart, R. S. (1972). Levels of processing: A framework for memory research. *Journal of Verbal Learning and Verbal Behavior, 11,* 671–684.

Cunningham, D., & Shablak, S. (1975). Selective reading guide-o-rama: The content teacher's best friend. *Journal of Reading, 18,* 380–382.

Durkin, D. (1978–1979). What classroom observations reveal about reading comprehension instruction. *Reading Research Quarterly, 14,* 481–533.

Earle, R. A. (1969). Developing and using study guides. In H. L. Herber & P. L. Sanders (Eds.), *Research in reading in the content areas: First year report* (pp. 71–80). Syracuse, NY: Syracuse University Reading and Language Arts Center.

Ericson, B., Hubler, M., Bean, T. W., Smith, C. C., & McKenzie, J. V. (1987). Increasing critical reading in junior high classrooms. *Journal of Reading, 30,* 430–439.

Facione, P. (1984). Toward a theory of critical thinking. *Liberal Education, 30,* 253–261.

Faw, H. W., & Waller, T. G. (1976). Mathemagenic behaviors and efficiency in learning from prose materials: Review, critique, and recommendations. *Review of Educational Research, 46,* 691–720.

Geva, E. (1983). Facilitating reading comprehension through flowcharting. *Reading Research Quarterly, 18,* 384–405.

Goodlad, J. I. (1983). A study of schooling: Some findings and hypotheses. *Phi Delta Kappan, 64,* 465–470.

Graves, M. F., Cooke, C. L., & LaBerge, M. L. (1983). The effects of previewing difficult short stories on low ability junior high school students' comprehension, recall, and attitudes. *Reading Research Quarterly, 18,* 262–276.

Guthrie, J. T. (1979). Research: How we understand the news. *Journal of Reading, 23,* 162–164.

Herber, H. L. (1978). *Teaching reading in content areas* (2nd ed.). Englewood Cliffs, NJ: Prentice-Hall.

Herber, H. L., & Nelson, J. B. (1986). Questioning is not the answer. In E. K. Dishner, T. W. Bean, J. E. Readence, & D. W. Moore (Eds.), *Reading in the content areas: Improving classroom instruction* (2nd ed., pp. 210–214). Dubuque, IA: Kendall/Hunt.

Kasparek, S. (1983). Selective reading guide-art. In T. W. Bean (Ed.), *Reading and learning from text course of study.* Anaheim, CA: Anaheim Union High School District.

Kleeman, C. (1983). Polar opposites guide for world geography. In T. W. Bean (Ed.), *Reading and learning from text course of study.* Anaheim, CA: Anaheim Union High School District.

Laffey, J. L., & Steele, J. L. (1979). Tell no teacher . . . In H. L. Herber & J. D. Riley (Eds.), *Research in reading in the content areas: The fourth report* (pp. 177–185). Syracuse, NY: Syracuse University Reading and Language Arts Center.

Larson, C. O., & Dansereau, D. F. (1986). Cooperative learning in dyads. *Journal of Reading, 29,* 516–520.

Manzo, A. V. (1969). The request procedure. *Journal of Reading, 13,* 123–126.

Manzo, A. V. (1975). Guided reading procedure. *Journal of Reading, 18,* 287–291.

Manzo, A. V., & Casale, U. P. (1985). Listen-read-discuss: A content heuristic. *Journal of Reading, 28,* 732–734.

McGee, L. M., & Richgels, D. J. (1986). Attending to text structure: A comprehension strategy. In E. K. Dishner, T. W. Bean, J. E. Readence, & D. W. Moore (Eds.), *Reading in the content areas: Improving classroom instruction* (2nd ed., pp. 234–245). Dubuque, IA: Kendall/Hunt.

Meyer, B. J. F., Brandt, D., & Bluth, G. J. (1980). Use of top-level structure in text: Key for reading comprehension of ninth-grade students. *Reading Research Quarterly, 16,* 72–103.

Meyer, B. J. F., & Freedle, R. O. (1984). Effects of discourse type on recall. *American Educational Research Journal, 21,* 121–143.

Nelson, G. (1971). *Ceramics: A potter's handbook.* New York: Holt, Rinehart and Winston.

Niles, O. S. (1965). Organization perceived. In H. L. Herber (Ed.), *Developing study skills in secondary schools.* Newark, DE: International Reading Association.

Niles, O. S., & Memory, D. (1977). Teacher's edition. *Reading tactics.* Glenview, IL: Scott Foresman.

Oram, R. F., Hummer, P. J., & Smoot, R. C. (1983). *Biology: Living systems.* Columbus, OH: Charles E. Merrill.

Pearson, P. D., & Johnson, D. D. (1978). *Teaching reading comprehension.* New York: Holt, Rinehart and Winston.

Raphael, T. E. (1984). Teaching learners about sources of information for answering comprehension questions. *Journal of Reading, 27,* 303–311.

Raphael, T. E. (1986). Teaching question answer relationships, revisited. *The Reading Teacher, 39,* 516–522.

Rayl, D. (1983). Physical fitness film anticipation guide. In T. W. Bean (Ed.), *Reading and learning from text course of study.* Anaheim, CA: Anaheim Union High School District.

Rumelhart, D. E. (1975). Notes on a schema for stories. In D. G. Bobrow & A. M. Collins (Eds.), *Representation and understanding: Studies in cognitive science.* New York: Academic Press.

Schwartz, M., & O'Connor, J. R. (1975). *New exploring a changing world.* New York: Globe Book.

Shablak, S., & Castallo, R. (1977). Curiosity arousal and motivation in the teaching/learning process. In H. L. Herber & R. T. Vacca (Eds.), *Reading in the content areas: The third report* (pp. 51–65). Syracuse, NY: Syracuse University Reading and Language Arts Center.

Shallert, D. L., & Vaughan, S. C. (1979). Author and reader: The communication connection. *Research on reading in secondary schools, 4,* 49–56.

Singer, H., & Bean, T. W. (1988). Three models for helping teachers to help students learn from text. In S. J. Samuels & P. D. Pearson (Eds.), *Changing school reading programs: Principles and case studies* (pp. 161–184). Newark, DE: International Reading Association.

Singer, H., & Rhodes, A. (1976). Learning from text: A review of theories, strategies, and research at the high school level. In W. D. Miller & G. H. McNinch (Eds.), *Reflections and investigations on reading* (pp. 22–51). Clemson, SC: National Reading Conference.

Smith, C. C. (1987). *Language across the curriculum: Learning from text.* Final report of California Academic Partnership Program Grant No. 4. Northridge, CA: Department of Secondary Education, California State University, Northridge.

Stauffer, R. (1969). *Directing reading maturity as a cognitive process.* New York: Harper & Row.

Stevens, R. J., Madden, N. A., Slavin, R. E., & Farnish, A. M. (1987). Cooperative integrated reading and composition: Two field experiments. *Reading Research Quarterly, 22,* 433–454.

Stockton, F. R. (1884). *The lady or the tiger and other stories.* New York: Charles Scribner and Sons.

Taylor, B. M., & Samuels, S. J. (1983). Children's use of text structure in the recall of expository material. *American Educational Research Journal, 20,* 517–528.

Thomas, K. J. (1979). Modified cloze: The intralocking guide. *Reading World, 19,* 19–27.

Tierney, R. J., & Lazansky, J. (1980). *The rights and responsibilities of readers and writers: A contractual agreement.* Reading Education Report No. 15. Urbana, IL: Center for the Study of Reading, University of Illinois.

Tierney, R. J., & Spiro, R. J. (1979). Some basic notions about reading comprehension: Implications for teachers. In J. Harste & R. Carey (Eds.), *New perspectives in comprehension.* Bloomington, IN: Indiana University.

Vacca, R. T. (1973). A means of building comprehension of social studies content. In H. L. Herber & R. L. Barron (Eds.), *Research in reading in the content areas: Second year report* (pp. 75–83). Syracuse, NY: Syracuse University Reading and Language Arts Center.

Vacca, R. T. (1977). An investigation of a functional reading strategy in seventh grade social studies. In H. L. Herber & R. T. Vacca (Eds.), *Research in reading in the content areas: The third report* (pp. 116–131). Syracuse, NY: Syracuse University Reading and Language Arts Center.

van Dijk, T., & Kintsch, W. (1983). *Strategies of discourse comprehension.* New York: Academic Press.

Ver Steeg, C. L. (1982). *American spirit.* Boston, MA: Allyn and Bacon.

Wallbank, T. W., Schrier, A., Maier, D., & Gutierrez-Smith, P. (1982). *History and life: The world and its people* (2nd ed.). Glenview, IL: Scott, Foresman.

Wood, K. D. (1987). Fostering cooperative learning in middle and secondary classrooms. *Journal of Reading, 31,* 10–18.

Yopp-Nolte, R., & Singer, H. (1985). Active comprehension: Teaching a process of reading comprehension and its effect on reading achievement. *The Reading Teacher, 39,* 24–33.

7

Anticipation　　　　**Reaction**

_____ 1.　　_____ 1. Writing activities belong only in English classrooms.

_____ 2.　　_____ 2. The teacher should collect and assess all
student writing.

_____ 3.　　_____ 3. Journal writing provides an opportunity for
students to reflect on concepts.

_____ 4.　　_____ 4. The teacher is the ideal audience for students' writing.

_____ 5.　　_____ 5. Writing enhances students' comprehension
of challenging texts.

Writing Strategies

Rationale

Writing is a powerful way of learning and questioning across content areas. Once the sole province of English classrooms, writing is now seen as an important bridge between students' prior knowledge and ideas expressed in science, social studies, mathematics, and other content area texts. You need to be well informed about the writing process and ways to ensure students' can use writing effectively in a variety of subjects. This chapter introduces you to contemporary thinking about the writing process and shows you how to use writing successfully to help students' learn and reflect on concepts in your classroom.

Chapter Objectives

After reading this chapter, you should:

1. Understand the distinction between composing and transcribing.
2. Be familiar with various teaching strategies that help students use writing to learn and writing to inform.
3. Be able to use various approaches to evaluate student's writing.

Graphic Organizer

The following graphic organizer is provided to give you some advance structure for the new vocabulary and concepts that will be presented in this chapter.

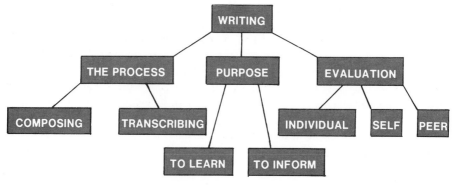

The Writing Process

Real writing, the forms of writing most of us use in our daily lives, consists of writing to schedule, rank, plan, map, inquire, record, recall, organize, evaluate, and report. We use writing to share our ideas with others. We use writing as a powerful, reflective means to "think about our thinking" (Calkins, 1986, p. 262). Since writing is such a powerful means of analyzing and interpreting experience, we might expect that content teachers would wholeheartedly embrace the use of writing to foster learning in their science, social science, mathematics, physical education, and arts classrooms. However, this is not the case.

Applebee's (1984) longitudinal studies of secondary classroom writing across various content areas found that students spent only three percent of their time writing selections that were paragraph length or longer. Rather, he found a preponderance of brief writing tasks consisting of filling in blanks on worksheets or writing short-answer responses to questions. Moreover, the typical audience for student writing was the teacher as examiner. When the teacher serves as students' main audience, writing may be less explicit because students are well aware that the teacher already possesses the information they, in the role of examinee, are imparting. Opportunities for students to engage in reflective journal writing were limited to about four percent of classroom time. Writing for larger audiences of peers or people outside the classroom occupied only six percent of the time.

Other undesirable features Applebee and his co-researchers found included an overemphasis on accuracy and correctness at the expense of adequate exploration of ideas and interpretation. Interestingly, the research on studying grammar indicates that when this effort is divorced from actual writing assignments and treated as a subject in its own right, it has little impact on the quality of students' writing (Smith, 1986).

Applebee also found that most writing assignments were expected to be completed in the brief span of a period. There was little emphasis on pre-writing exploratory activities. When longer papers were assigned, writing guidance typically consisted of a specified topic, due date, and paper length.

Yet for most of us, writing is a craft. And like any craft, our writing progresses, sometimes haltingly and in small increments, through many stages (Graves, 1983). We may let ideas incubate for a time, simply tossing scraps of hastily written notes in a folder, collecting articles, and throwing them in the pile. Eventually, we are ready to organize this disorganized collection into categories having a tentative structure. The structure may be a narrative or one of the expository patterns introduced earlier in the text. Writing a draft, revising as we one of the expository patterns introduced earlier in the text. Writing a draft, revising as we go, and sharing our draft with others eventually lead to a finished piece of writing we can feel good about. Students need to see some of their writing evolve in this fashion. Other writing may be more exploratory, much like a diary that is not intended for public reading but may contribute to learning in your classroom. Thus, some writing that you engage students in will be designed to help them inform others about a topic; other writing activities will assist their learning. There should be room for both forms of writing in content classrooms.

Before exploring specific strategies that help students use writing to learn and to inform, we want to define and consider two important aspects of the writing process, composing and transcribing.

Composing and Transcribing

Composing is the ongoing process of generating and shaping ideas before writing and as the actual writing unfolds. Calkins (1986) describes it this way:

> Like an artist at a sketch pad, we begin to find the contours of our subject. We make light, quick lines; nothing is permanent. Each writer has his or her own style. Some bolt quickly down the page, their momentum building, their pencil leading in unexpected directions. Others work in smaller units, toying with their beginnings, trying a line one way and then another. (p. 17)

Composing involves thinking about ideas, weighing them, and putting them in some kind of order (Christen, Searfoss, & Bean, 1984). Brainstorming, creating, clustering, and categorizing are some of the processes students use in composing. Out of these pre-reading musings come new ways of looking at topics in content classrooms. Stafford (1986, p. 25) said, "A writer is not so much someone who has something to say as he is someone who has found a process that will bring about new things he would not have thought of if he had not started to say them."

As a student gets started composing at a word processor or simply begins writing on a piece of paper, transcribing facilitates or inhibits the development of a finished product. *Transcribing* is a term that describes the mechanics of writing, including spelling, punctuation, capitalization, handwriting, formatting, and neatness. During the early draft stages of writing, when composing dominates a student's thoughts, placing too much emphasis on the conventions of transcribing may interfere with the development of ideas. Certainly when students are engaged in reflective journal writing, which they do primarily for their own purposes, transcribing should be less of a concern than when they are preparing a final draft of a paper for a larger audience. As we look at the practice of journal writing in content classrooms, remember that composing issues are at the forefront. Personal journal writing is one of the best ways for students to explore ideas without feeling pressed to produce perfect spelling and grammar. In addition, it is a powerful way for you to carry on a dialogue about the class with individual students. Journal writing is the first writing to learn strategy we will consider.

Writing to Learn

In many content classrooms, students feel that the authority for their learning resides exclusively with the teacher. Yet in classes where students write often, as much as four and five times a week, they feel like they are in the driver's seat (Hansen, 1987). Writing becomes a powerful vehicle for guiding their learning—a filter through which they can sift and examine concepts and see how these sometimes obscure notions may connect with their lives. Writing-to-learn activities initiate students to various methods for using writing to explore and integrate ideas arising from a content area.

Journal Writing

Observational studies of classrooms reveal far too little sustained writing of a personal nature (Fulwiler, 1986). Yet in our day-to-day world, we see teachers, business people, scientists, and artists frequently jotting down random ideas or notes in a journal for their own purposes. When ideas wing briefly into short-term memory, a journal is an ideal place to pin them down for later consideration. In social studies, a student's journal may consider how the Bill of Rights might relate to student's rights in a high school environment. In science, a journal entry might wonder about gene splicing and its impact on future generations. In art, a journal comment may state how a student interprets a surrealistic painting. Or, a journal entry may have no higher purpose than to state, "I stayed up late last night. Today I'm having a lot of trouble concentrating on your lecture about the Roman Empire." In this way, *journal writing* can communicate a student's feelings and emotions, and provide you with some sense of how your lessons are progressing for individual students on various days. In our crowded classrooms, journals can serve the important need to communicate attitudes and interests beyond the typical rapid fire charge through endless facts and concepts.

As you begin to use journal writing in your own subject area, consider the following principles (Bean, 1989; Fulwiler, 1986):

1. Journal writing should become a regular part of your teaching. Students need to write in their journals on a daily basis.

During the first five minutes of class, journals can be an ideal way to enter a topic or recap a previous day's lesson. For example, in a social studies classroom, on the first day of a unit students worked through an anticipation-reaction guide activity on the Bill of Rights. One of the statements read: "Students should have the right to select the classes they take." At the beginning of the next day's class, the teacher gives students an opportunity to comment further in their journals on this idea. Jeff writes:

> I think it's a good idea. But only if we pick our class schedule every other week. That way, at least some of the time we have to take classes that are good for us, even though we may not like them. Like math. Math would be okay every other week. But I know this isn't going to happen. We have to do whatever the government tells us to do. It's depressing.

Jeff was undoubtedly reluctant to express these opinions in the large class discussion the previous day. But in the privacy of his journal, he is free to explore divergent proposals. Journals can be used to explore content area concepts from a personal perspective, so it is important for students to have opportunities to pick what they want to write about. Therefore, you may want to alternate days devoted to some commentary on previous or upcoming lessons with days devoted to reflections on general topics students choose individually. The next principle suggests how you can demonstrate the range of topics students may wish to explore in their journals.

2. You should model journal writing by keeping your own journal and sharing entries aloud with students.

Just as sustained silent reading works best when you join in by reading a novel of your choice, journal writing takes on real importance in student's eyes when you also participate. For example, your entries may range from commentaries on how a unit is progressing to entries that chronicle your efforts to reduce your 10 kilometer running time.

3. You should look at students' journals and respond to their thoughts.

We recognize that it is unrealistic to expect a teacher to collect endless stacks of journals every day and respond to them. Rather, collect journals randomly so that you see every student's journal a few times in the course of a semester. In order to keep some parts of the journal completely private, you may have students use a looseleaf notebook with dividers labeled "public" and "private" (Fulwiler, 1986). In this way you can at least respond to those sections marked "public" while not inhibiting opportunities for private comment.

How much time should students spend each day writing in their journals?

4. Allot five to ten minutes for journal writing.

These four principles should not imply that journals be used in a rigid, formulaic fashion that may become stultifying over time. Rather, we recommend that you make them a flexible and creative regular part of your teaching repertoire. You can even use journals as a way to interrupt a lecture, lab, or activity in order to let students reflect on what they understand at that intermediate phase of a lesson. Using journals will do much to foster students' enthusiasm and personal investment in the content you are trying to teach.

Activity

Think about the most challenging group of students you have taught. Write a journal entry describing your feelings now as you think back on the impact your teaching may or may not have had on these students. Exchange your entry with a colleague in class. Discuss the teaching experience you wrote about and your views on journal writing in a content classroom.

Possible Sentences

Possible Sentences is another writing-to-learn strategy that helps students use technical vocabulary and related concepts in your content area. This strategy places students in an active role in which they predict an author's use of language in a text and evaluate their written predictions against the actual text passage (Moore & Moore, 1986). Possible Sentences engages students in higher order reasoning to identify examples in the text that support their pre-reading sentences or to revise their sentences after considering the text version. This exercise gives students a vested interest in reading the text to check their pre-reading possible sentence predictions. A Possible Sentences lesson has four steps.

Step One

List on the board or overhead key terms from a chapter or reading selection. The words should be well defined by the context and pronounced several times for the students. For example:

Target Words
> pigment
> albinism
> enzymes
> melanin
> suntan
> albino

Passage

Albinism*

> The absence of pigmentation in the skin, hair, and eyes in albinos is the result of a deficiency in the manufacture of pigment (melanin) by the body. Albinism is a metabolic disorder resulting from the absence or inactivity of a specific enzyme. Enzymes are complex compounds which act as catalytic agents or mediators of chemical changes in living forms. This enzyme is involved in the formation of melanin. The condition is not restricted to humans and it has been found in many animals: snakes, salamanders, gorillas, rats, mice, Easter bunnies, and even ravens, to name a few.
>
> Human albinos are characterized by white translucent skin and white hair. Because of the lack of pigment in the iris, the eyes are red due to blood vessels. There is no way to overcome albinism. The necessary information to produce the right enzyme has not been inherited and will never be acquired. The specific enzyme or the melanin pigment would have to be injected continuously into each and every pigment cell of the skin, scalp, and eyes in order to produce a normally pigmented individual.
>
> Albinos need continuous protection from sunlight since they burn very easily. Their skin cannot develop a suntan since tans are nothing more than the accumulation of melanin as a response to an increase in the ultraviolet radiation of sunlight. They are also more susceptible to skin diseases and tend to have poor vision. They are otherwise perfectly normal people.

Step Two

Individual students select any two of the words and dictate or *write a sentence* using them. The teacher writes the sentences on the board exactly as dictated, whether the information in them is accurate or not. For instance:

*Brum, G. D., Castro, P., & Quinn, R. D. *Biology and Man.* Dubuque, Iowa: Kendall/Hunt, 1978, p. 57.

Possible Sentences

a. Suntans come from having a lot of enzymes in your skin.
b. A albino is a person who has no melanin.
c. An albino can never get a suntan.
d. Albinism is the missing of pigment in the skin.

Step Three

After an arbitrary number of sentences have been generated, the students search through the passage to *verify the sentences* on the board. A game twist can be added to this by having teams that are supposed to generate as many sentences as possible with unique pairs of the words listed. In this example there are 15 different possible pairs of words that can be used. Once each team generates its sentences, the opposing teams challenge (with books closed, of course) the accuracy of each set of individuals sentences. Points can be given for each accurate sentence. Penalty points can be deducted for inaccurate challenges.

Step Four

The *"possible sentences" are corrected* on the board and students are given an opportunity to enter them into their notebooks. For instance:

Revised Possible Sentences

a. Suntans come from having a lot of melanin in your skin.
b. An albino is a person who has no melanin.
c. An albino can never get a suntan.
d. Albinism is the absence of pigment in the skin.

Possible Sentences will tease out any misconceptions students have about a topic. Writing sentences is generally a nonthreatening activity, even for second language learners. We have found that students enjoy Possible Sentences. They enthusiastically pursue text reading to verify their predictions.

Probable Passages

Probable Passages (Wood, 1984), a writing strategy that is similar to Possible Sentences, involves larger, paragraph length sections of a text. Although Probable Passages was developed for use with predictable story patterns, it works equally well with many of the expository text patterns introduced earlier in the text. Probable Passages is especially appropriate for those text patterns that branch into cause-effect, compare-contrast, and problem-solution structures. As in the Possible Sentences strategy, Probable Passages capitalizes on prediction and verification of student-authored text passages that are compared with the original text.

The following steps should be followed in developing a Probable Passages lesson.

Step One

Carefully analyze the text selection for the most significant concepts and identify vocabulary that may need special emphasis. If the text has a clear pattern of organization (e.g., problem-solution), categorize the vocabulary under these text structure labels. Present the words you have identified on the board or overhead projector. For example, the Probable Passages lesson that follows accompanies a problem-solution reading selection from a health class on hypothermia (adapted from Dutton, 1988).

Problem	*Solution*
hypothermia	moving muscles
body temperature	protection
shivering	heater
numbness	eating
hallucinations	stamina

Step Two

Tell students about the text structure categories that you have used to label the key words. If students are not already familiar with the text structure of the passage, you can introduce this concept through a cartoon or other concrete visual.

Step Three

Students receive a copy of an incomplete text selection. Only the problem portion of the selection is provided with blanks for those words listed under this category (i.e., hypothermia, body temperature, shivering, etc.). The second part of the text frame should give students an opening sentence that foreshadows the second half of the text passage, in this case, the solution part. The following incomplete text frame demonstrates this step.

Hypothermia

_____ is a drop in the normal _____ _____ below 98.6 degrees. Anyone exposed to very cold temperatures for too long can experience this condition. Your body burns up its food resources, resulting in a loss of heat. It is a particularly dangerous problem for surfers and skiers during the winter months.

Although the symptoms of hypothermia include _____ and _____ of the extremities, these symptoms may not be heeded because people lapse into _____ . High up on a mountain or far out in the surf, hypothermia can lead to a loss of strength and coordination, endangering the life of a skier or surfer.

Hypothermia can be avoided through a common-sense approach to sports like surfing in cold water and skiing. (*Now use the words from the* "problem" *side of the list to write the rest of this probable passage the way you think an author might.*)

Step Four

Before students attempt to write their probable passage by filling in the words from the problem column in the passage, and then writing the solution section, go over each word, discussing definitions as needed. Then *ask students to construct a probable passage.* Here is one a student wrote.

Hypothermia

(Hypothermia) is a drop in the normal *(body temperature)* below 98.6 degrees. Anyone exposed to very cold temperatures for too long can experience this condition. Your body burns up its food resources, resulting in a loss of heat. It is a particularly dangerous problem for surfers and skiers during the winter months.

Although the symptoms of hypothermia include *(shivering)* and *(numbness)* of the extremities, these symptoms may not be heeded because people lapse into *(hallucinations)*. High up on a mountain or far out in the surf, hypothermia can lead to a loss of strength and coordination, endangering the life of a skier or surfer.

Hypothermia can be avoided through a common sense approach to sports like surfing in cold water and skiing. The clothes you wear surfing and skiing should give *protection* from the elements. If you surf, wear a wetsuit. If you ski, wear a parka and ski pants. *Moving* your *muscles* by flexing your arms and legs on the chair lift keeps up your *stamina*. If these steps don't work out and you do get hypothermia, warm up in the lodge next to a *heater* or by a fire at the beach. *Eating* and drinking warm foods will help. Better yet, stay inside and be a couch potato when it's cold outside!

Step Five

Have students read the original selection so they can evaluate how close their probable passage came to the original passage. Notice that this student's composition included all of the words from the solution side of the list. Moreover, the passage addresses the reader directly, referring to "you." The original passage contained a few more details but it is actually not as vibrant as this student's creation. After they have had a chance to compare their passage with the original, you may want to have students exchange their probable passages. Here is the solution half of the original text.

Hypothermia

Hypothermia can be avoided through a common-sense approach to sports like surfing in cold water and skiing. Keeping in good physical shape helps increase *stamina* and wards off the effects of the cold. Wearing adequate *protection* from the elements in the form of a good three to five millimeter wetsuit and boots for surfing or gore-tex fabrics for high mountain skiing keeps out the cold. *Moving muscles* vigorously generates heat as well.

If a surfer or skier does experience hypothermia, the best solution is to warm up as soon as possible. Hot non-alcoholic beverages and a car *heater* help. *Eating* to build up the store of caloric energy in the body also helps. But the best approach is to take preventive steps before this condition develops.

Step Six

Once they have had a chance to compare their probable passage to the original text, *students should edit their passage to include any missing or contradictory information.*

A Probable Passage lesson helps students anchor concepts within a pattern of organization that fosters comprehension and recall. Writing about concepts from their own perspective is an opportunity students' experience far too rarely. In addition, because of its highly structured format, Probable Passages provides a good basis for easing students into writing summaries of text information, which we take up next.

Summarization: The GIST Procedure

The ability to distill a lengthy paragraph, passage, or article into its essential ideas is the mark of a proficient reader in any content area. Moreover, writing a summary enhances students' reading comprehension.

During the last few years, strategies for teaching students to summarize text effectively have been developed and explored. A strategy called *GIST* (Cunningham 1982), which denotes "generating interactions between schemata and text," can effectively improve students' reading comprehension and summary writing (Bean & Steenwyk, 1984).

GIST entails careful teacher modeling and guidance at the reading stage of a lesson. The reader is interrupted and directed to record selectively a gist summary of the material just read. GIST involves the following steps:

Step One

Select a short passage in a chapter that has an important main idea. A passage of three to five paragraphs is ideal. These paragraphs should be typed on an overhead transparency.

Step Two

Place the transparency on the overhead and display only the first paragraph (cover the other paragraphs). Put 20 blanks on the chalk board. *Have students read the paragraph and instruct them to write a 20 word (or less) summary* in their own words.

Step Three

As a class, *have students generate a composite summary* on the board in 20 or fewer words. Their individual summaries will function as guides for this process.

Step Four

Reveal the next paragraph of the text and *have students generate a summary statement of 20 or fewer words that encompasses both of the first two paragraphs.*

Step Five

Continue this procedure paragraph by paragraph, until students have produced a gist statement for the entire passage under consideration. In time, they will be able to generate gist statements across paragraphs without the intermediate steps.

The following example from industrial education demonstrates the use of GIST in a content area (Casucci, 1983). The passage contains two paragraphs from *Metalwork Technology and Practice* on "Why the Lathe is Important" (Ludwig, McCarthy, & Repp, 1975, pp. 499–500).

> We are living in the age of the mechanic. The airplane, steamship, locomotive, electric motor, computer, transfer machine, and automobile are among the outstanding inventions. All these wonders were made possible through the development of the lathe. It is the oldest and most important tool in industry.
>
> The lathe helped the development
> of all our other machines
>
> ____ ____ ____ ____ ____
>
> ____ ____ ____ ____ ____
>
> The modern lathe can perform many different operations. In studying the history of other machines, we find that the idea of their operation comes from the lathe. There are more lathes in this country than any other kind of metal working machine tool.
>
> The lathe is the father
> of other machines and continues
> to be the most often
> used metal working tool _____ .

The second series of 20 blanks contains a summary statement encapsulating the two paragraphs. In addition, students should have a good grasp of this section. They might expect that the remainder of the chapter will expand on functions of the lathe.

By restricting the length of students' GIST summaries, the teacher compels the students to use the three major strategies necessary for comprehension and retention of key ideas in any text. They must delete trivial information, select key ideas, and generalize in their own words (van Dijk & Kintsch, 1983). Thus, GIST produces dual benefits by advancing students reading comprehension and writing fluency.

Semantic Mapping, which we introduced in chapter six as a vocabulary strategy, can also serve as a means of brainstorming and organizing students' ideas about a topic before or after reading. These important ideas and details can then become the basis for a written summary.

Semantic Mapping

A semantic map is a "categorical structuring of information in a graphic form" (Heimlich & Pittelman, 1986, p. 1). Unlike graphic organizers, which generally correspond to the hierarchical structure of a passage, semantic maps are more free-flowing. They represent a student's idiosyncratic approach to reconstructing ideas.

Most semantic maps contain three levels of information:

1. The main topic in a central hub
2. Branches labeled to indicate major ideas or categories
3. Branches containing specific supporting details

Since semantic maps usually contain a substantial number of lower level supporting details, often written out in phrases, they provide a good foundation for summarizing text information. The following semantic map is a student's post-reading reconstruction of a science article about cockroaches (Westcott, 1987).

This student produced the following summary based on her map of the cockroach passage. It contains most of the important ideas and supporting details in the original passage with her own views about this formidable pest.

Cockroaches

Cockroaches are an even bigger menace than I originally thought. The article describes how they survive and reproduce. It also gives some ideas about exterminating cockroaches and making sure they don't get in your house. But from what the article says, I think the roaches have the upper hand.

First, the German Cockroach can survive on things we don't think of as food. They eat glue in books, starch in shirts, bath soap and shoe polish, and grease and leftovers. You can reduce their source of food by washing dishes right away but they can still survive.

Second, cockroaches reproduce like crazy. The female lives just 140 days but she can lay six to eight egg capsules. This may not sound like much, but each capsule has 140 offspring. She can produce 160 to 180 females!

Third, cockroaches are very hard to exterminate. Most pesticides won't work. Boric acid works too slowly compared to how fast they reproduce. Most of the baits don't work. Some new pesticides are being created for use in agriculture. These may work for a while.

How should you keep cockroaches away from your house? You should keep a clean house and look in any boxes or newspaper you bring in. But I still think the cockroaches will win!

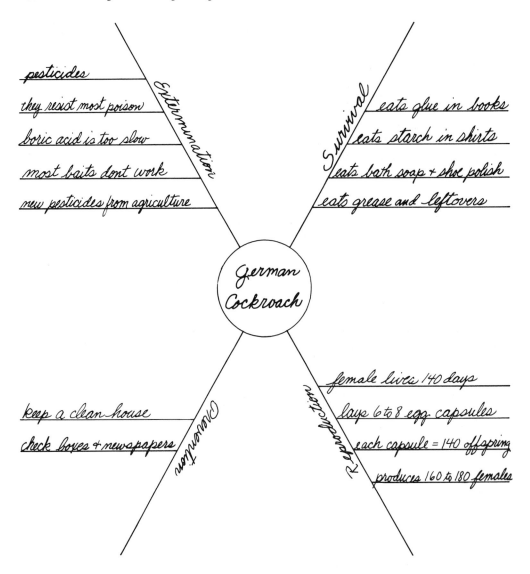

This student's summary is a well-structured informational account of the major points and key details from the original article. You can introduce this form of summary writing by providing students with a partially completed map and having them read and discuss a text passage to fill in the missing branches on the map. You can then think aloud as you write a model summary on the board or overhead, using the map to structure your writing.

A prototypical map that you construct for a passage can serve as a good template for scoring students' summaries. For example, the cockroach article contains four major ideas about how cockroaches survive, reproduce, are exterminated, and how to prevent them from entering a home. These major ideas could be worth five points each. The supporting details might be scored at one point each. Thus, the student summary included here would receive 35 points. She mentioned all four category labels for five points, or 20 points total, and all the supporting details. For example, the survival category has four supporting details, for four points. Naturally, if a student produces an incomplete map, the resulting summary is likely to be missing crucial information as well.

Activity

Pair-up with a colleague in a class from a different content area than your own (e.g., biology and English). Select a passage from your text and guide your partner through either a GIST lesson or a Semantic Mapping/Summary lesson.

Writing Roulette

The next writing-to-learn strategy we are going to explore is *Writing Roulette.* This strategy was originally created to help students become more fluent in writing by having them write about anything at all for a specific period of time (Shuman, 1979). A kitchen timer would be set for five minutes or so, and when it went off, students would pass their writing on to a peer who continues developing the passage for another five minutes or so. Writing Roulette helped students' overcome worries about perfect grammar and spelling and moved them into a composing mode.

Bean (1986) modified the original Writing Roulette strategy for use in content learning. First, instead of writing whatever comes to mind, students are told to use a simple three-part story structure for the activity so that three different students write each distinct part of the story. Second, they review content material within the framework of the story by selecting key vocabulary words from their expository reading and including these words in each section they write. The process of conducting a Writing Roulette session is as follows.

Step One

Provide a simple structure for the story, consisting of three major elements or divisions.

a) A setting and characters
b) A problem or goal for the main character
c) A resolution

Step Two

Advise students that each section of the story must use at least two words from the lesson or unit they have been studying. These words should be underlined in the story. You can have students review their vocabulary collections, or you can simply supply a list of technical terminology from which they can choose six words.

Step Three

Set a specific time limit for the first story section (e.g., five minutes for the setting). You can use a kitchen timer for this.

Step Four

When time is up, have students exchange papers or collect and shuffle them so that a second author writes the problem or goal section. Advise students to read the paper they receive and continue the story. Set a time limit for this writing as well.

Step Five

Exchange papers one last time so a third author can provide a resolution for the story. Then, have students return the story to the original author and share aloud those stories that are particularly interesting or that use content vocabulary in creative ways.

Writing Roulette is a good way to have students review important vocabulary and concepts before an essay exam or quiz. It is best introduced after students have used other strategies such as graphic organizers and list-group-label, so that they have a good understanding of content vocabulary. The example that follows is a Writing Roulette story developed by three preservice content teachers. The words are taken from the glossary of our text.

Student 1

Gertrude and Susie were on their way home from school. "Gertrude," said Susie, "that *anticipation guide* we use in class was really great."

"Yeh," replied Gertrude. "And didn't you just love the *graphic organizers?* I can't wait to get home and call all our friends and let them know about our class."

Gertrude and Susie continue down the street, chatting happily.

Student 2

The big history test was rapidly approaching. Gertrude reread her graphic organizer and called Susie on the phone to discuss *study strategies.* She felt her *comprehension* had suffered because she did all of her reading in front of the television. She had never missed an episode of "Dance Fever" since the show's inception. Susie tried to help Gertrude fill in the blank spaces their teacher had left in the graphic organizer. They stayed on the phone for three hours in anticipation of the big *test.*

Student 3

The next day, Gertrude entered the classroom to face the test. She whispered to Susie, "I hope he gives us an *anticipation-reaction guide* to help us with this test."

The teacher came around and placed a *cloze test* on each student's desk. Gertrude took a look at it and almost died. Every other word has been deleted. Gertrude whispered to Susie, "Do you have any idea how to do this test?"

Susie said, "Sure, use your knowledge of *morphemic analysis* to *slice* the *response mode,* which will require you to have fewer pieces of information. Then the *scope of information* search will be halved.

Gertrude gave Susie a blank stare. Susie said, "guess!"

Gertrude knew she would fail, but, fortunately for her, the teacher pulled down the overhead screen, knocking down the wall clock, and a large plastic potted fern onto his big toe. Class was immediately terminated, and Gertrude went whistling out of the classroom, knowing she had escaped a fate worse than death.

Students find Writing Roulette a pleasurable and creative approach to reviewing technical vocabulary and concepts. Since it takes a full period to conduct a Writing Roulette session, you should plan to allot this time just to the activity. Once students have completed their stories, they enjoy exchanging and reading each other's creations in the small group setting. Writing Roulette capitalizes on a familiar narrative structure to review concepts presented in expository material.

The last writing-to-learn strategy we are going to consider is the Guided Writing Procedure. The GWP guides students through pre-reading and post-reading stages of a lesson.

The Guided Writing Procedure

The *Guided Writing Procedure* (GWP) gives students practice in developing a coherent written account of a topic they are studying in the text (Bean, 1989; Christen, Searfoss, & Bean, 1984; Searfoss, Smith, & Bean, 1981; Smith & Bean, 1980). The GWP helps students examine their prior knowledge of a topic. They can then modify their previous knowledge based on the text reading. In contrast to the strategies we have introduced up to this point, the GWP entails editing writing for both content and form. The GWP is designed to achieve the following teaching objectives:

1. To activate and sample students' prior knowledge of a topic before they do any text reading.
2. To sample and evaluate students' written expression in a content area.
3. To improve students' written expression through guided instruction.
4. To facilitate the synthesis and retention of content area material.

Research designed to gauge the impact of the GWP on students' content learning and writing shows that using the GWP significantly improves the quality of the writing that students produce. They are more adept at integrating information from text and prior knowledge, and these students produce writing that is carefully edited and readable (Konopak, Martin, & Martin, 1987; Martin, Konopak, & Martin, 1986).

The GWP usually spans three days of content instruction and involves the following steps.

Day One

Step One

Write the topic heading you are introducing on the board and have *students brainstorm words or phrases* that come to mind when they think about this topic. For example, social studies students who were about to read a chapter describing conditions during the Depression of 1929 (Ver Steeg, 1982), generated six ideas based on their prior knowledge of this topic.

Step Two

Record students ideas verbatim on the board or overhead. Engage students in a discussion of their ideas, and ask them to explain how they are related to the topic being considered. Students produced the following list for the causes of the Depression of 1929.

no jobs	stocks crash
no money	everything is cheap
poverty	bad investments

Step Three

Guide students in constructing an outline, graphic organizer, or semantic map of these ideas with appropriate category labels. For example:

Causes and Effects of the Depression

   I. Causes
      a. bad investments
      b. stocks crash
  II. Effects
      a. no jobs
      b. no money
      c. poverty
      d. everything is cheap

Step Four

Tell students to individually write a short paragraph or two as a "first draft," with the outline as a guide to content and organization. You should tell them to direct this draft to a specific audience. A reasonable audience for this information is another class member or a classmate who is absent for this lesson.

Step Five

Collect students' first drafts and rapidly analyze the paragraphs, using the GWP checklist that follows. You should *not* make any marks on students' papers. The first draft that follows was written by a student based on the six ideas generated in the brainstorming on the Depression.

Causes and Effects of the Depression

     The awful Depression of 1929 was caused by the stock market crash. People made bad investments and lost all their money. Some people bought too much stock on credit. They went to far into det.

     When the stock market crashed people lost a lot of money. There wasn't money to pay people for work. People without jobs sunk into poverty. Everything was dirt cheap. You could probably go to a movie for a dime!

GWP Checklist

(✓ = okay; 0 = needs revision; ? = can't tell)

Criteria

Organization of Ideas

Clear topic ✓

Supporting details/examples 0

Logical flow ✓

Comments: *Good organization of ideas. The text will give you details and examples.*

Style

Shows variety in
Word choice ✓

Sentence length 0

Comments: *Short sentences need to be balanced by some that are longer.*

Mechanics

Complete sentences ✓

Capitalization ✓

Punctuation ✓

Spelling 0

Comments: *too much (vs. to); sank (vs. sunk); debt (vs. det)*

This student constructed a first draft that has a clear topic sentence and good organization. At this pre-reading stage, students' had only limited knowledge of the causes and effects of the Depression, so the draft is understandably brief. He made some fairly common spelling errors that the teacher simply pointed out in the mechanics section of the GWP checklist. We are now ready for day two.

Day Two

Step Six

Return students' drafts and checklists. Have students make necessary edits and polish their first drafts, based on the guidelines you offered on the checklist. You can circulate among students to provide extra help. You can also use this time for individual conferences with students' experiencing real difficulty with the writing process. For example, second language learners generally benefit from extra, one-on-one discussion of their writing efforts. You may want to display some sample drafts on the overhead and model the process of editing for organization of ideas, style, and mechanics.

Step Seven

Have students turn-in their second draft and the original GWP checklist they used to guide their editing. You can then record any comments, particularly praise, on the bottom of the original checklist.

Step Eight

Assign text reading, explaining to students that the purpose of this reading is to locate additional information, especially supporting details and examples, that they can include in a final draft of their writing.

Day Three

Step Nine

Now that they have acquired additional knowledge about the topic (in this case, The Depression), *engage students in a group discussion to revise the original outline to include this text information.* Any misconceptions can be cleared up as well. Here, the text that students read added little to their basic understanding of the causes of Depression. However, it did expand on the effects of the Depression on workers in the cities and on farmers. Thus, their new outline contained a blend of their original ideas about the Depression and the new information discussed in the text.

Causes and Effects of the Depression

I. Causes
   a. bad investments by people and banks
   b. the stock market crash
   c. business downturn for 10 years
II. Effects
   a. people stopped buying goods
   b. factories closed
   c. by 1932, 13 million jobless workers (one of every four)
   d. young people hopped trains to find work
   e. homeless people lived on the outskirts of town in shacks called "Hoovervilles," after President Hoover
   f. farmers had too much surplus corn, which they could not sell
   g. farmers lost their farms—droughts also led to the Dust Bowl in the early 1930s
   h. poverty was common

Step Ten

Students should then revise and expand their compositions, based on new information from the text. You may want to have them include lecture and discussion information if the text is limited in its coverage of the topic. Students can work in pairs or small groups while you come around to help them link text and prior knowledge concepts. Then have students turn in these final drafts for a grade or give a quiz on this information. These compositions can be used as a lead-in to a unit (in this case, on the New Deal). They can also become part of the guide material you use with future classes, creating a very real audience for students' efforts.

The student who wrote the original draft on the Depression produced the following final version.

Causes and Effects of the Depression

The awful Depression of 1929 was caused by bad investments in the stock market. People took great risks with money, stringing themselves out in debt by buying too much stock on credit. The banks also made bad investments and many had to close after the stock market crashed. The Depression that started with the stock market crash of 1929 was a business downturn that, different from the ones before it, lasted for 10 years!

The effects of the Depression were many. Because people lost so much money, they stopped buying goods. The factories had to close and by 1932, 13 million people, or one in four, were out of work. Young people hopped trains to seek work in other towns. Homeless people lived on the edge of the big cities in tiny shacks called Hoovervilles, after President Hoover. Even the farms suffered. Farmers grew too much corn, which they couldn't sell. Since they couldn't sell the corn, they couldn't pay for their tractors and other equipment. They lost their farms, and droughts made things even worse. The Dust Bowl in the early 1930s wiped out even more farmers. People sank into poverty. Everything was dirt cheap. You could probably go to a movie for a dime, but I would rather live now!

This student's final version now contains supporting details from the text. Furthermore, he includes his own views about living during that era.

The GWP is an in-depth exploration of a text reading assignment. Since it is time consuming, you should plan on using it as a lead-in to a unit so that students approach their reading with some power over the text. For example, in the Depression outline stage, students begin to see the text as a cause-effect organizational pattern, which helped them read fluently and selectively for key ideas and details to revise their original GWP compositions.

Writing to Inform

Writing for an audience of peers, especially to argue a particular point of view, can help students become analytical readers. The strategies considered next emphasize both analytical reading and writing.

Read-Encode-Annotate-Ponder (REAP)

Each part of this acronym, *REAP* (Eanet & Manzo, 1976), denotes a step in a sequence of writing annotations about a story or expository text. R = read reconstruct the writer's message; E = encode the message in one's own words; A = annotate by recording the message in writing; and, P = ponder the author's message through a discussion with others. We emphasize just four of Eanet and Manzo's original seven annotations based on our experience in using this strategy with students. These four annotations provide enough background for students to critique a reading selection. It should be noted that while REAP can be applied to expository text that is not controversial, it lends itself to topics that encourage students to adopt and defend a particular position.

Students are asked to read a selection and write the following four annotations:

1. Key Quote
   Ask students to select a quote that captures the essence of the text passage.

2. Thesis
   Have students use this quote to write, in their own words, a statement of the author's major argument (non-fiction) or theme (fiction).

3. Motivation
   Students should then write a comment on the author's purpose (e.g., to persuade) and motive for writing a selection (e.g., ideological position, financial gain, etc.).

4. Critique
   This final annotation should express students' critique of the selection. They should agree, disagree, or agree in part with the author's thesis and present a short defense of the chosen position.

You may want to model the process of writing annotations before students attempt this independently. You can highlight key quotes in the early stages of REAP. The following example shows a student writing the four annotations in response to a newspaper article on sugar entitled "It's all sweet. It's all sugar" (Squires, 1985) for a health class. Just a brief excerpt of the article precedes the student's writing.

It's All Sweet. It's All Sugar

Despite widespread consumption, myths stick to sugar like chocolate coats an ice cream bar.

Chief among these misconceptions is the idea that certain forms of sugar—honey, for instance—are more nutritious than others. The fact is, for the most part, sugar is sugar is sugar, be it corn syrup, brown sugar, processed white sugar, honey, or maple syrup.

In terms of calories, sugar ranks surprisingly low. One teaspoon contains about 16 calories. And one form of sugar—molasses—contains a significant amount of iron, plus lesser amounts of calcium, potassium, and the B-vitamin niacin.

1. Key Quote
"The fact is, for the most part, sugar is sugar is sugar, be it corn syrup, brown sugar, processed white sugar, honey, or maple syrup."

2. Thesis
Sugar has gotten a bad reputation while honey and other forms of sugar are seen by people as more healthy.

3. Motivation
I think Squires wrote this to set the record straight on sugar. Sugar is in healthy foods like broccoli and green beans as well as junk food.

4. Critique
I agree with the author. Health food fanatics think just because they are eating honey it is somehow better for them. Sugar is actually a fairly low calorie food. After reading this I'm going to buy a candy bar during nutrition break!

Not all the students in this health class agreed with this individual or the author. One student pointed out that the article was featured in a newspaper in Hawaii, where sugar cane is grown and sold. This student also argued that if sugar was so healthy, why did her dentist tell her it contributed to cavities?

REAP can be a good starting point for a research paper that explores a topic in greater depth. This single news article would need to be checked against the views of other health authorities.

Free-Response and Opinion-Proof

This strategy, like REAP, is best applied to reading selections that generate diverse opinions. *Free-Response and Opinion-Proof* encourages students to read and write in an analytical fashion that goes beyond simply summarizing information (Santa, Dailey, & Nelson, 1985). It can be applied to stories or expository texts. We will demonstrate this strategy with an expository passage on the topic of poltergeist.

The following steps comprise a Free-Response and Opinion-Proof lesson:

Step One

Prepare the reading selection by underlining key sections of the text that signal some response from the reader. For example, if the author chronicles a major event in history, or strongly asserts an opinion, these sections should be underlined. In conventional texts, important sections may already be highlighted and italicized, or, the author may have margin notes that alert the reader to important ideas.

Step Two

Ask students questions that prompt their background knowledge about the topic to be considered. For example, you might say, "Have any of you seen the movie *Poltergeist?*" And, "What happened to the family in that film?" "Do you believe that this can happen?"

Step Three

Ask students to read the selection, stopping to reflect and write their reactions following each underlined or signaled section of the text. They can write these on a separate piece of paper, or, if you are using a paper copy, in the margin. Provide some general guidelines for these written reactions. The following questions usually stimulate students' thinking:

- Do you agree or disagree with what the author is saying?
- Why do you agree or disagree?
- Can you think of any experiences you have had that are like the one being described?
- Do you like or dislike these events, characters, etc.?

Step Four

Once they have finished reading and jotting down their reaction notes, *have students meet in pairs or small groups to discuss their particular view of the selection.* Students should be able to substantiate their opinions with reference to background knowledge or instances in the text that support their arguments. This discussion and the accumulated notes can then form the basis for a longer research paper exploring the topic under consideration, in this case poltergeist.

In the section that follows, we illustrate steps one through three of this lesson structure in a psychology class, along with a student's reaction notes. Her comments on the selection are in parentheses after the first two paragraphs of the article on poltergeist (Christen, Searfoss, & Bean, 1984, pp. 134–137).

Poltergeist

The German word "poltergeist" denotes "noisy spirit" but has come to connote the movement of objects by some mysterious means. Parapsychologists prefer the more scientific term: "Recurrent Spontaneous Psychokinesis" or RSPK.

There are many arguments supporting the existence of poltergeist or RSPK. First, *the number of reported cases,* well in excess of 100 dating back to 1858, show that this is not an isolated phenomenon.

(What a joke. Most of these so-called "cases" are reports made by a single individual without any scientists present. There are over 100 UFO sightings too, that doesn't mean we know, without a doubt, that they exist)

Second, instances of poltergeist are not confined to any one region of the world. Cases have been reported in Europe, America, India, and Indonesia. Thus, RSPK appears to be *a universal phenomenon.*

(If poltergeist is such a universal event, why can't scientists cause it to happen in a controlled experiment? From what I understand about parapsychologists, they have been unable to directly observe RSPK or to induce this event in a person who supposedly demonstrated the ability to move furniture and objects about a room or shake a house)

When Free-Response and Opinion-Proof is applied to controversial material such as the poltergeist passage, it helps students read critically and analytically. Analytical writing comprises the major form of writing students are asked to use in developing research papers in science and social science, yet they often approach this form of writing as if they are writing a lengthy summary, devoid of opinions (Durst, 1987). Both REAP and Free-Response and Opinion-Proof are good precursors to writing the research paper.

Research Papers

At its worst, a research paper assignment may amount to no more than students engaged in the busywork of copying facts laboriously cataloged for a teacher who knows this information in the first place. In this instance, the paper is put off as long as possible and hurriedly thrown together the night before it is due. The teacher then pays an inordinate amount of attention to the form of the paper, poison pen in hand to circle in red any grammar and spelling errors.

At its best, a research paper is the culmination of a student's efforts to become an expert in some subtopic of a field so this knowledge can be shared with an audience of peers (Calkins, 1986). This may range from developing an insider's knowledge of sharks in science to an understanding of how parapsychologists explore phenomena such as poltergeist in a psychology class. You can probably recall writing papers of this sort a few times during your years in school. But notice we said "a few times." Opportunities to become actively involved in pursuing a topic of genuine personal interest are all too rare.

Research papers involve students in the intense scrutiny of a topic and call on many of the independent study strategies discussed in chapter eight. Many writing texts offer detailed guidelines and examples for developing research paper assignments (e.g., Christen, Searfoss, & Bean, 1984), but in this section we simply want to mention some general steps to consider as you assign research papers in your content classroom.

Step One

Selecting and narrowing a topic is often a difficult task for teachers and students alike. Davey (1987) recommends having students form cooperative research groups for this stage of the process. A research team of two to five students with a recorder can brainstorm subtopics within the general area you suggest. For example, if the topic was "earthquakes," students might narrow this to a list consisting of "famous earthquakes, California earthquakes, science of earthquakes," and so on.

Step Two

Once the topic has been chosen, *the research team can then meet to plan how they are going to tackle the topic.* They can brainstorm possible questions for their topic and place them on notecards. For example, if the topic were "the science of earthquakes," possible questions might include: "What causes earthquakes? Can scientists predict when they will occur? Where do they occur most often?" Davey (1987) recommends that all questions be considered at this brainstorming stage. Once all possible questions have been elicited, they should be categorized and transformed into statements that will guide the research and note-taking stage.

Step Three

The research team should identify potential sources of information, including encyclopedias, textbooks, films, and experts who may be interviewed. If your school has access to computer data-bases that contain up-to-date encyclopedias, these may also be a good place to locate information.

Once each research team has identified their resources for the paper, they should develop a time line that delineates specific dates when they will finish each task. Thus, they need a date for completing the collection of information in the form of notes, another date for a paper outline, one for the first draft, and a date for the second draft. The search for information can be divided among team members so that a portion of the team reads and annotates encyclopedia information while another dyad interviews an expert on earthquakes.

Step Four

Once information has been collected, *students should regroup in their teams to categorize and consider the ideas they have.* This is a good time to transform the headings that guided the information search into a tentative outline. The "Science of Earthquakes" outline might look like this.

I. Earthquake
   A. Definition
II. Cause of earthquakes
   A. Early myths
   B. Modern tectonic theory

    III. Where they occur the most
        A. Pacific belt
        B. Mediterranean belt
    IV. Effect of earthquakes
        A. Landslides
        B. Tsunamis
     V. How they are studied
        A. Seismographs
        B. Earthquake waves

Once the outline is prepared, students can begin writing their individual reports. Be sure they realize that the outline is merely a tentative guide—it may be altered as the writing progresses and new insights develop.

Step Five

The first draft of the paper can now be written. Once the first draft is completed, students should exchange papers and use the writing guide checklist that accompanied the Guided Writing Procedure to peer-edit the papers (Christen, Searfoss, & Bean, 1984).

Step Six

Based on suggested edits by their peers as well as yourself, students can now complete the second and final draft. Naturally, this process takes time. Students need adequate class time to meet in their groups, and they need enough time to allow for two drafts of the paper. Davey (1987) recommends providing student groups with a form where they can list team members, the topic, categories to be explored, resources, and the timeline proposed. The teacher then reviews this material for each group and signs-off to indicate topic approval. Students may also need a checklist, particularly for the group recorder, that indicates the various stages of the process (e.g., brainstorming, researching, organizing, and writing), along with the sub-steps for each procedure (e.g., for brainstorming: generate questions, categorize the questions and write them as statements; identify sources; and set timelines). This will help focus the group effort on the various steps in the process.

In addition to carefully describing the parameters of a writing assignment as extensive as a research paper, you may want to share with students some model papers that were completed in a previous class. More importantly, papers written by former students can become important sources of information for the present class, giving students a functional audience for their writing aside from the usual teacher as examiner-audience. At their best, research papers should be memorable experiences for students that result in in-depth knowledge and appreciation of subtopics that might otherwise go unnoticed in a frenetic effort to cover too much content in too short a time.

Imaginative Writing to Inform Assignments

Annotating and discussing text reading, and writing an in-depth research report are mainstays of content learning. But it is equally important to provide a variety of writing opportunities, especially opportunities for imaginative writing. In this section we offer some imaginative writing assignments that lend themselves to a variety of content areas. You can undoubtedly think of other possibilities.

Students can project themselves into the lives of people in historical contexts or animals in various habitats by writing a diary entry from a unique perspective (Hansen, 1987). For example, have social studies students write a diary entry as if they were hobos riding the rail during the Depression. In the area of ecology, they could write a diary entry from the perspective of a whale or dolphin passing through an ocean channel near one of our polluted city harbors.

Similarly, have students write a "Who Am I?" piece in which they portray topics such as "I am your heart, I am your lungs, I am President Roosevelt, I am a camera," and so on. This exercise can require researching on a topic in detail to transform what might otherwise be dull expository prose into a lively, personal account (Hansen, 1987).

Activity

Write a brief "I am" piece describing some aspect of your own content area. For example, in biology you could write "I am the cell." In physical education, you might write "I am a gymnast." When you have completed the description, exchange yours with a colleague from another content area.

Imaginative writing expands students' sense of audience and encourages creativity. Smith (1986) offers a number of suggestions for imaginative writing that informs the reader. In business education, students can write real letters to a newspaper column or the Small Business Association, asking for advice about their business interests. They can write a business plan for a small business they wish to start, such as yard cleaning or car detailing. Some students may want to interview a small business owner and create an oral history of the trials and tribulations of business ownership.

In social studies, students can write about a historical event from the perspective of a person experiencing it. For example, what was it like to be a woman on a ranch during cattle drives, isolated from other women, responsible for a family and livestock? Students can write fictional accounts about historical events, transforming expository prose into a more lively narrative form. In mathematics, students can create a story using math symbols in place of some words. In science, defending an unpopular theory, such as the notion that there is such a thing as "earthquake weather," and directing this defense to a newspaper or a peer audience requires both research and imagination. In foreign language classes, acting in the role of a visiting student writing a diary entry about the first day in the United States can illuminate cultural diversity.

In music, drama, and art, writing a critical review of a concert or interviewing an artist for the newspaper helps broaden the audience for student writing. Finally, in health and physical education, keeping a sports diary that chronicles jogging or swimming progress and diet strategies demonstrates the day-to-day usefulness of writing to inform.

Responding to Writing

As students develop research papers and lengthy pieces of writing in your content area, your skill at responding to their writing becomes crucial. You may remember having a paper returned from a teacher covered with red marks attesting to your ability to produce sentences that were "awk" (i.e., awkward), and phrases that were, in the teacher's eyes, "frags" (i.e., fragments) (Stanford, 1979). When students receive a barrage of negative criticism for their writing efforts, they come to associate writing with frustration, depression, self-doubt, and avoidance. In contrast, we believe that students need to be able to take risks in portraying their ideas in writing without simultaneously balancing total attention to the mechanics of grammar and spelling, except in the revision stage of the second draft. You should avoid riddling a student's paper with red marks that focus on mechanical errors and consider alternate means of responding to students' writing. This is especially important in working with second language learners who may be very intimidated by writing in English.

Beaven (1977) recommended various ways to respond to students' writing that avoid the pitfalls of the poison red pen approach. First, taping comments you have, referring to particular parts of a student's paper, provides a more positive approach than marking every error. Second, beginning any comments about a student's paper with some positive praise alleviates anxiety and opens the door for revision. Third, writing marginal questions that probe areas of the paper that need revision directs the student to take responsibility for this process. Fourth, using an analytical checklist like the GWP checklist provides a means of guiding revision without marking up a student's paper. Fifth, individual conferences in combination with the checklist can be more productive than merely returning a paper with marginal comments. Finally, helping students use effective self-evaluation to revise their writing based on a series of generic questions will also lessen your paper load and encourage independence.

We want to discuss three of these six response schemes in detail. Individual conferences, self-evaluation, and peer evaluation deserve attention.

Individual Conferences

An individual conference is a conversation between a teacher and student for the purpose of evaluating and pointing out areas for revision of a draft of a paper (Newkirk, 1986). These conferences can be organized with a sign-up sheet on a first-come, first-served basis, or you can circulate about the room meeting with students as needed. The conversations you have with students should be purposeful, resulting in specific ideas for revision of a draft. Having a series of generic questions in mind to guide the individual conference will help the student participate actively in these sessions rather than passively by hoping you will do the revising. The following questions are recommended (Newkirk, 1986, p. 121):

1. What do you like best about this draft?
2. What do you like least?
3. What gave you the most trouble in writing this?
4. What kind of reaction do you want your readers to have—amusement, anger, increased understanding?
5. What surprised you when you wrote this? What came out differently than you expected?
6. What is the most important thing you learned about your topic in writing this?

These questions, in combination with the Writing Guide Checklist, should place the emphasis on the student's ideas, but there is always a tendency in teaching for the teacher to do most of the talking. Listening carefully and holding back your natural desire to grab the paper and revise in a way *you* think appropriate gives a student responsibility for this important process. Calkins (1986, p. 119) says, "I find that my own writing block vanishes the instant I see someone else's draft. My fingers begin to itch. I envision my ideal version of the text, and I know exactly what changes I would make to bridge the gap between what the student has written and what I would write." But she goes on to say that we need to keep in mind that this paper belongs to the student, not us. If they are to become what she calls "critical readers of their own texts," they are the ones who need to hold the paper in their hands and make the necessary revisions.

Ideally, students need to learn effective means of self-evaluation. The individual conferences you conduct using a series of generic questions can form the basis for effective self-evaluation.

Self-Evaluation

The Writing Guide Checklist introduced with the Guided Writing Procedure can serve as a guide for self-evaluation. Similarly, a series of questions like the following may also focus the writer on areas needing revision (Bean, 1989).

1. What makes you happy about this writing?
2. Do you excite your reader with a good beginning?
3. Is there a clear topic sentence?
4. Do you back up your ideas with details and examples?
5. Do you use a variety of words to express your ideas?
6. Are your sentences different lengths?
7. Do you use complete sentences?
8. Did you check your writing for correct capitalization, punctuation, and spelling?

Although checklists and questions can help students detect areas needing revision, a writer's distinct "style" is more difficult to define. Writing that expresses each student's individual interest in his or her own unique style is often a pleasure to read. However, many of the expository texts students read seem to have had the author's voice edited out of them. If these are the only models of writing students read in a content area, their own writing may have this same bland quality. In addition to texts, students need to read tradebooks in science, social studies, mathematics, and business that demonstrate the author's enthusiasm for a topic and unique voice.

In addition to self-evaluation, peer evaluation can play an important role in the revision process. If you have ever tried to evaluate your own writing objectively, you know how hard this process can be. You know what you meant to say, even if the actual version you produced on paper is incoherent. A peer reader will quickly find these problem areas.

Peer Evaluation

Teams of two students can become skilled at evaluating each other's writing when they have some practice and clear guidelines for the process. We have found that students can comfortably practice peer editing by starting with some writing samples from a lower grade. They can apply the Writing Guide Checklist to these samples without feeling self-conscious about critiquing a classmate's writing. Once they are skilled at responding to these papers, they can then exchange papers with a peer and collaborate to polish their first drafts.

The Writing Guide Checklist offers a good general series of composing and transcribing considerations for any content area writing. However, students should begin a peer editing session by first complimenting their partner on some aspect of the paper. The following general comments help students grasp this important first step (Moore, Moore, Cunningham, & Cunningham, 1986, p. 125): (1) "I thought the most interesting part of your paper was . . .", (2) "You gave the most complete information about . . ."

Moore et al. (1986) also suggested that students phrase any negative comments as questions. For example, "Can you tell me more about . . ." The approach avoids engendering any defensive feelings as a peer helps in the revision process.

In peer editing, merely finding problems in a paper is not enough. Unlike the red pen "awks" and "frags" we all remember trying to decipher and resolve, a peer reader should offer some solutions to the problems that have been identified. For example, the reader can suggest alternative organizational structures, revised sentences, correct spellings, and format changes. With the increased use of word processing among student writers, these changes should be less overwhelming than they were in the cut-and-paste era. Kinzer, Sherwood, and Bransford (1986) discuss microcomputer use across various content areas, with sections on database searches and word processing.

Individual conferences, self-evaluation, and peer evaluation all help content teachers manage the paper load, the biggest single obstacle to writing assignments in many content classrooms. You can also spot check shorter writing-to-inform (e.g., REAP and Free-Response and Opinion-Proof) and writing-to-learn activities.

The fact that you can probably remember those content area papers you have written over the years where *you* became the class expert on some topic, whether it was sharks or the stock market, attests to the power of writing as a mode of learning and reflection. It is worth the trouble. It takes real effort to guide students through various drafts for longer papers and real restraint to resist overcorrecting writing that is intended only for the writer's eyes as a bridge to learning.

Calkins (1986) says this about writing, and we agree:

> By articulating experience, we reclaim it for ourselves. Writing allows us to turn the chaos into something beautiful, to frame selected moments in our lives, to uncover and to celebrate the organizing patterns of our existence. (p. 3)

Summary

In this chapter we briefly discussed the writing process with an emphasis on the distinction between composing, where the writer places attention on ideas, and transcribing activities, including editing for appropriate grammar and spelling. Two major forms of writing in the content areas were considered: (a) writing-to-learn and (b) writing-to-inform. We examined seven writing-to-learn strategies: (1) journal writing; (2) possible sentences; (3) probable passages; (4) GIST; (5) semantic mapping; (6) writing roulette; and, (7) the guided writing procedure.

In the writing-to-inform section, we explored four topic areas: (1) read-encode-annotate-ponder (REAP); (2) free-response and opinion-proof; (3) research papers; and, (4) imaginative writing to inform.

Finally, we discussed responding to students' writing with an emphasis on three approaches: (1) individual conferences; (2) self-evaluation; and, (3) peer evaluation.

Now go back to the anticipation guide at the beginning of the chapter. React again to the statements, this time recording your answers in the column entitled "Reaction." Compare your answers with those you made in the Anticipation column.

Miniprojects

1. Visit a content area classroom for at least a week. Keep a log of writing activities you observe. Categorize these activities according to the major headings on the graphic organizer for this chapter: writing-to-learn, writing-to-inform, and responding to students' writing. Compare your findings to those of other students in your class.
2. Examine the writing activities recommended in a major student text in your content area. Using the headings from this chapter, determine what types of writing are being emphasized. Compare your findings to those of colleagues in class.
3. Select one of the writing-to-learn strategies, and conduct a lesson with students in your content area. Write a description and evaluation of this lesson and share it with colleagues in class.
4. Select one of the writing-to-inform activities and conduct a lesson with students in your content area. Respond to students' writing using the writing guide checklist, and conduct at least one individual conference or peer editing session, using the guidelines in this chapter. Write a description of your experience and share it with colleagues.

Additional Recommended Readings

Applebee, A. N. (Ed.). (1984). *Contexts for learning to write. Studies of secondary school instruction.* Norwood, NJ: Ablex.
This book reports a detailed descriptive study of writing assignments across content areas. The authors call for improving the quantity and quality of writing activities at the secondary level.

Calkins, L. M. (1986). *The art of teaching writing.* Portsmouth, NH: Heinemann.
This is a powerful book that chronicles the author's many years of helping students and teachers to appreciate the subtleties of teaching writing.

Christen, W. L., Searfoss, L. W., & Bean, T. W. (1984). *Improving communication through writing and reading.* Dubuque, IA: Kendall/Hunt.
Chapter six in this book for students is devoted to modeling the process of writing a major research paper.

Dishner, E. K., Bean, T. W., Readence, J. E., & Moore, D. W. (Eds.). (1986). *Reading in the content areas: Improving classroom instruction.* Dubuque, IA: Kendall/Hunt.
Chapter nine is devoted to the topic of composition strategies and chapter six features a good description on using writing to teach text structure awareness.

Romano, T. (1987). *Clearing the way: Working with teenage writers.* Portsmouth, NH: Heinemann.
This book recounts the author's work with secondary students through case studies of student writers as they struggle to find their own unique voices.

Smith, T. R. (Ed.). (1986). *Handbook for planning an effective writing program: Kinder-garten through grade twelve.* (4th ed.) Sacramento, CA: The California State Department of Education.

Chapter three features a comprehensive description of how to implement a schoolwide writing program.

References

Applebee, A. N. (Ed.). (1984). *Contexts for learning to write: Studies of secondary school instruction.* Norwood, NJ: Ablex.

Bean, T. W. (1986). Combining writing fluency and vocabulary development through writing roulette. In E. K. Dishner, T. W. Bean, J. E. Readence, & D. W. Moore (Eds.), *Reading in the content areas: Improving classroom instruction* (2nd ed., pp. 349–351). Dubuque, IA: Kendall/Hunt.

Bean, T. W. (1989). Writing in the content areas. In L. W. Searfoss & J. E. Readence (Eds.), *Helping children learn to read* (2nd ed.). Englewood Cliffs, NJ: Prentice-Hall.

Bean, T. W., & Steenwyk, F. (1984). The effect of three forms of summarization on sixth graders summary writing and comprehension. *Journal of Reading Behavior, 16,* 297–306.

Beaven, M. H. (1977). Individualized goal setting, self-evaluation, and peer evaluation. In C. R. Cooper & L. Odell (Eds.), *Evaluating writing: Describing, measuring, judging* (pp. 135–156). Urbana, IL: National Council of Teachers of English.

Calkins, L. M. (1986). *The art of teaching writing.* Portsmouth, NH: Heinemann.

Casucci, C. (1983). GIST in industrial education. In T. W. Bean (Ed.), *Reading and learning from text course of study.* Anaheim, CA: Anaheim Union High School District.

Christen, W. L., Searfoss, L. W., & Bean, T. W. (1984). *Improving communication through writing and reading.* Dubuque, IA: Kendall/Hunt.

Cunningham, J. W. (1982). Generating interactions between schemata and text. In J. A. Niles & L. A. Harris (Eds.), *New inquiries in reading research and instruction* (pp. 42–47). Thirty-First Yearbook of the National Reading Conference. Rochester, NY: National Reading Conference.

Davey, B. (1987). Team for success: Guided practice in study skills through cooperative research reports. *Journal of Reading, 31.* 701–705.

Durst, R. K. (1987). Cognitive and linguistic demands of analytic writing. *Research in the Teaching of English, 21,* 347–376.

Dutton, J. (1988). Hypothermia, the killer cold. *Surfer, 29,* 38.

Eanet, M. G., & Manzo, A. V. (1976). REAP—a strategy for improving reading/writing/study skills. *Journal of Reading, 19,* 647–652.

Fulwiler, T. (1986). Journals across the disciplines. In E. K. Dishner, T. W. Bean, J. E. Readence, & D. W. Moore (Eds.), *Reading in the content areas: Improving classroom instruction* (2nd ed., pp. 360–366). Dubuque, IA: Kendall/Hunt.

Graves, D. H. (1983). *Writing: Teachers & children at work.* Portsmouth, NH: Heinemann.

Hansen, J. (1987). *When writers read.* Portsmouth, NH: Heinemann.

Heimlich, J. E., & Pittelman, S. D. (1986). *Semantic mapping: Classroom applications.* Newark, DE: International Reading Association.

Kinzer, C. K., Sherwood, R. D., & Bransford, J. D. (1986). *Computer strategies for education.* Columbus, OH: Charles Merrill.

Konopak, B. C., Martin, S. H., & Martin, M. A. (1987). An integrated communication arts approach for enhancing students' learning in the content areas. *Reading Research and Instruction, 26,* 275–289.

Ludwig, D., McCarthy, W. J., & Repp, V. E. (1975). *Metalwork technology and practice* (6th ed.). Bloomington, IL: McKnight Publishing.

Martin, M. A., Konopak, B. C., & Martin, S. H. (1986). Use of the guided writing procedure to facilitate reading comprehension of high school text material. In J. A. Niles, & R. V. Lalik (Eds.), *Solving problems in literacy: Learners, teachers, and researchers.* Thirty-fifth Yearbook of the National Reading Conference (pp. 66–72). Rochester, NY: National Reading Conference.

Moore, D. W., & Moore, S. A. (1986). Possible sentences. In E. K. Dishner, T. W. Bean, J. E. Readence, & D. W. Moore (Eds.), *Reading in the content areas: Improving classroom instruction* (2nd ed., pp. 174–178). Dubuque, IA: Kendall/Hunt.

Moore, D. W., Moore, S. A., Cunningham, P. M., & Cunningham, J. W. (1986). *Developing readers and writers in the content areas.* White Plains, NY: Longman.

Newkirk, T. (1986). Time for questions: Responding to writing. In T. Newkirk (Ed.), *To compose* (pp. 121–124). Portsmouth, NH: Heinemann.

Santa, C., Dailey, S., & Nelson, M. (1985). Free-response and opinion-proof: A reading and writing strategy for middle grade and secondary teachers. *Journal of Reading, 28,* 346–351.

Searfoss, L. W., Smith, C. C., & Bean, T. W. (1981). An integrated language strategy for second language learners. *TESOL Quarterly, 15,* 383–389.

Shuman, R. B. (1979). Writing roulette: Taking a chance on not grading. In G. Stanford (Ed.), *How to handle the paper load* (pp. 3–5). Urbana, IL: National Council of Teachers of English.

Smith, C. C., & Bean, T. W. (1980). The guided writing procedure: Integrating content teaching and writing improvement. *Reading World, 19,* 290–294.

Smith, T. R. (1986). *Handbook for planning an effective writing program: Kindergarten through grade twelve* (4th ed.). Sacramento, CA: California State Department of Education.

Squires, S. (1985, June 26). It's all sweet. It's all sugar. *The Honolulu Advertiser.* Honolulu, HI.

Stafford, W. (1986). A way of writing. In T. Newkirk (Ed.), *To compose* (pp. 25–27). Portsmouth, NH: Heinemann.

Stanford, B. (Ed.). (1979). *How to handle the paper load.* Urbana, IL: National Council of Teachers of English.

van Dijk, T. A., & Kintsch, W. (1983). *Strategies of discourse comprehension.* New York: Academic Press.

Ver Steeg, C. L. (1982). *American spirit.* Boston, MA: Allyn and Bacon.

Westcott, J. (1987, October 14). Cockroaches make formidable foes for humans. *The Orange County Register,* p. B2. Santa Ana, CA.

Wood, K. D. (1984). Probable passages: A writing strategy. *The Reading Teacher, 37,* 496–499.

CHAPTER

8

Anticipation Guide/Reaction Guide

Directions: Before you begin reading this chapter, take a moment to put a check
mark by any of the statements with which you agree. Use the column
entitled "Anticipation."

Anticipation   **Reaction**

_____ 1.   _____ 1. It is impossible for human beings to focus
                                           their conscious attention on two things at the
                                           same time.

_____ 2.   _____ 2. The grade you get on a test is largely de-
                                           termined by your existing knowledge of the
                                           subject.

_____ 3.   _____ 3. In general, a little bit of practice each day is
                                           better than a lot of practice all at one time.

_____ 4.   _____ 4. It is impossible for the average person to re-
                                           member a 100-digit number.

_____ 5.   _____ 5. Writing comments and underlining in text-
                                           books is an essential study skill for sec-
                                           ondary students.

Study Strategies

Rationale

As teachers, the fruit of your labors will be *learning,* which can be defined broadly as ". . . a change in the organism that occurs at a particular time as a function of experience" (Crowder, 1976, p. 3). Hopefully, what your students learn will have much to do with math, English, or the sciences, and little to do with accuracy in hurling paper projectiles—although both entail learning. To put it in different words, any experience-based modification of schemata involves learning, whether or not one would consider the modification beneficial.

In a much narrower sense, learning can be defined in terms of the acquisition of specific information in content areas, and the preceding chapters of this text have dealt primarily with the means by which this acquisition process can be facilitated. One focus of the present chapter is on study strategies that help students retain and retrieve information.

Everyone has had the experience of walking into an examination, such as the SAT or GRE, only to find the answers to certain questions elusive due to memory failure. For example, the solution to a simple geometry problem may require knowing the formula for finding the circumference of a circle. (Let's see, is that πr^2, $2 \pi r$, or $2 \pi r^2$?) A failure to extract the necessary information from memory may result because: (1) you never bothered to learn the formula in the first place; (2) you learned it at one time but have for some reason failed to retain the formula in your memory; or (3) you did learn the formula and it is still locked in your memory, but you are unable to retrieve or recall the formula. In any event, the net effect is the same, a wrong answer on the test. Clearly, the ability to retain and recall information is as important as the ability to learn it in the first place. For this reason, study strategies are the business of every content teacher.

A second reason for teaching study strategies in content area classes is to develop in students those habits that encourage and assist independent learning. To the extent that students learn to study effectively on their own, they will be capable of continued reading and learning in the absence of explicit external guidance.

Study strategies (the traditional study skills curriculum) have included aspects of instruction as diverse as notetaking, map reading, uses of the card catalog, and speed reading. It has been the hodgepodge of the reading profession and the dumping ground for miscellaneous skills that everyone wants their students to know but no one wants to teach. The purpose of this chapter is not to cover all bases. Rather, we want to introduce some carefully selected independent study strategies and instructional procedures that will help students retain and recall information directly related to reading assignments.

Chapter Objectives

After reading this chapter, you should be able to:

1. Justify the time required to guide students toward effective study strategies in your content area.

2. Understand the general learning principles that underlie the study strategies described in this chapter.

3. Guide students in developing study strategies that improve retention and recall of material from your content area.

Graphic Organizer

The following graphic organizer is provided to give you some advance structure for new vocabulary and concepts that will be presented in this chapter.

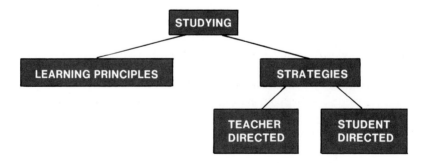

Principles of Effective Study Strategies

"If I were compelled to sum up in a single word all that is embraced in the expression 'a good memory', I should use the word attention. Indeed, I would define education, moral and intellectual, as attention." (Aiken, 1896, p. 74).

Attention

Read through the following passage one time, and be prepared to answer a single question:

> An *empty* hotel elevator stops and one person enters. The elevator goes up two floors and six people get on; up three more floors and three people get on. The elevator goes down one floor and seven people get off; down one more floor and one person gets off. The elevator then shoots up ten floors and two people get on. Now, without looking back, how many times did the elevator stop?

The answer is six; you probably got it wrong. Why? The second word in this old joke is a distractor. The fact that the elevator is empty has no bearing on the answer to the question. However, the reader, not knowing the question in advance, guesses or assumes that keeping track of numbers of people is the pertinent task. The real rub lies in the fact that tallying the number of elevator stops is much easier than calculating how many people get on and off.

The principle in this is that comprehension and learning/memory are not at all the same thing. It is quite possible to read with good comprehension and at the same time fail to retain the information. In most instances, the individual's active attention is a powerful factor in placing information in a durable memory store. It is a matter of common sense and common experience. Everyone remembers Miss Frock (the fourth grade teacher) who said, "If you don't pay attention, you won't remember anything."

There is, however, another aspect of attention which has less to do with willingness or appropriateness of attention than capacity to attend. Generally, human beings are capable of attending consciously to only one task at a time (LaBerge & Samuels, 1974). For instance, it is quite impossible to attend to two conversations at precisely the same time, although it is possible to quickly switch attention back and forth between conversations or other tasks which require conscious attention. This principle of *capacity limitation* for attention will be a critical consideration in discussion of specific study strategies later in the chapter.

Goal Orientation

One of the most serious and frequent impediments to learning is the counterproductive study goal. Students often read a textbook assignment for the sake of completing it, i.e., to be able to tell the teacher, without fibbing, that they have in fact read the assignment. When the student's attention is focused on getting through X number of pages rather than on comprehending and retaining information, the result is almost certain to be inferior comprehension and retention. Students who fail to read the last two paragraphs of a chapter because the teacher accidentally designated reading pages 79–93 instead of 79–94 demonstrate a counterproductive study goal. They meet the letter of the assignment but not its spirit. Constructive purpose, given by the teacher and embraced by the students, is essential to effective study.

Organization

Pronounce each digit in the following number one time, and then try to recall the number from memory:

1248163264128

Difficult, wasn't it? Now, try again.

1　2　4　8　16　32　64　128

The second time should have been much easier. If you sensed the geometric progression, you should have been able to reproduce the original number sequence with minimal strain on memory. It is much easier to remember one number (in this case, 1) and one rule (in this case, digits are produced by doubling the preceding number) than it is to recall what appears to be a random series of digits. This is *organization,* the arrangement of parts of a whole in such a manner that the parts are related to each other. The analogy to study strategies is obvious; whenever information can be organized into meaningful patterns, retention and retrieval of information will be facilitated.

A second type of mental organization is *chunking.* Bits of information are said to be chunked when they are transformed into one large bit of information. For example, the letters *h c r a o* can be transformed into the word "roach." The advantage in chunking is that a larger bit of information, e.g., "roach," requires no more memory than a smaller bit of information, e.g., *c,* (Miller, 1956). Because it permits the storage of large amounts of information without placing a corresponding strain on memory, chunking is an efficient means of organizing information.

A third type of mental organization is *mnemonics,* association devices for triggering recall. Perhaps the most familiar mnemonic device is the *acronym.* The process of acronymy is one in which words are formed by combining the initial letters or segments of a series of words. AWOL (absent without leave), VIP (very important person), and radar (radio detecting and ranging) are common examples of acronyms. Tying a string around your finger, remembering how to spell "piece" with the phrase "piece of pie," or improving recall of names by distorting them (e.g., "Baldwin" becomes "bald one") represent other types of mnemonic devices.

Activity

Directions: Develop a set of at least ten specific mnemonic devices that could be used to assist in the recall of specific information in your content area. Include acronyms but do not limit your devices to them.

Rehearsal

The acquisition, retention, and recall of information are all assisted by rehearsal or practice. *Rehearsal* is a natural strategy that people use to keep information in memory. In the case of short-term memory, information is repeated over and over until the immediate need for information desists. For instance, it is normal to look up a telephone number, rehearse it rapidly during the act of dialing, and then forget the number as soon as the dialing has been completed.

In the case of long-term memory, recall of information is improved most through *distributed* practice, in which rehearsals are separated by some break (Crowder, 1976). For example, the retention and recall of specific facts and historical trends derived from a social studies lecture will be better with frequent, spaced, and brief periods of study (rehearsal) than with a single massive study session.

Time On Task

While it is almost certainly true that the organization of practice affects retention and recall (e.g., distributed versus massed practice), it is equally true of the raw amount of time spent practicing. In fact, it has been argued that some strategies or teaching techniques appear to improve learning primarily because they result in students spending more time on learning tasks, and not because the techniques are better than others (Carver, 1972, 1987; Dyer, Riley, & Yekovich, 1979). For example, which of the following strategies would result in the best recall: (1) reading and then outlining a textbook chapter; or (2) reading and then answering teacher-prepared questions over the content? To some degree, the answer would be dependent upon the amount of time each technique caused students to study.

Depth of Processing

Most college graduates are capable of solving an algebra problem such as (a):

$$a. \ x - 14 = 23$$

On the other hand most college graduates probably could not solve an equation like (b), in spite of the fact that they were undoubtedly forced in high school to work problems at this level of difficulty:

$$b. \ Q(x) = \frac{x^3 \times 5x^2 + 6x}{x + 3}$$

One justification for introducing difficult material is that it helps to guarantee the long-term retention of basic principles and processes. In other words, it is possible that people retain the ability to solve problem (a), not because it is easy but because they were made to expend great mental energies solving problems like (b). This is the principle of *depth of processing,* which asserts that there is a greater liklihood of long-term retention and recall when: (1) the mental activity demands a deeper level of thinking, (2) more schemata are committed to the task, and (3) the degree of semantic analysis is high (Anderson & Armbruster, 1984; Craik & Lockhart, 1972). The depth of processing principle also explains why a new vocabulary word and its definition will be remembered longer and with greater accuracy by most people if the word is introduced with such elements as context, morphemic analysis, and an etymology. You guarantee better memory for the word and its fundamental meaning by forcing a deeper, more expansive mental processing of the word and its associations.

Specific Strategies

Strategy implies intent. A strategy is not an accident but is rather the planned means to an end. In general, it is best to plan study strategies that have the following characteristics:

1. They help students focus attention on *important* information.
2. They provide students with meaningful study goals.

3. They help students organize information.
4. They cause students to practice.
5. They encourage deep processing of information.

The study strategies that follow are plans that teachers and students can implement cooperatively to further the acquisition, retention, and recall of information.

Listening and Taking Notes

Notetaking during lectures and discussions is one of the most common events in the classroom, yet there is considerable confusion over the purposes and best methods of taking notes. In fact, there are many notetaking systems but none of them have empirical documentation (Heinrichs & LaBranche, 1986; Norton, 1981).

Notetaking has two presumed functions, external storage and encoding. The *external storage* (the notes themselves) of information serves as a substitute for memory and gives students an opportunity to review material that might otherwise have been forgotten. The *encoding* function presumably improves the comprehension and retention of information by forcing the notetaker to transform lecture material into personally meaningful language (depth of processing principle). The difference between external storage and encoding is often described as a contrast between taking and having notes. The validity of the encoding function is based on the assumption that during the course of a lecture students will be able to mentally transform what they are hearing. Pauk (1979) rejects this assumption on the grounds that fast presentation rates during lectures preclude the reflective thought necessary for such encoding. In fact, it is quite possible that taking any kind of notes is detrimental to learning if the material is presented too quickly (Peters, 1972). The consensus is that the external storage function in notetaking is more important than the encoding function (Kiewra, 1984).

In addition to the question of notetaking purposes, there is also disagreement regarding the "best" procedures for notetaking. For instance, it is customary for students to take notes in *parallel,* i.e., to be writing and listening at the same time. However, research (Aiken, Thomas, & Shennum, 1975) suggests that *spaced* notetaking improves recall of lecture material. A spaced presentation is one in which the lecture is broken into segments, followed by intervals of silence several minutes long. Students listen during each lecture segment and then make notes at the interval which follows. Why this should be an effective notetaking procedure is explained in part by the limits of human attention. If people can concentrate on only one task at a time, why should we expect students to write and listen effectively at the same time? Most notetakers probably switch back and forth; i.e., they listen for a few seconds and then hear, perhaps, but do not listen during those seconds in which individual notes are recorded. The result for many notetakers is incomplete lecture information that has been received in bits and pieces. In contrast, a spaced notetaking procedure permits students to focus their complete attention on listening to the teacher and on encoding lecture information into meaningful notes.

The following statements, based on research, summarize what is presently hypothesized about notetaking (Faw & Waller, 1976; McAndrew, 1983):

1. The external storage of notes is more important than the act of taking notes (encoding).
2. Parallel notetaking may interfere with the reception of forthcoming lecture information.

3. Teachers should use a spaced lecture format.
4. The rate at which notes are delivered appears to affect the value of notes.
5. The value of notes is much reduced if the notes are not used for practice.
6. Teachers should place important information on the blackboard to cue notetaking.
7. Teachers should use handouts to supplement notetaking.

Teacher Strategies. It is easy to assume that the quality of student notes is nothing more than a function of students' intelligence and other attributes. However, the lecture situation is a meeting of minds, and the organization and presentation format of the lecture can affect the quality of the notes radically. Here is a list of suggestions that will make notetaking easier and more efficient for students in your lectures and class presentations.

1. Do not lecture if students are expected to write down and remember everything you say. Instead, type the material and hand it out. Lectures are more interesting if they include elements of discussion.
2. Lectures typically follow the same organizational patterns found in texts (Lopate, 1987), e.g., cause/effect and comparison/contrast. Point these patterns out to students while you are lecturing, and tell them about how you have organized your notes. For example, if you have three points to make under each of two headings, let students know so that they can make appropriate room in their notes.
3. Notetaking should not be a game in which the student has to guess about what is important. It is absurd to assume that novices in chemistry or political science should, without guidance, instantly sort essential ideas from trivial details. Write important information on the board, or just tell students when to take notes and when not to.
4. Speak slowly.
5. Use a spaced notetaking procedure. Allow students to listen to your lecture for ten minutes or so. Then give them time to write and ask you questions. This will prevent the students from having to write and listen at the same time (capacity limitation problem).
6. Give students a few minutes at the end of class to revise and/or supplement their notes, and make them do it!
7. Give students distributed practice with their notes. Encourage them to review their notes on a nightly basis or in class. You can give students frequent quizzes over lecture material, allowing them to review their notes before the quiz or even allowing an open-notebook quiz. Another review possibility is to have students create questions strictly from their notes for a class review. In general, anything you can do to get the students to modify and refer back to their notes will boost their recall and retention.
8. Have open-note, but closed-book, quizzes to give students an idea of the quality of their notes. Students who take the time to revise notes and to review will perform better; this in turn will encourage others to revise and review.

Student Strategies. We believe that it is a good idea for students to learn to take good notes, and we define good notes as any notes, however disorganized, sloppy, or idiosyncratic, that will serve as a successful warehouse for lecture information. We know of no one best notetaking procedure for all people of all ages in all subject areas. Therefore, we recommend considerable latitude in individual notetaking systems.

The notetaking procedure we recommend for students is the *Verbatim Split Page Procedure*. VSPP is a blend of various notetaking systems and is comprised of recording, organizing, and studying from notes.

1. *Recording Notes.* Begin teaching VSPP by having students divide their notebook paper so that 40 percent of each page lies to the left and 60 percent to the right. Instruct students to take notes only on the lefthand side during lectures. All notes should be verbatim and clipped. The idea is to expend minimum amounts of mental energy on writing in order that full attention can be focused on listening to the lecture.

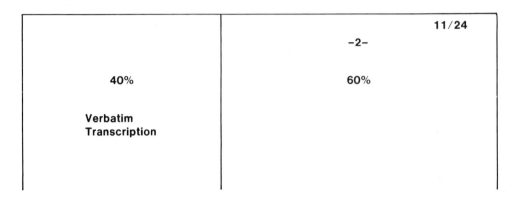

2. *Organizing Notes.* Nearly everyone has had the experience of taking abundant notes for a class, only to find those notes either unreadable or bizarre when it came time to study for the final exam. Abbreviated words, telegraphic sentences, and hasty scribbles may seem quite lucid to the notetaker at the time they are written; however, as the context in which the idiosyncratic shorthand was produced fades, notes of this sort rapidly lose meaning and integrity. For this reason, it is necessary to reorganize notes during significant pauses within the lecture or immediately following the lecture.

The right side of the notebook paper is used for reorganizing and expanding upon the scribbles to the left. Students should be encouraged to:

1. Place lecture information in an outline format;
2. Interpret notes and then encode them in their own words;
3. Expand notes to include lecture information that the student didn't have time to note; and
4. Write out whole words, phrases, and sentences so that notes will be clear in the future. (See Figure 1.)

It is sometimes recommended that students take notes in an outline format. This is an extremely difficult task for two reasons. First, deciding which ideas are superordinate and which are subordinate requires attention that notetakers can't spare as they play the role of listener. Secondly, lectures are hardly ever organized and presented in ways which immediately lend themselves to outline notetaking. In Figure 1 it is clear that the lecture on space phenomena began with an overview of superordinate concepts and then later presented subordinate bits of information. In reality, most lectures and other teacher presentations are

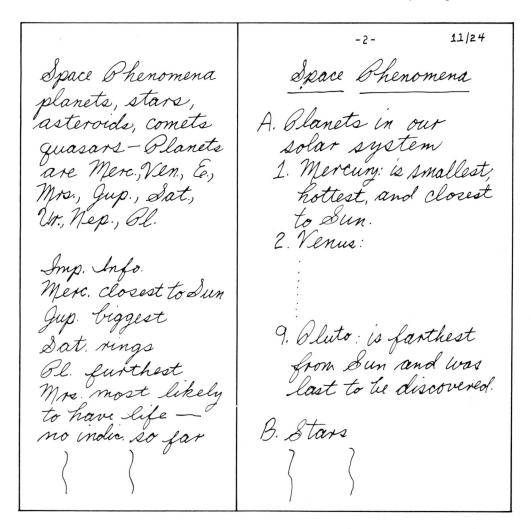

Figure 1. Organizing Notes.

punctuated frequently with digressions and slices of knowledge that are improperly layered within the lecture. With the help of limited verbatim notes, students should be able to rethink and reorganize the lecture material AFTER the lecture is over and when the entire presentation is fresh in their minds.

Metacognition

Broadly defined, *metacognition* refers to awareness of one's own mental processes, that is, knowing how you know what to do. It entails an effort to manage one's own thoughts through conscious planning. People who have good metacognitive skills understand their own behaviors, employ mental strategies that they can verbalize, and evaluate the quality of their thinking (Paris, Wasik, & Van der Westhuizen, 1988). Metacognition is thinking about thinking.

Most children do not have good metacognitive skills. The most common response children give when asked why they have done something is: "I don't know." Sometimes they hide behind the "I don't know" when they do not wish to respond to parents, teachers, or other authority figures. For example:

Dad to teenage Daughter: "I told you to be home at 12 last night. Why did you come home at 3 A.M.?"

Teenage Daughter to Dad: "I don't know."

Of course, the real thought of the teenage daughter is: "Jimmy and I were too busy kissing to pay attention to your stupid rule." On the other hand, young people frequently do not understand or even attempt to monitor their own thought processes, and this is often true in the area of reading comprehension. Too many students rove mindlessly through a textbook assignment without any clearly defined purposes or conscious strategies for learning. Current research in the area of metacognition indicates that students who have good metacognitive skills are better comprehenders (Forrest-Pressley & Waller, 1984). Therefore, helping your students to develop their metacognitive awareness is fundamental to study strategies.

Teacher Strategies. One current approach to developing metacognition in students is the *think-aloud* technique (Nist & Kirby, 1986; Randall, Fairbanks, & Kennedy, 1986). The think-aloud technique is a teacher-modeling strategy in which the teacher reads aloud from a text and verbalizes whatever comes to mind in an effort to show students how to reason during reading. The teacher's verbalized thoughts may include questions, predictions, paraphrases, evaluative statements, and even text-irrelevant comments. Here are the steps in the strategy:

1. Select a passage between 100 and 300 words long in your subject area. The passage should be fairly difficult so that your reasoning is actually useful to the students. If the passage is too easy the students will not see the value of what you are doing.
2. Prepare your comments for the think-aloud based on your experiences. Because the material will not really be difficult for you, you need to plan an idealized set of think-aloud responses. You will be acting the part of a student with good metacognitive skills.
3. Explain to the students exactly what you are doing, e.g., "I am going to show you how I think when I read."
4. Read the passage to the class and insert your planned think-alouds as you go.
5. When you are finished, give students a chance to ask you questions about how you think or about the think-aloud procedure itself.
6. Have students practice thinking aloud with smaller segments of the text.

The paragraph below exemplifies a think-aloud for a biology text. The teacher's questions and statements are indicated by superscripts within the paragraph and referenced below the paragraph.

Amniocentesis[1] is a technique used by fetologists[2] when the parents are known or suspected to carry one of several types of genetic disease or when the woman is over age 40.[3] Older women are more likely to have a fetus with Down's syndrome.[4] The diseases specifically tested for are caused by having an extra or missing chromosome, a chromosome which has been broken,[5] or a metabolic disease such as phenylketonuria.[6] A hypodermic needle is inserted through the abdomen of the pregnant woman[7] and into the amnion.[8] A small amount of amniotic fluid, containing fetal cells,[9] is drawn into the syringe. These cells are then cultured (grown) for a period of time; when enough culture cells are available, they can be tested for many metabolic defects. Cells can also be specially stained and prepared so that the chromosomes can be seen under a microscope.[10] (Brum, 1978, p. 105).

1. Looks like this is the topic. I better remember this word.
2. What's this? Someone who studies feet?
3. I didn't know people that old could have babies.
4. OK, I know about that. A boy in our church has it.
5. How do you lose a chromosome or get it broken? Could it happen to me if I play football or get in an accident? How will I know?
6. I wonder what nerd made up this word.
7. Ouch!
8. Better ask the teacher what this is.
9. I get it now. Fetal refers to fetus, an unborn baby. That explains what a fetologist is, an unborn baby doctor.
10. Sounds cool; I'd like to see it.

Student Strategies: Most of the strategies in this text will improve metacognitive skills to some extent. However, students needs a guiding mental strategy for studying. *PLAE* (Simpson & Nist, 1984) is an acronym that stands for *P*replan, *L*ist, *A*ctivate, *E*valuate.

Preplan: Plan how to study. This may entail asking questions such as:
"Should I summarize, take notes, or reread?" "What kind of a test is the instructor going to give?" "Do I want to study by myself or in a small group?"
List: The answers to such questions should result in planned behaviors rather than thoughtless or reflexive ones. The planned behaviors should be written down. For example: "I will read this chapter twice." "I will ask my teacher whether the test will be essay or multiple-choice." "I will ask Marty and Beth if they want to study with me tomorrow."
Activate: This is a monitoring behavior. Basically the student needs to regularly ask, "Am I following my plan?"
Evaluate: Students assess whether or not the plan has worked. For example: "Was it worth studying with Marty and Beth?" "Would I do it again?"

PLAE is deceptively simple, so much so that you may be tempted to dismiss it as superfluous. Yet we believe that a strategy as simple as this is fundamental and not at all too obvious to bother with as you are teaching. How many times have you gotten to school or the office only to discover that you had forgotten your lunch, house keys, wallet, purse, term paper, or other important item? If the average American adult simply stopped at the front door before leaving and asked, "Do I have everything I need to take with me?" it would probably save millions in gasoline and aspirin.

Activity

Select a textbook from your content area and develop a think-aloud lesson that you can demonstrate for the rest of the class.

Reading Daily Assignments

One of the content teacher's ever-present problems is how to get students to comprehend better and retain more information from textbook reading assignments. How does the teacher convert the passive page-watcher into a reader who is actively engaged in reconstructing and evaluating the author's thoughts?

Unfortunately, the best method of responding while reading, writing in the text, is not an option for most students because the books belong to the school. Underlining main ideas, starring important terms, asking and answering questions, and making evaluative comments in the margins combine to make a highly personal and convenient response mode during reading. In the absence of this option, however, it is necessary to consider alternative study strategies.

Teacher Strategies. In addition to the comprehension techniques presented in chapter six, we recommend having students generate questions when they read. Questions can be used for purposes of in-class review or they may be questions that the student truly does not know the answer to. We highly recommend using the ReQuest procedure (chapter six) to teach students how to ask questions at different levels: text-explicit (reading the lines), text-implicit (reading between the lines), and experience-based (reading beyond the lines). Be patient; some students will have a very difficult time formulating questions that involve inferences (text-implicit). There are three basic strategies to give students for deriving questions from reading assignments:

1. *Personal Review.* Students should ask questions in order to eliminate confusions left over from their reading assignment. Each question should have a page number along with it so that you and the class can refer directly to the source of the confusion. In many cases, students with the greatest comprehension problems will be the least likely to volunteer questions. Praise these reluctant students for asking questions, even if the questions seem superfluous or oblique.
2. *Class Review.* Assign students to write a set number of questions based on a reading assignment. You might, for example, assign them to create three text-explicit questions, two experience-based questions, and one text-implicit question. During the following class you can have students take turns asking and answering questions, or you might create teams for a question-and-answer showdown. In any case give lots of praise for good questions, especially if they are text-implicit.
3. *Stump the Teacher.* Students will enjoy creating questions to test you. Again, try to get them to generate legitimate questions at a variety of levels by modeling for them the kinds of questions you might ask one of your college professors. Students may at first be inclined to ask trivial, text-explicit questions, e.g., "How many words are on page 144?" However, with guidance from you the students should begin to ask the kinds of questions that will stimulate class discussions.

Student Strategies. There are two strategies that we recommend teaching to your students: *summarizing* and *SQ3R*. Both of these strategies can help students become better comprehenders in your class and independent learners elsewhere.

1. *Summarizing.* This is a strategy that will improve comprehension, especially if the type of comprehension you want from students is an understanding of superordinate concepts as opposed to the memorization of details (Bretzing & Kulhavy, 1979). For this reason summary writing is perhaps a better strategy for the humanities and social sciences than

for the physical sciences and mathematics, where broad generalizations are frequently less important than the precise application of specific and detailed information. We suggest the following:

a. You should model summarizing because many students have a vague notion of what a summary is and no notion at all of how to create one. Take a short section from the class text and have the students read it in class. Then write a summary on the board, speaking out loud as you construct it so that students can observe the process. From you they can discover how to distinguish supporting details from important generalizations, how long a summary should be, and where to look in the text for information that should be included.

b. Assign a brief reading selection to the entire class and ask them to write a summary. If you do this in class, it makes an excellent project for small groups because so many students will get stuck trying to figure out how to complete the task.

c. Have students write brief summaries in their notebooks after each major subheading in reading assignments. Or, assign summarizing for sections of the text assignments you feel are particularly important or are amenable to summarizing.

d. On exams, include appropriate essay questions or objective questions that tap superordinate concepts relevant to the summarizing activities of students.

2. *SQ3R and Variations.* The *SQ3R* procedure (Survey, Question, Read, Recite, Review) is over forty years old (Robinson, 1946), and in recent years there have been numerous imitations and variations of the old SQ3R themes; e.g., PQRST (Preview, Questions, Read, Summarize, Text), and EVOKER (Explore, Vocabulary, Oral reading, Key ideas, Evaluation, Recapitulation). In the authors' opinion, there are few significant differences among them. All of them seek to make reading more meaningful by: (a) giving the reader some purpose for reading; (b) getting the reader to search for information or the answers to questions instead of being passively manipulated by the print; (c) encouraging review; and (d) causing students to spend more time on task. The following describes SQ3R:

a. *Survey:* This initial preview step encourages the reader to skim the reading assignment in order to answer broad questions about its content. The reader should spend several minutes quickly reading the opening paragraphs of the chapter, major headings and subheadings, and possibly the chapter summary. Attention should also be directed briefly to pictures, charts, and italicized words. At the conclusion of the survey, the reader should be able to answer questions such as "What is this chapter about, basically?" or "Is this chapter going to require more study time than usual?"

b. *Question:* In this second stage of SQ3R the reader begins to progress sequentially through the text, mentally or in writing, converting chapter headings into questions. For instance, the heading "Characteristics of Emulsions" would be transformed to "What are the characteristics of emulsions?"

c. *Read:* As readers create questions (step b), they read to find answers to their questions.

d. *Recite:* After each section of the chapter is read, the reader pauses briefly to: (1) determine whether or not the questions posed in step b has been answered satisfactorily, and (2) rehearse the answer. In this manner, steps b, c, and d are repeated as the reader progresses through the text.

e. *Review:* At the end of the chapter the reader spends a few minutes trying to recall main ideas and important supporting details from the entire reading assignment. The review may also entail paging through the chapter using each heading as a focus. Reviews distributed frequently are recommended to promote long-term recall.

Whatever you do as a teacher that causes students to spend more time on daily assignments, to see purpose in their reading, and to review will increase learning, retention, and recall of information. The tactic can be SQ3R, one of its variations, or some other device.

In any event, avoid giving assignments such as, "OK, read pages 24–43 for Monday." Assignments like this make the completion of page 43 the objective of the assignment. A much better assignment would be "OK, read pages 27–43. When you are finished you should be able to answer these questions . . ." or "As you are reading, write down at least ten words, facts, procedures, or explanations you didn't understand." By the time you have finished detailing the reading assignment, your students should be able to answer the following questions:

1. What is this reading assignment about?
2. Why am I reading this?
3. What should I know when I have finished?

In fact, students have a right to this information and should be encouraged to ask for it whenever they find themselves facing purposeless reading assignments.

Graphic Comprehension

Graphic comprehension, or *graphic literacy,* refers to the ability to interpret charts, maps, graphs, and other visual presentations that are commonly used to supplement the prose of textbooks, nonfiction trade books, and newspapers. These visual representations of concepts in nonverbal or semiverbal form tend to be difficult for students, yet are ignored as specific instructional objectives in basals and other school texts. The following taxonomy shows the tremendous diversity of graphs (Fry, 1981).

Teacher Strategies. Do not assume that your students will understand even simple pie graphs. If the purposes and designs of graphs have never been explained to them, many students will automatically skip graphs, an unfortunate behavior, since graphs are designed to improve comprehension—not create interference.

As a prereading activity, you should introduce graphs as you would new and important vocabulary. Have students open their texts to the graphs. Then explain the purposes of the graphs to them and demonstrate correct procedures for their interpretations, e.g., how to plot points on a complex quantitative graph. We also recommend that you try the *Graphic Information Lesson* (Reinking, 1986). The GIL has three stages:

1. In the *introductory stage* the teacher shows the students a graph and explains the mechanics of its use. Then the teacher asks text-explicit, text-implicit, and experience-based questions that are designed to enlighten the students as to the relationship between the graph and the rest of the text. Students can also learn to judge whether the graph is supplemental, redundant, or complementary to the text.

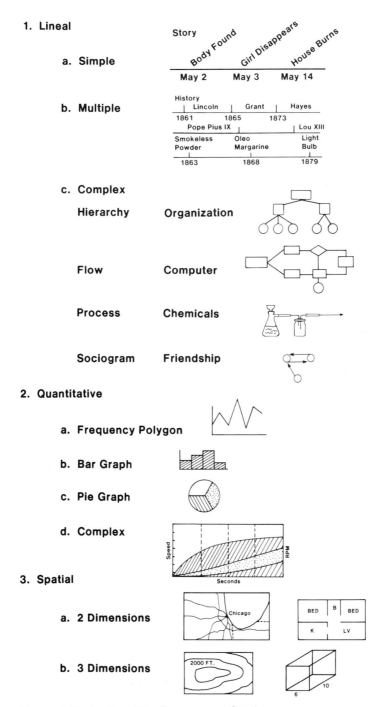

Figure 1. Illustration of the Taxonomy of Graphs.

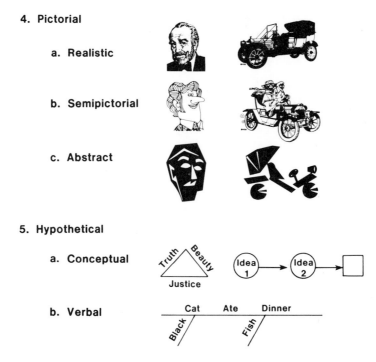

4. Pictorial

    a. Realistic

    b. Semipictorial

    c. Abstract

5. Hypothetical

    a. Conceptual

    b. Verbal

Figure 1. Continued.

2. In the *synthesizing stage* the teacher presents teacher-made *pseudographics,* graphs that are related to current text material but which may or may not be accurate or believeable. The students have to be able to relate the new graph to what they have learned from the text in order to judge its validity. Two examples of pseudographs follows. Notice that students must document their decision with a page number from the text.
3. In the *application stage* students are asked to: a) develop their own pseudographs to accompany the text, or b) critique the author's use of graphic aids.

    Student Strategies: Encourage students to use the summarizing strategy previously introduced when they have reading assignments containing graphs. Because graphs are non-verbal presentations of concepts, a verbal summary provides a translation that will help to ensure comprehension as well as long-term retention of the concept.

Activity

    Select a textbook, and, using Fry's taxonomy, catalog all of the different types of graphs in the text and their frequency of occurrence. Make a graph to show your results to the class.

A.

Number of Acres Planted in Cotton
(Old South—Virginia, North and South Carolina)

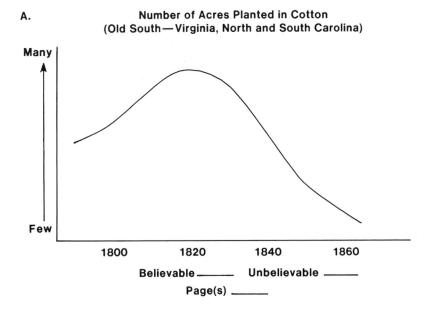

Believable _____ Unbelievable _____

Page(s) _____

B.

Ad in a Virginia
Newspaper 1790

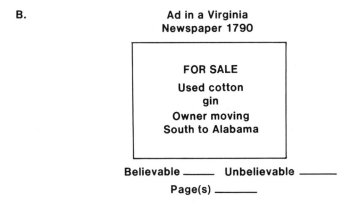

Believable _____ Unbelievable _____

Page(s) _____

Figure 2. Two examples of a teacher's pseudographics.

Test Preparation

Evaluation tends to be an anxiety-producing situation for teachers or students. Anxiety can be reduced and learning maximized if teachers prepare students for specific examinations and if students learn how to study for and take tests intelligently.

Teacher Strategies. Middle and secondary students typically fear examinations and mistrust teachers' motivations. Many students develop a neurosis over tests because they have stereotyped teachers as a group of ogres who try to trick them with unfair questions or who purposely do not reveal what material a test will cover so that they can have the pleasure of doling out bad grades. To prove to your students that you are not a test-ogre we suggest that you: a) give students precise information about what material an exam will cover, and b) give students ungraded practice in taking the kinds of tests they will later have to negotiate for grades. We recommend the *Fake Pop Quiz* (FPQ).

The FPQ is a quiz which is designed to reinforce rather than test recently introduced information. The purpose of the quiz format is to stimulate interest. Students are considerably more alert following, "Get your pencils ready; it's time for a fake pop quiz," than they are after hearing, "Get your pencils ready; it's time to do some review exercises." Tests are really a lot of fun once the anxiety over being externally evaluated has been neutralized. In addition, students appreciate test simulations because they know that the teacher is trying to prepare them for the true evaluation that inevitably follows.

FPQ's can be brief interludes in daily lessons (placed on the blackboard) or comprehensive reviews prepared on dittos. In either case, the quiz should be preceded by general directions, either verbal or written, along the lines of the following:

> "Today we are having a fake pop quiz on earth science vocabulary. Obviously, the score you get on this quiz won't affect your grade in the course, but it will give you some practice and an idea of how well prepared you are for a real test. When everyone has finished the quiz, you will score your own and get two points for each correct answer. Good luck!" (The FPQ may be open- or closed-book depending upon the teacher's objectives and the nature of the exercises.)

Once students have finished the quiz, specific questions can serve as guides to classroom discussion. The FPQ offers a golden opportunity to focus on text-implicit and experience-based kinds of questions.

Student Strategies. Students can acquire confidence in their own test-taking abilities if they learn how to prepare for exams and how to cope with them logically. The following information can help your students meet these objectives.

Test-taking skills refer to long-term study strategies as well as to strategies that students can use while taking exams, often referred to as testwiseness. You should be doing frequent reviews of text material, class notes, and other assigned materials. Remember, lots of short study sessions are better than a few giant cramming sessions. Students can be given the following advice for preparing for content area exams:

> *When you hear about the test.*

1. Find out as much as you can about the test itself.
2. Find out exactly when the test will be given.
3. Ask your teachers to discuss the kinds of questions that will be on the test, e.g., multiple choice, true-false, or essay.
4. If your teachers give essay tests, ask them what they look for in a good essay answer.
5. Ask your teachers to give you examples of test items and good test answers. Many will be willing to do this, but almost none will do it if you don't ask.
6. Try to guess which questions your teacher will ask.

The night before the test.

1. A light study session should be enough. Do not cram!
2. Make sure you have pencils, pens, paper, a watch, a calculator (if permissible), and any other materials you may need for the exam.
3. Get a good night's sleep.

The day of the test.

1. Eat a good breakfast.
2. Tell yourself that you will do well on the exam.
3. Make sure you have all the materials you need for the exam.
4. Do not cram right before the test. That is the worst thing you can do. Cramming can cause students to forget important information. Cramming also causes needless test anxiety.

Testwiseness refers to a series of principles that can be applied to exams independently of subject area knowledge. To be testwise is to be able to (1) exploit the flaws in teacher-made exams, and (2) apply logic, common sense, and good organization in test-taking situations. Testwiseness by itself will not guarantee good grades in grade school or college. There is no substitute for studying hard and being knowledgeable. However, testwiseness skills can help students to do a better job on classroom tests (Sherman & Wildman, 1982).

The present discussion will be limited to the most common types of exams: multiple choice, true/false, and essay.

Multiple Choice Tests

Students probably take more multiple choice tests than any other kind. The most usual variety of multiple choice item consists of a stem and several options. For example:

World War II ended in   (Stem)
  1. 1960
  2. 1944   (Options)
  3. 1945
  4. 1955

The following strategies will help students to be testwise on multiple choice tests.

1. Read all directions carefully. It is not unusual for students to get poor grades on exams simply because they fail to read and follow directions.
2. Budget your time so that you are certain to finish the test. Students sometimes spend too much time on one part of the test and then fail to finish another. Nothing hurts a test grade worse than leaving items blank.
3. Do not waste time on items which are very difficult. Come back to them at the end of the exam.
4. Assume that each item has a correct answer and that you are smart enough to figure it out one way or another.

5. Always guess if you don't know the answer. Never leave a multiple choice question blank.
6. If the right answer is not obvious to you right away, try to eliminate obvious wrong or silly answers and then guess from among those that remain. For example,

The speed of sound is

    A. 3700 feet per second
    B. 1087 feet per second
    C. 0
    D. 186 miles per second

You should be able to eliminate answer C right away. That would give you a 1/3 chance of guessing right instead of 1/4 chance.

7. Whenever two of the options are identical, both answers must be wrong. For example,

The universal donor is

    A. O −
    B. H_2O
    C. AB
    D. water

8. Whenever two of the options are opposites, one of them is always wrong and the other is often, but not always, right. For example,

A proton is a

    A. positively charged particle
    B. free atom
    C. negatively charged particle
    D. displaced neutron

9. Be aware that the answer to a question may appear in the stem of another question. For example, the answer to item *I* can be found in the stem of item II.

    I. A z-score is a

        A. percentile equivalent
        B. concept in criterion referenced testing
        C. measure of standard error
        D. standardized score

    II. Standardized scores such as z-scores and t-scores are based on

        A. standard deviations
        B. stanines
        C. chi squares
        D. grade equivalents

10. Be alert for alternatives that do not match the stem grammatically. Teachers sometimes make this mistake. For example,

The smallest unit of sound capable of making a meaning distinction in language is a

    A. morpheme
    B. allophone
    C. phoneme
    D. tagmeme

11. When alternatives seem equally good, select the one that is longest and seems to hold the most information. For example,

In the United States, inferior intellectual development is most often caused by

A. poor nutrition
B. divorce
C. the combined effects of heritability and environmental deprivation
D. television

12. When all else fails, select an option which is not the first choice or the last. For example,

The probability of rolling a 12 with two dice is

A. 3 in 12
B. 1 in 12
C. 1 in 36
D. 2 in 19

Activity

Identify a course outside your area of expertise. Ask the instructor if you can take one of his or her multiple choice exams to practice your test-taking strategies.

True-False Tests

True-false questions are actually statements that students must decide are true or untrue. Major examinations are seldom composed entirely of true-false questions. However, many teachers like to include a section of these on their tests. True-false tests are feared by many students, who believe that teachers are trying to trick them into a lower grade. In reality most teachers are just interested in finding out how much the students know. Here are some testwise principles for true-false tests.

1. Read all directions carefully.
2. Budget your time so that you are certain to finish the test.
3. Always guess if you don't know the answer. Never leave a true-false question blank.
4. If any part of the statement is false, the correct answer for the item is "false." For example, the following item is false because the second part of the statement is false.

The United States entered World War II after the Japanese attacked San Francisco.

5. Be alert for the words "never" and "always." These absolutes often indicate a wrong answer. For example, item *A* is false because it does occasionally rain in the desert. On the other hand, item *B* is true because the word "never" is qualified.

A. It never rains in the Sahara Desert.
B. It almost never rains in the Sahara Desert.

6. Long statements are somewhat more likely to be true than short statements. For example, *A* is true and *B* is false.

A. In the poem *Ozymandias* Shelley uses irony to make a statement about the mortality of man.
B. Ozymandias was a monk.

7. Assume that the teacher is asking straightforward questions. In other words, do not turn an obviously true statement into a false one by creating wild possible exceptions in your mind. For example, item *A* is true in spite of the fact that *B, C,* and *D* are, if you have a strong imagination, contradictions to the statement.

   A. Shoes are an important part of the business person's physical appearance.
   B. Business people don't wear horse shoes.
   C. Brake shoes are not part of the business person's appearance.
   D. If your pants are too long and cover your shoes, then the shoes won't make any difference.

Essay Tests

Essay tests are among the most difficult exams because they require recall of information, good writing skills, and good organization. Here are some testwise principles for essay tests.

1. Read all directions carefully. Essay tests often use in their directions key words that you must clearly understand. Here are some of the key words and their meanings:

Key Word	Meaning
enumerate	to name one at a time
illustrate	to explain with examples
trace	to tell the history or development of something from the earliest to the most recent time
compare	to point out similarities and differences
contrast	to point out differences
summarize	to give a brief version of the most important points
evaluate	to judge the merit of
justify	to give reasons for
critique	to summarize and evaluate

Two answers (A and B) are given below for the same essay question. Answer B is a better answer because the writer followed directions and "compared" (noted similarities and differences) the topics under discussion.

Directions: Compare saccadic and pursuit eye movements.
Answer A: There are two basic kinds of eye movements: saccadic and pursuit. Saccadic movements are used when you go from object to object when the objects are at rest. Pursuit movements follow a moving target. During the act of reading saccadic movements allow the reader to stop on a line of print and pick up information. The word saccade means little jerk.
Answer B: There are two basic kinds of eye movements: saccadic and pursuit. They are the same in the sense that both of them are used to locate visual information. However, they are physically different. Saccadic movements are jumps while the pursuit movement is smooth. Another difference is that saccadic movements let the eyes go from one still object to another while pursuit movement follows a moving target.

2. Budget your time so that you are certain to finish the test. Check to see how much each essay question is worth. Spend the most time on the questions that are worth the most points.
3. Always give some kind of an answer, even if you don't understand the question.

4. Unless the directions say otherwise, never give a minimal answer. Teachers will expect you to elaborate and to give full explanations on an essay. For the essay question below, responses *A, B,* and *C* technically answer the question, but only *C* meets the spirit of the essay exam by giving an explanation.

> *Questions:* Do you believe that American troops should fight in foreign wars?
> *Answer A:* No.
> *Answer B:* No. I don't think that Americans should fight in foreign wars.
> *Answer C:* No. I think war is immoral. We should not fight unless we are attacked. Besides, when we sent troops to other countries it makes us look like fascist-capitalistic dogs.

5. Use the technical language of the course when writing an essay. Remember, the teacher wants to find out how much you know. And that includes your knowledge of the appropriate vocabulary. Compare answers *A* and *B* for the essay question below. *B* is a better answer because it uses more technical language.

> *Question:* Summarize the process of conception and the initial stage of prenatal development.
> *Answer A:* The male cell goes up to the egg and digs its way inside. Once this happens the genetic material from the man and the woman mix to form the genetic pattern for the baby. After this happens the cell begins to split up again and again as the fertilized egg works its way down to the uterus where it will attach itself to the woman's body.
> *Answer B:* The male sperm cell digs its way into the ovum and the egg is fertilized. Once this happens the chromosomes from the sperm cell and the chromosomes from the ovum mix to form the genetic pattern for the baby. After this happens the fertilized ovum begins to reproduce itself through a process called mitosis. As this process continues, the fertilized egg, now called a zygote, works its way down the fallopian tube to the uterus where it will attach itself to the wall of the uterus.

6. Pay attention to capitalization, punctuation, spelling, grammar, and neatness. Proof for these things as you reread your answers. Remember, the grading of essays is largely subjective. A careless presentation of your answer can only reduce your grade.

Summary

In this chapter we have provided a rationale for introducing study strategies in content area classrooms. Time on task, distributed practice, organization, attention, and depth of processing have been described in terms of how they affect retention and recall of information. Strategies that exploit these principles of learning have been introduced: VSPP, SQ3R, think-aloud, summarizing, PLAE, GIL, and FPQ. In addition, the chapter has presented basic information on graphic literacy and test-taking skills.

Now go back to the anticipation guide at the beginning of the chapter. React to the statement as you did before, but this time record your answers in the column labeled "Reaction." Compare your responses with those you made earlier.

Miniprojects

1. Try the VSPP notetaking procedure for a lecture in a class you are presently attending. Prepare a written evaluation of the method.
2. Interview a small group of college students to determine the test-taking strategies they use. List the different strategies they report and then provide a written evaluation indicating the quality of their metacognitive skills in test-taking.

Additional Recommended Readings

Baldwin, R. S., Schatz, E. K., & Weiss, A. S. (1985). *Passports to college success.* Dubuque, IA: Kendall/Hunt.

A comprehensive study strategies guide for high school and college students.

Paris, S. G., Wasik, B. A., & Van der Westhuizen, G. (1988). Metametacognition: A review of research on metacognition and reading. In J. E. Readence & R. S. Baldwin (Eds.), *Dialogues in literacy research.* Thirty-seventh Yearbook of the National Reading Conference. Chicago, IL: National Reading Conference.

A methodical, comprehensive, and readable review of the literature of metacognition.

References

Aiken, C. (1896). *Methods of mind training.* New York: Harper.

Aiken, E. G., Thomas, G. S., & Shennum, W. A. (1975). Memory for a lecture: Effects of notes, lecture rates, and informational density. *Journal of Educational Psychology, 67,* 439–444.

Anderson, T. H., & Armbruster, B. B. (1984). Studying. P. D. Pearson (Ed.), *Handbook of reading research* (pp. 657–679). New York: Longman.

Bretzing, B. B., & Kulhavy, R. W. (1979). Note taking and depth of processing. *Contemporary Educational Psychology, 4,* 145–153.

Brum, G. D. (1978). *Biology and man.* Dubuque, IA: Kendall/Hunt.

Carver, R. P. (1972). A critical review of mathemagenic behaviors and the effect of questions upon the retention of prose materials. *Journal of Reading Behavior, 4,* 93–119.

Carver, R. P. (1987). Should reading comprehension skills be taught? In J. E. Readence & R. S. Baldwin (Eds.), *Research in literacy: Merging Perspectives* (pp. 115–126), Thirty-sixth Yearbook of the National Reading Conference. Rochester, NY: National Reading Conference.

Craik, F. I. M., & Lockhart, R. S. (1972). Levels of processing: A framework for memory research. *Journal of Verbal Learning and Verbal Behavior, 11,* 671–684.

Crowder, R. G. (1976). *Principles of learning and memory.* Hillsdale, NJ: Erlbaum.

Dyer, J. W., Riley, J., & Yekovich, R. R. (1979). An analysis of three study skills: Notetaking, summarizing and rereading. *Journal of Educational Research, 73,* 3–7.

Faw, H. W., & Waller, T. G. (1976). Mathemagenic behaviors and efficiency in learning from prose materials: Review, critique, and recommendations. *Review of Educational Research, 46,* 691–720.

Forrest-Pressley, D. L., & Waller, T. G. (1984). *Metecognition, cognition, and reading.* New York: Springer-Verlag.

Fry, E. (1981). Graphical literacy. *Journal of Reading, 24,* 383–390.

Heinrichs, A. S., & LaBranche, S. P. (1986). Content analysis of 47 college learning skill textbooks. *Reading Research and Instruction, 25,* 277–287.

Kiewra, K. A. (1984). Acquiring effective notetaking skills: An alternative to professional notetaking. *Journal of Reading, 27,* 299–302.

LaBerge, D., & Samuels, S. J. (1974). Toward a theory of automatic information processing in reading. *Cognitive Psychology, 6,* 293–323.

Lopate, K. (1987). *The organization of college lectures in selected introductory level courses.* Unpublished doctoral dissertation, University of Miami, Coral Gables, FL.

McAndrew, D. A. (1983). Underlining and notetaking: Some suggestions from research. *Journal of Reading, 27,* 103–108.

Miller, G. A. (1956). The magical number seven plus or minus two: Some limits on our capacity for processing information. *Psychological Review, 63,* 81–97.

Nist, S. L., & Kirby, K. (1986). Teaching comprehension and study strategies through modeling and thinking aloud. *Reading Research and Instruction, 25,* 254–264.

Norton, L. (1981). Patterned notetaking: An evaluation. *Visible Language, 15,* 76–85.

Paris, S. G., Wasik, B. A., & Van der Westhuizen, G. (1988). Meta-metacognition: A review of research on metacognition and reading. In J. E. Readence & R. S. Baldwin (Eds.), *Dialogues in literacy research,* Thirty-seventh Yearbook of the National Reading Conference. Chicago, IL: National Reading Conference.

Pauk, W. (1979). Notetaking: More bad advice exploded. *Reading World, 18,* 300–303.

Peters, D. L. (1972). Effects of notetaking and rate of presentation on short-term objective test performance. *Journal of Educational Psychology, 63,* 276–280.

Randall, A., Fairbanks, M. M., & Kennedy, M. L. (1986). Using think-aloud protocols diagnostically with college readers. *Reading Research and Instruction, 25,* 240–253.

Reinking, D. (1986). Integrating graphic aids into content area instruction: The graphic information lesson. *Journal of Reading, 30,* 146–151.

Robinson, F. P. (1946). *Effective study.* New York: Harper & Bros.

Sherman, T. M., & Wildman, T. M. (1982). *Proven strategies for successful test taking.* Columbus, OH: Charles Merrill.

Simpson, M. L., & Nist, S. L. (1984). PLAE: A model for planning successful independent learning. *Journal of Reading, 28,* 218–223.

Assessment and Accommodation of Individual Differences

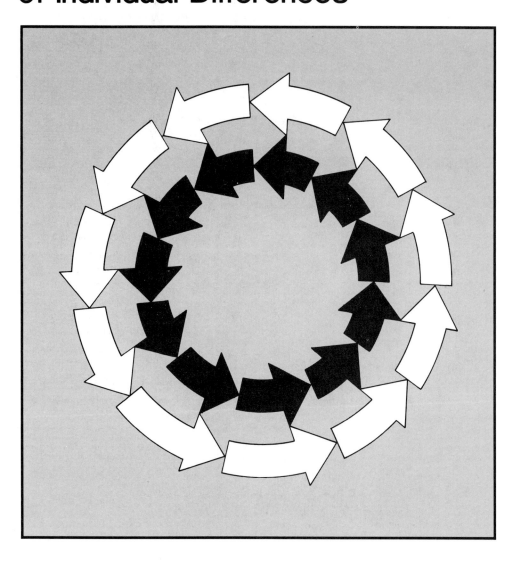

CHAPTER

Anticipation Guide/Reaction Guide

Directions: Before you begin reading this chapter, take a moment to put a check mark by any of the statements with which you agree. Use the column entitled "Anticipation."

Anticipation   **Reaction**

—————— 1.   —————— 1. Assessment is a day-to-day occurrence.

—————— 2.   —————— 2. Strict adherence to stated course objectives will provide students with effective instruction in content areas.

—————— 3.   —————— 3. Standardized tests provide teachers enough information concerning students' abilities to begin instruction.

—————— 4.   —————— 4. The best reading tests to administer to students are those which compare them with other students across the nation.

—————— 5.   —————— 5. Diagnosis is necessary for effective instruction.

Assessing Students' Abilities

Rationale

Instruction is the means by which teachers bridge the gap between what students already know and what they need to know. For instruction to be maximally effective, teachers must possess a knowledge of techniques to assess just what students do know. Assessment information about students' abilities and levels of achievement provides a foundation for selecting appropriate teaching strategies. On the other hand, without assessment information teachers are forced to make hazardous assumptions about what students do and do not know.

This chapter describes the role of assessment in order to promote the instructional match between student and text. Specifically, formal and informal types of assessment will be discussed and placed in proper perspective in the total instructional program. Various types of informal assessment strategies will be described and recommended for use by content teachers. Suggestions will also be offered for instruction based upon results obtained from administration of these informal assessments.

Chapter Objectives

After reading this chapter, you should be able to:

1. Understand the need for assessment in the content classroom.
2. Describe the differences between formal and informal testing.
3. Utilize various types of informal tests as the basis for beginning instruction.

Graphic Organizer

The following graphic organizer is provided to give you some advance structure for the vocabulary and concepts that will be presented in this chapter.

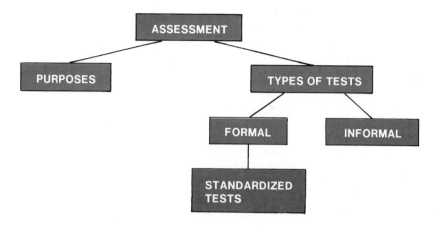

Purposes for Assessment

The end product of assessment in the content classroom, or any classroom for that matter, is decision-making concerning the kind of instruction to be provided students. Assessment is purposeless if it does not lead to intelligent instructional decisions. Content area teachers should keep this goal clearly in mind as they conduct assessment procedures.

In general, assessment in reading is conducted through the use of various types of tests. As such, tests are administered for two major purposes: (1) program evaluation, and (2) student diagnosis. Program evaluation is usually conducted for accountability purposes, and formal tests are usually the devices used. Formal testing instruments, i.e., standardized reading tests, are administered at regular yearly intervals, usually in the fall or spring of the school year. This function is to monitor student progress in reading. With the help of this assessment, school administrators are able to compare the reading levels of their students with those of other students across the nation at the same or similar grade levels. Although such comparisons may help a particular school district justify its need for federal support for its instructional programs, they are virtually useless for instructional decision-making by teachers with regard to the individual needs of students.

Formal testing may also be used to identify weaknesses in the instructional program. If students in school district A as a whole score low relative to the national average on a particular type of test such as vocabulary or comprehension, that district may decide to examine the emphasis placed on that portion of the reading program. Finally, formal testing may serve as a screening device for those students not performing up to reading program expectations. This should indicate to the school district the need for more intensive diagnostic testing to pinpoint areas of skill weakness in individual students. Unfortunately, the results of these tests may be inappropriately used to refer students to special programs without the benefit of further testing. Once labeled as "special," it may be very difficult for such students to escape that stigma.

The second major purpose for reading assessment is student diagnosis. Student diagnosis can provide teachers with the kind of information necessary to make instructional decisions. Informal assessment tools are usually utilized to gather such information. Specifically, informal tests can be used to diagnose possible reading and learning problems of students.

Additionally, such tests can be used to determine the reading levels of students. Knowledge of students' reading and learning problems and reading levels provides a **starting** point for good teaching. This knowledge eliminates the need to presuppose any learning on the part of the students and provides the essential foundation for instructional decision-making.

Descriptive Terminology of Assessment

Before launching into a discussion of the advantages and disadvantages of particular types of tests, a discussion of some basic distinctions between types of tests is necessary. The distinction between "formal" and "informal" tests has already been mentioned. *Formal tests* are often called *standardized,* norm-referenced tests. The major characteristic of these tests is that one can only interpret the quality of a given score by comparing it with scores acquired by others. The scores of those "others" are called *norms.* The norms represent a standard against which the performance of others may be compared. Norms are created by administering a test to large groups of students at a variety of grade levels. On the basis of the results of the testing, an average score is calculated for students at each grade level. These averages become the norm, and all students who take the test later are compared with the norming group. For example, the norms established for sixth and seventh grade students, respectively, are forty and forty-four items correct on a particular standardized test. School district A administers this instrument to its seventh grade students resulting in an average of forty items correct. In comparison to the standard set, it can then be said that school district A's students achieved on a par with sixth graders and that their group performance was below the average for seventh graders.

Informal assessment tools differ from standardized tests. *Informal tests* do not employ the use of norms as standards for comparison. Rather they employ a relative standard, or *criterion,* which implies adequate achievement for a given task or assignment. The score itself has meaning, even without reference to the performances of others. For instance, if the criterion has been set at sixty-percent correct, a student must meet that figure to progress to another level of instruction; otherwise the student might need to work through the unit again and may require some special help to do so. Finally, informal tests are often teacher-made, though some are published. Thus, they can be designed to obtain information specifically related to an individual school's reading program.

A second distinction used in describing tests involves *survey* and *diagnostic* tests. A survey test does what its name implies; it surveys global areas of achievement such as vocabulary and comprehension. *Survey tests* are usually standardized tests and therefore are useful for purposes of group comparisons but not for individual instructional guidelines. No specifics with regard to the global areas of the survey are provided. That is, we are unable to determine what the specific areas of weaknesses in vocabulary and comprehension may be. That is what a diagnostic test endeavors to measure. Scores from a *diagnostic test* can indicate strengths and weaknesses in specific skill areas. For example diagnostic tests provide scores for recognizing main ideas, details, inferences, etc.—the specifics of comprehension. Therefore, it might readily be seen that a standardized, survey-type instrument can be used as a screening device to tell a reading teacher, for instance, in which global areas a student might be experiencing difficulty. The reading teacher can then employ diagnostic tests to ascertain which specific areas are causing the difficulty.

Two other distinctions can be made in discussing testing instruments, neither of which requires a lengthy explanation. These are *group* and *individual* tests. As the names imply, tests may be group-administered or individually administered. The other distinction is between "silent" and "oral" tests. Again, as the names imply, tests may be silently or orally administered or employ some combination of the two.

Usually, standardized tests utilize a format which requires a group, silent administration. Examples of such tests are the *Nelson Reading Test* (1977) and the *Stanford Achievement Test* (1982) which provide global scores for vocabulary and comprehension and in which administration is accomplished through the group, silent format. At the other end of the continuum are informal tests which are diagnostic in scope and are administered in an individual, oral format. Examples of this type of instrument are the *Basic Reading Inventory* (Johns, 1985) and the *Classroom Reading Inventory* (Silvaroli, 1982). It must be emphasized that even though examples have been provided at opposite ends of the continuum, many testing instruments fall somewhere in between.

Cautions Concerning Formal Testing

Standardized tests offer some advantages in a total reading assessment program. Because they are administered in a group setting, they do not take the great amount of time that individual testing requires. Additionally, since formal tests are administered silently instead of orally, confusion is kept to a minimum. Finally, the scores achieved by students allow school districts to compare the performance levels of their students with other students across the nation.

The ease of administration of standardized tests and their use of norms also present some disadvantages. It is essential that content teachers be cognizant of these disadvantages. It is all too easy to obtain students' standardized test scores from their permanent files and make decisions about their abilites based on those scores. Questions content teachers should ask themselves concerning standardized test scores might include the following:

1. What exactly does a score, such as 7.0, on reading mean?
2. What exactly are standardized tests measuring?
3. How accurate a picture do I obtain about the reading ability of students from examining their test scores?

The following discussion of cautions concerning standardized tests will attempt to answer those questions and other questions you may have in mind.

1. *Inappropriate Norms.* Even though great care is taken by test makers in standardizing a test, the norms established for comparison may be inappropriate for a particular class. The norms may be based on students with whom your students should not be compared. For instance, how could one compare a score of 7.0 achieved by a low socioeconomic group member with norms that may have been calculated from a group of students from a different socioeconomic group? How accurate an indication of achievement could you get out of a student such as this? Certainly, the norming population needs to be considered.

2. *Extraneous Factors.* It must be emphasized that the scores achieved by a student on a formal test are only a measure of that student's performance at that particular point in time. They may not necessarily be indicative of a student's true ability. An individual's performance may vary radically from day to day depending on extraneous factors which can

complicate matters. Factors as simple as the amount of sleep students had the night before, to factors as complex as the emotional stability of their homes may interfere with students' daily performance in school as well as their performance in testing situations.

3. *Timed Testing.* Most standardized tests employ a time limitation in their administration procedures. Thus, a premium is placed on speed in completing the test. We are all probably reminded of personal experiences with friends or students who may be categorized as slow, but accurate: i.e., students who lack speed in completing tasks, but thoroughly weigh alternatives before responding accurately. The slow but thorough reader may fail to complete the comprehension section of a test and thus get a low score when compared to the established norm. In reality, the student's comprehension could be excellent.

4. *Prior Knowledge.* Since comprehension occurs when students are able to associate the unknown with the known, prior knowledge may be a factor in test performance. In fact, there is a question as to whether standardized instruments actually measure reading comprehension or prior knowledge (Johnston, 1983). Test items which may be answered from prior knowledge without the aid of a reading selection are said to be "passage independent." Items which require students to read a selection in order to answer them correctly are termed "passage dependent." It may be virtually impossible to eliminate the effect of prior knowledge on test performance. However, depending on the degree to which prior knowledge is a factor in particular test questions, the resulting scores can yield an unfair comparison between individuals.

5. *Comprehension Skills.* Standardized tests of reading comprehension, in many cases, emphasize factual recall of relatively insignificant facts. Is this the type of comprehension utilized in most reading situations? Certainly factual recall is important, but it is only one dimension of comprehension.

6. *Interest.* Everyone is aware of the effect of interest in reading. In fact, reading comprehension is better when the topic of a passage interests the reader. On the other hand, lack of interest may militate against the completion of a reading task. If the passages to be read on a standardized test are of little or no interest to students, it is bound to affect the students' ability to answer comprehension questions based on the passage.

7. *Guessing.* Most standardized tests employ a multiple choice format for their questions. They are designed in this manner to facilitate scoring by machines and for convenience (Readence & Moore, 1986). With such a limited format, guessing can unduly raise test scores. If four choices are offered, chances are one in four that a correct guess can be made. On any given test situation, two people with identical reading skills could get different test scores simply because one person happened to guess better that day. In fact, on most standardized tests, it is possible to receive grade-level equivalents, e.g., fourth-grade level, by guessing. Fry (1972) has described these pure-chance scores as "orangutan scores."

8. *Test Floors and Ceilings.* When formal tests are standardized through averaging scores of students at a particular grade level, limits are placed on the range of performance at that grade level. Students are not supposed to score below a certain grade-level norm or, for that matter, above a certain norm in their performance. In effect, the use of *test floors* and *ceilings* may affect the validity of test scores. Specifically, the ceiling of the test may underestimate a more competent student's performance, while the floor may overestimate a

less competent student's ability. In effect, the ceiling may penalize better readers because tests cannot truly measure their ability while the floor may place a poorer reader at a level where success cannot be achieved. Standardization is designed to predict average performance, not performance at the extremes.

9. *Standard Error of Measurement.* This term indicates the variation in test scores that one might expect if that test were administered repeatedly to an individual student. By adding or subtracting this built-in error to a student's obtained test score, one obtains a range of scores within which the student might actually score. For example, if the standard error of measurement is five months and a student's resulting score is 7.0, the range of scores within which the student might actually have scored is 6.5 to 7.5. Awareness of this factor of built-in error is essential when examining scores on standardized tests.

10. *Fallacy of Grade-Level Reporting.* So what does a score of 7.0 mean? First of all, it is an estimation of performance. Second, it really says little with regard to the students' performance; yet it is commonplace to use such scores when discussing reading ability of students. Just because two students both score 7.0 does not mean they are equivalent in reading ability. There are countless ways in which individuals may perform to attain a score of 7.0, yet each performance may be unique. Grade-level scores obscure differential performances of individuals with like scores in the same grade, or in different grades. Further analysis of each student's performance is necessary.

Content teachers must keep these cautions in mind when examining standardized test scores or when provided information concerning them by other school personnel. Such scores provide the basis for comparing group performances and for program evaluation. Many of the factors which cause standardized tests to provide inaccurate scores for individuals (e.g., guessing and personal interests) balance out in group situations, thus making results far more accurate for groups than for individuals. However, they do not provide the kind of information necessary for making instructional decisions. Informal testing provides content teachers with that type of information.

Informal Testing

Informal testing, as stated earlier, can more readily provide content teachers with diagnostic information from which to begin instruction. Informal tests which are administered individually and orally can provide the necessary information content teachers are seeking, but they also pose some problems. First, and foremost, it would be too time-consuming to test each student in a content teacher's classroom individually. Of course, a teacher aide or paraprofessional would be of great benefit in this situation. Testing could be accomplished with minimal sacrifice of the teacher's instructional time. However, the availability of aides in subject matter classrooms would be a luxury for most schools and is really not a feasible solution to the problem. Second, oral testing does produce noise which could disrupt other class members. Additionally, with the normal level of activity, a typical classroom is not the best atmosphere for a testing situation. A solution to that dilemma might be using some other space in the building to provide an appropriate atmosphere for testing. However, the availability of such space is limited in most schools.

What content teachers need is some form of assessment that combines the advantages of both informal and standardized testing. In other words, content teachers need to combine the advantages of group and silent administration of formal testing with the diagnostic advantage of informal testing. *The resultant combination of informal-group-silent-diagnostic emphases is probably the best means available for content teachers to utilize in testing situations.*

Numerous advantages are inherent in these types of tests. First, they are quick and easy to administer in a group setting. Second, since they are teacher-made, informal tests can be designed to obtain the kind of diagnostic information content teachers desire of their students. Specifically, they can be designed to obtain information concerning the reading levels of students and their reading and learning skills. This information, as stated previously, is most relevant for effective instruction by the teacher. Third, these types of informal instruments can be textbook-based. This makes the diagnostic information relevant since it is taken directly from the major source of instruction in the subject matter area. Fourth, since the tests are teacher-made and textbook-based, they provide for ease in scoring. Criteria for judging test answers are objective, eliminating subjectivity as a deterrent in effective scoring. Finally, these instruments later may become the basis for teaching. Once the teacher has obtained the essential diagnostic information, the tests may become instructional instruments with which the teacher can begin to acquaint students with the author's style and the organization of the textbook.

To reemphasize, perhaps the greatest advantage of informal-group-silent-diagnostic tests is that they use real content materials instead of materials which may not be relevant for instruction. Testing can be accomplished by using materials taken from actual instruction in the classroom. These instruments are designed to determine how well students can construct meaning from print. Therefore, the textbook, the major unit of instruction, is the best and most relevant means to obtain this information. Additionally, since these types of tests are also used to appraise reading levels of students, what better means to assess this than through the textbook?

In the following sections two types of informal-group-silent measures will be described, the *cloze procedure* and the *content reading inventory*. These measures are recommended by the authors for the advantages discussed earlier and because they provide content teachers with knowledge concerning students' reading levels and ability to use the textbook as a learning aid.

The Cloze Procedure

The *cloze procedure* provides the content teacher with a simple, economical method of determining the reading levels of students. It is designed to determine whether a match exists between the reading level of the student and the level of the textbook. Using the cloze procedure the teacher can make instructional adjustments by identifying those students whose performances indicate that the text is either too easy or too difficult.

Originally designed by Taylor (1953) as a measure of readability, the cloze procedure involves the systematic deletion of words from a text selection. Students are then asked to supply the deleted words. Their ability to correctly supply the missing words is an indicator of how well they can read and construct meaning from print. Thus, cloze functions as a measure of the process of reading, or what happens when one reads, rather than just a measure of the product of reading.

The following cloze testing exercise is designed specifically as a model for content teachers to follow when constructing, administering, and scoring a cloze test they design for use with their students. Additionally, the authors are of the opinion that a good way to understand a technique or strategy is through direct exposure to it.

Activity

Complete the following "recipe for cloze testing." It has been designed as you, the content teacher, would construct and present a cloze test to your students. Your task now, just as your students' would be, is to supply the deleted words.

A Recipe for Cloze Testing

A. *Constructing the Cloze Test*

1. *Select passage.* From the content textbook select a passage of approximately three hundred words of continuous text. The passage should be representative of the read-

    ability level of the entire _____ . The material must not _____ been pre-

    viously read by _____ students. Complete paragraphs should _____ used.

2. *Identify words to* _____ *deleted.* Approximately 25 words _____ be left

    intact as _____ lead-in to the selection. _____ underline every fifth word

    _____ 50 words have been _____ . These words will comprise _____

    missing words to be _____ by the students. Words _____ after the fiftieth

    deletion _____ be left intact.

3. *Prepare* _____ *stencil.* Type the selection _____ a stencil, double-space

    format, _____ blanks for words previously _____ . Care should be taken

    _____ make all blanks of _____ length.

B. *Administering the Cloze Test*

Duplicate the test _____ distribute one mimeographed copy _____ each stu-

dent. Emphasize the _____ oral directions to your _____ .

1. Supply one word _____ each blank.

2. Encourage guessing, _____ students should attempt to _____ all blanks.

3. Misspellings will _____ scored as correct as _____ as they are recogniz-
    able.

4. _____ cloze test will not _____ timed.

5. Before beginning, silently _____ through the entire test. _____ will then

    read it _____ to you before you _____ .

C. *Scoring the Cloze Test*

Determine each student's raw _____ in the following manner:

1. _____ only exact replacements as _____ . Synonyms are incorrect.

2. Misspellings _____ the only exception to _____ above rule. Do not ____ the student for spelling _____ .

3. Inappropriate word endings are _____ .

4. The raw score will _____ the number of correct _____ for each student.

D. *Classifying Student Performance*

It _____ generally been found that _____ who score between 40 _____ 60 percent would benefit _____ use of that textbook. _____ scoring at this level are said to be performing at their instructional reading level. The textbook might be too difficult for those students scoring below 40 percent. It may be too easy for those scoring above 60 percent.

Now that you have completed this cloze test, turn to the end of the chapter for the answers. Classify your performance according to the criteria specified in the cloze test. The majority of individuals taking this test will score at the instructional level. A few of you may score either above or below this level. In the next section the construction, administration, and scoring of the cloze test will be reexamined and explored in depth.

A Further Look at the Cloze Procedure. In constructing your cloze test, choose a passage as close to the beginning of the text as possible. Later parts of a text will be too heavily laden with concepts built on previously read material and will not provide an adequate sample for cloze testing. Remember that using complete paragraphs is essential. Students need the benefit of complete thought units within the selection to insure the best possible performances. It also is recommended that cloze tests be administered before students begin to read and learn from the textbook. If students have previously read the textbook selection, it will invalidate their performance due to their familiarity with the material. The cloze test should be administered on a one-time only basis at the very beginning of the school year or during the year if major new text material is introduced.

In order to make an accurate determination of which terms should be deleted, the teacher must leave a lead-in of at least 25 words intact. Part of the rationale behind the use of the cloze procedure is that students must be able to effectively cope with an author's language structure, vocabulary, and meaning. The lead-in of at least 25 words seems sufficient to serve this function. Likewise, a lead-out of at least 25 words serves also to promote continuity in processing the author's writing style.

Finally, in constructing the cloze test all blanks replacing words must be uniform. Differential length of blanks, related to word length, provide unnecessary, additional clues for readers in completing the cloze test. Fifteen typed spaces is recommended, as this length should be long enough for students to write in the longest word deleted.

In administering the cloze test, the greatest difficulty students may face in successfully completing it may be their unfamiliarity with its design. After all, students are usually provided a test format that demands correctness, not guessing. Additionally, test questions are usually multiple-choice, short answer, or essay type. The lack of this structure and the presence of a "mutilated" text may present some problems for certain students.

To alleviate this potential problem, the authors recommend some guided, group exercises utilizing a cloze format. Students can first be shown sentences with a deleted word and then asked to supply the missing word. It is imperative that those students offering suggestions for the missing word justify their guess. In this way all students may hear the rationale for the guess. In initiating these exercises group discussions are recommended. Once students see that "informed" guesses based upon the syntax and meaning are encouraged, they then can be provided groups of sentences or a paragraph in which to perform the same task. Breaking the class into small groups will encourage students to interact with their peers and to explore feasible alternatives for deleted words. This procedure to familiarize students with the structure of cloze tasks will not take that much time—and it is an active learning situation that can be fun, and most importantly, will provide students an acquaintance with the structure of cloze tests.

Then the teacher may supply students with the oral directions for the cloze test as specified earlier. Care should be taken that students silently read through the entire cloze passage before marking any answers. Combining this silent reading with the teacher's oral reading of the cloze passage should make the students familiar enough with the author's language structure, vocabulary, and meaning to insure their maximum performances.

Finally, in planning the administration of the cloze test, teachers should be aware that students will be completing the task at different times because there is no time limit. It is recommended that some alternative activity be scheduled for those students finishing early. The activity should involve some type of quiet independent work to allow other students an undisturbed opportunity to finish.

For those teachers concerned about the exact replacement scoring of the cloze test, the following rationale is offered. Objective scoring of the cloze test is one of the advantages this informal test provides. It is easy to score the deletions as correct or incorrect to obtain an idea of how well students can complete the cloze test. However, if you begin to weigh the possibilities of considering synonyms in lieu of exact replacements for deleted words, you may encounter some problems.

There might be no doubt that synonyms indicate that readers may be effectively comprehending the text material, and it is recommended that the cloze technique be considered a possible strategy for comprehension development. However, for purposes of evaluating the possibilities of the instructional match between the students and the textbook only exact replacement must be credited. Synonyms are too difficult to evaluate. What may be a synonym for teacher A may not be one for teacher B. Additionally, Henk (1981), in a study exploring synonymic versus exact replacement scoring on cloze tests, found virtually no advantage in counting synonyms correct; i.e., exact replacement was found equally valid and much simpler to score. Further, Henk and Selders (1984) found that synonymic scoring of cloze tests by independent raters was highly variable.

To close the issue of exact replacement scoring, the authors emphasize that cloze is a conservative measure for initially matching students and materials. Scores achieved in cloze testing serve as starting points for teachers to begin effective instruction with the students.

The authors do **not** view cloze test performance as a definitive measure of comprehensibility for all students; rather, it allows teachers to begin to adjust their instruction with students. Those instructional methods may be subsequently reevaluated.

After cloze tests have been scored, teachers need to classify student performance. The cloze percentages the authors recommend for the instructional reading level are scores which fall between 40 and 60 percent. There is nothing magical about this range of scores, as various research studies have indicated other ranges of percentages to establish the instructional reading level (e.g., 44–57%, Bormuth, 1968). However, since the research is conflicting with regard to this range, the authors view the 40–60% range as a valid compromise for teachers to use in interpreting students' cloze test performance. Additionally, it can be easily seen that calculating scores for the instructional reading level would be much easier using a 40–60% range than a 44–57% range.

Students may be classified according to their cloze test performance in the following manner:

Using Cloze with Text Material

Reading Level	Cloze %	Difficulty Level	Solution
Independent	61+	Too easy	A. Supplementary materials B. Independent research projects C. More difficult text
Instructional	40–60	Adequate	A. Structured reading B. Teacher guidance
Frustration	39–	Too difficult	A. Structured listening B. Easier text

Specifically, for those students who score between 40 and 60 percent, the text material is said to be at their *instructional reading level*. Teachers can be fairly sure that a match exists between the difficulty level of the text and the ability level of the students. The text material should challenge these students without being too difficult if the teacher provides sufficent guidance for them to be successful in learning from the text.

Students scoring above 60 percent or below 40 percent present teachers with other instructional problems, and alternative methodology is recommended for those students. For students scoring above 60 percent the textbook is said to be at their *independent reading level*. At this level the text is probably too easy and will not provide sufficient challenge. These students may be able to read and learn from the text without teacher assistance. One solution to this dilemma may be to seek a more difficult text. If this is not feasible, supplementary materials should be sought in order to provide a challenge for these students. Another alternative is to assign independent research projects for which these students will use library source materials to explore topics in more depth.

Finally, the text material is said to be at the *frustration level* of those students scoring below 40 percent. Teachers will have to do an especially good job of instruction with these students because the text may be too difficult for them. These students may use the text with generous amounts of teacher guidance and structured reading activities. However, if after a short period of instruction teachers see that these students are not effectively learning from the text, it is recommended an easier text be found for them. It is additionally recommended that teachers utilize some structured listening activities with these students. This will ease their burden in learning from the textbook.

The proper match between the difficulty level of the text material and the ability level of the students is extremely important in considering the type and quality of instruction the teacher provides. The goal is to maximize the ability of students to learn from the text. The range of ability levels in a content classroom is a real situation which all teachers must face. Such a situation requires differential instruction suited to the abilities and needs of students. The cloze procedure is recommended as one means of obtaining information which will assist teachers in meeting differential instructional needs of students.

Cloze for Readability Purposes. Before moving on to a discussion of the content reading inventory, an alternative use of the cloze procedure for readability purposes should be mentioned. In a previous chapter the Raygor Readability Estimate was recommended as a quick means by which teachers could get an approximate idea of a textbook's readability level. Used as either a substitute for the Raygor or to corroborate the results of the formula, the cloze technique presents considerable advantages in estimating readability. As discussed previously, the Raygor method bases the readability estimate upon the average sentence length and average number of long words; i.e., upon text variables only. A more viable consideration in readability measurement is the interaction of students with the textbook. In this way readability of the textbook is based upon how well the students' schemata—their experiential backgrounds and language knowledge—mesh with those of the author. The cloze technique presents teachers with just such an opportunity.

To illustrate the use of cloze for readability purposes, the following example is provided. A group of social studies teachers has been assigned the task of considering three different textbooks in American History for whole school adoption for a specified length of time. In examining the textbooks for comprehensibility, each seemingly presents the desired readability level as measured by the Raygor and also possesses the desired text characteristics to aid students' reading. In a quandry as to which textbook to adopt and knowing they will have to live with their decision for some time, the teachers decide to seek student input to aid them in making their decision. Knowing that the cloze technique presents the most systematic means to obtain such input, the teachers decide to construct a cloze passage from each textbook and administer the tests to the students over a period of two weeks. The data are collected and the results of each cloze passage are averaged for each of the four American History classes that eventually will use one of the textbooks. Knowing the average readability score will indicate the ability of most students to read each textbook at the instructional reading level, the teachers compare the following scores:

Class	Book A	Book B	Book C
1	54%	47%	38%
2	60%	53%	47%
3	47%	41%	30%
4	65%	57%	51%
TOTAL	56.5%	49.5%	41.5%

Activity

Before reading any further, decide which textbook would be the most viable one for the social studies teachers to adopt. Justify your decision.

Let's examine this problem. First of all, the total average readability for each textbook falls within the range for the instructional reading level, 40% to 60%. Potentially then, each textbook could be used with these students. If the school has the necessary funds, the best solution may be to adopt an individual text for each class. For instance, Book A could be adopting for Class 3; Book B for Class 1; and Book C for Classes 2 and 4. There certainly is merit to multiple adoption but it is not feasible for most schools. Realistically, the decision facing this group of teachers is which book presents the best fit for all the students for instructional purposes. Book A, in general, seems to be the easiest for the students to read. However, two of the classes generally seem to find Book A too easy. Using that textbook may require teachers to do extra planning to cope with the needs of those students. Supplementary materials and independent projects would have to be used to challenge these students.

Book C, on the other hand, presents an opposite problem as it seems to be the most difficult of the three textbooks. Two classes, in fact, generally find Book C too difficult. Again, extra planning and an especially good job of instruction would be necessary in order to help those students learn effectively from this textbook.

Book B seems to present the best match between students and textbook. All four classes fall within the instructional range for the text. Even though classes 3 and 4 fall near the extremes of the instructional reading range for Book B and may require some additional planning for teachers, the textbook does seem to make the best fit for most of the students.

Using cloze in this manner can provide the additional information to aid teachers in adopting textbooks for instruction. The cloze technique provides a systematic means to utilize student input in their decision-making by using their eventual content materials to make judgments as to the ability of students to construct meaning from print. The more information that can be gathered concerning the merits of a textbook, the better the final decision should be.

The Maze Technique—A Cloze Alternative. Another technique which might be considered for assessment purposes is the *maze technique* (Guthrie, Seifert, Burham, & Caplan, 1974). The maze technique might be considered in lieu of the cloze technique when teachers desire to provide a more structured assessment task for students. The maze technique seems to present a simplification of the cloze technique. An example of one sentence incorporating the use of the maze technique is provided below:

delete

Example: To modify the text using the maze procedure, substitute

data

grouping

three alternative words instead of innocently only a blank.

providing

It was probably fairly obvious to you, a fluent reader, what the correct choices were. Guthrie et al. (1974) recommended altering the text by substituting three alternatives:

1. The correct word,
2. A syntactically correct (same part of speech) but semantically incorrect (it doesn't make sense) word,
3. A syntactically incorrect word (different part of speech).

To construct a maze passage, follow the "recipe for cloze testing" discussed earlier in this chapter except for the text modification system described earlier. A system of random ordering of alternatives should be employed. Caution students to circle their desired choice and encourage them to guess if they are unsure. The correct choices are totaled and the percentage correct for each student is determined. Student performance is classifed using the following criteria (Bradley, Ackerson, & Ames, 1978):

% Correct	Text Difficulty
85%+	Too easy
50–85%	Adequate for instruction
50%−	Too difficult

As with the cloze technique, successful completion of the maze technique is based upon the ability of readers to use their knowledge of the syntactic and semantic constraints of language.

The Content Reading Inventory

Whether the cloze technique or the maze alternative is employed, content teachers need to consider the use of the content reading inventory in conjunction with them. Though the cloze or maze technique can provide information concerning the instructional reading level, it does not provide specific diagnostic information about the ability of students to utilize the various reading/learning skills necessary to understand the text. It is the intent of the content reading inventory to provide teachers with that kind of information.

The *content reading inventory* provides a means by which to obtain additional information about the ability of students to learn successfully from text material. When this information is coupled with the information obtained through the use of the cloze technique, teachers are provided a valuable package of diagnostic information concerning the abilities of students in relation to classroom materials. Effective instruction can then begin.

The content reading inventory is an informal-group-silent-diagnostic test. Inherent in the inventory, then, is the ease of administration and scoring as well as the relevancy of the diagnostic information obtained. The content reading inventory consists of three major sections. The first section of the inventory concerns knowledge of, and ability to utilize, the various aids within the textbook or supplemental to it. Specifically, the test covers book parts common to most textbooks such as the table of contents, index, and pictorial aids. The students' ability to use resource aids which supplement the textbook such as the encyclopedia or card catalog are also examined. The premise behind this section of the content reading inventory is that the ability to effectively utilize the internal and external aids of the text is critical to learning from it.

In the last two sections of this inventory, students are asked to read a short three- to four-page selection from the text. Section two then determines the ability to deal with the technical and specialized vocabulary encountered in the reading. Both vocabulary through recall and in context are examined. Section three examines the ability to comprehend text explicit and implicit information as well as to grasp an author's text structure. A representative content reading inventory, therefore, should contain the following sections:

Section I: *Textual Reading/Study Aids*
    A. Internal Aids
        1. Table of Contents
        2. Index
        3. Glossary
        4. Chapter Introduction/Summaries
        5. Pictorial Information
        6. Other Pertinent Aids
    B. External Aids
        1. Card Catalog
        2. Reader's Guide
        3. Encyclopedias
        4. Other Pertinent Aids

Section II: *Vocabulary Knowledge*
    A. Recall
    B. Contextual Meanings

Section III: *Comprehension*
    A. Text-Explicit Information
    B. Text-Implicit Information
    C. Text Structure

Content Reading Inventory Guidelines. To construct, administer, and score a content reading inventory, the following guidelines are offered:

1. Plan to construct approximately 20 to 25 questions. It is recommended that eight to ten questions be constructed for section I, four to six for section II, and seven to nine for section III.
2. Choose a short three- to four-page selection for students to read.
3. Explain to students the rationale for using the content reading inventory. Administer the inventory in two sections being careful to orally read each question to the students before they begin.
4. Section I is administered first, as the ability to use the various parts of the total text is examined.
5. Sections II and III are administered next. Care is given that appropriate readiness is established for students to read the selection. Questions for these sections are based solely on the short selection, not the entire text.

6. The completed content reading inventory is scored using the following criteria:

% *Correct*	*Text Difficulty*
86%–100%	Too easy
64%–85%	Adequate for instruction
63%–	Too difficult

It is cautioned that students who miss a majority of the questions within a particular category might need help in that area.

Activity

Complete the following example of a content reading inventory. It is designed just like you, as the content teacher, would construct and present a content reading inventory to your students. Your task, just as that of your students would be, is to answer the questions. Section I is based on the total text; sections II and III are based upon chapter 5.

Content Reading Inventory

Section I: Textual Reading/Study Aids

Directions: Using your textbook or your previous knowledge, answer each of the following questions on a separate sheet of paper.

A. Internal Aids
   1. On what page does Chapter Three begin? What is the title of the section of which it is a part?
   2. On what page(s) would you find information regarding the Guided Listening Procedure?
   3. Where would you look in the text to find the definition of "slicing?"
   4. Of what use is the section entitled "Rationale" at the beginning of Chapter Eight?
   5. Using the checklist on page 193, what recommendations would you make concerning the student's writing?
   6. Where would you look to find out how this text is organized?
B. External Aids
   7. What library guide would aid you in locating a book on attitudes and attitude development?
   8. If you were to give an oral report in class about content area reading and you knew that much of the information you needed would be in current periodicals, what guide would you use to help you find the information?
   9. Name one set of encyclopedias. How are the topics in it arranged?

Directions: Read the sections in your text entitled "Words" and "Vocabularies" on pp. 83–85. Based upon what you have read, answer the questions in sections II and III on a separate sheet of paper.

Section II: Vocabulary Knowledge

10. Define the concept of "word" as used in this text.
11. Compare and contrast denotations and connotations. Provide an example.
12. Define the italicized word as it is used in this sentence: "A vocabulary is a *corpus* of many thousands of words and their associated meanings."
13. What term refers to the process by which new information is incorporated into existing schemata?
14. Define the italicized word as used in this sentence:
    "Technical vocabulary presents labels for unfamiliar concepts which must be accommodated by modifying *extant* schemata."

Section III: Comprehension

15. Why do adult language users have little difficulty agreeing whether or not a particular sequence of sounds or symbols is a word?
16. Learning new words (concepts) requires more than a simple explanation by the teacher. Why?
17. What are the largest vocabularies for literate adults?
18. Describe the differences between the words (concepts), "Cold War" and "crass."
19. Describe the process involved with regard to the schemata of students when the word "secant" is presented them.
20. Explain the role of the school with regard to the development of the expressive and receptive vocabularies of students.
21. How is the section entitled "Vocabularies" organized?

Now that you have completed this content inventory, turn to the end of the chapter for the answers. Classify your performance according to the criteria specified previously for the content reading inventory. The majority of individuals taking this test will find this text adequate for instruction. A few of you may score above or below that level.

As can be seen, the content reading inventory can provide the teacher with information concerning the difficulty level of the text as well as specific information concerning students' ability to effectively utilize the textbook. The following checklist is provided as a format for teachers to record the information gathered from the content reading inventory.

Using a format such as specified above will make information obtained from the performances of students easily accessible. However, since only a few items are assessed in each area, this checklist is **only** a beginning—a point of departure—for assessing students' abilities. As teachers observe students interacting with text in their daily reading and writing assignments, they will acquire additional information that will corroborate or refute the initial findings.

Classroom Summary

Subject _____   Title of Text _____

Grade and Section _____   Teacher _____

Student Name	Table of Contents	Index	Glossary	Chapter Introduction/Summary	Pictorial Information	Other Internal Aids	Card Catalog	Reader's Guide	Encyclopedia	Other External Aids	Vocabulary-Recall	Vocabulary-Context	Text-Explicit	Text-Implicit	Text Structure
1. John Bead	✔		✔	✔	✔		✔		✔			✔	✔		
2. Tom Rean	✔	✔		✔			✔		✔		✔	✔	✔		✔
3. Scott Bee		✔	✔	✔			✔	✔	✔		✔		✔		✔
4.															
5.															
6.															
7.															

Getting Started: Using the Textbook Diagnostically

To "get instruction off on the right foot," the authors recommend that informal-group-silent-diagnostic tests be administered in content classrooms at the beginning of the year. Specifically, the authors recommend that teachers administer the cloze technique and content reading inventory to ascertain how effectively students can learn from a textbook. The following checklist is offered as a means for analyzing student performance on the cloze and content reading inventory:

Class Profile

Subject _____   Title of Text _____

Grade and Section _____   Teacher _____

Student Name	Text Difficulty*	
	Cloze	Content Reading Inventory
1. John Bead	2	2
2. Tom Rean	1	2
3. Scott Bee	3	2
4.		
5.		
6.		
7.		

* 1 = Too easy
  2 = Adequate for instruction
  3 = Too difficult

Analyzing the combined results of these two measures can provide the starting point for teachers to make instructional decisions. Do the combined results indicate that the textbook is too easy? too difficult? With this information teachers will not make inappropriate assumptions about the abilities of students.

If the results of the content reading inventory indicate student deficiencies in certain areas, teachers may want to use the inventory as an instructional tool. Since the questions asked on the inventory are probably similar to those teachers ask in the classroom, they can expect the students' responses to be similar to those they would make in class discussions. Therefore, the content reading inventory provides the framework for teachers to initiate a preview of the text, as described in chapter four. The premise behind this strategy is that the teacher will model the use of the various text parts and efficient use of the author's organizational structure. In this way all students can be effectively introduced to their textbook in a systematic manner. The preview also offers students an introduction to proper utilization of the various reading/study aids authors incorporate into textbooks.

Students may also break into small groups and be given the task of arriving at a consensus of opinion as to the correct responses on the content reading inventory. Students having difficulties coping with the various aspects of the textbook will be afforded the opportunity to experience how other students arrived at their responses to the questions. Again, teachers should follow these task group discussions with a whole-group discussion insuring an effective introduction to the textbook.

Task groups may also be utilized to provide additional practice in areas of need as indicated by the analysis of the summary information sheet that tabulates the results of the inventory. For instance, if the class as a whole seems to have difficulty processing text-implicit information, the teacher can construct a series of questions emphasizing the use of this skill and assign them to the task groups. Through peer interaction and a whole-group discussion/followup, the teacher can provide students experience with some of the processes necessary to enhance learning from text.

The diagnostic use of the textbook enables content teachers to **initiate** instruction in their classrooms on an informed basis. No assumptions are made about what is already known; therefore, instruction is based upon establishing the background necessary for effective comprehension of new material. Thus, knowledge of the students' ability to successfully cope with their text material is essential.

Assessing Prior Knowledge

Throughout this book we have stressed the importance of prior knowledge to reading and learning from text. In essence, the more knowledge students bring to the printed page, the more likely they will successfully comprehend the text, particularly if they or the teacher activate the appropriate prior knowledge. Conversely, if students lack, or fail to select, the appropriate prior knowledge, their comprehension may suffer. Therefore, teachers may wish to assess students' knowledge about a topic before they encounter it in a learning situation. In this way, teachers can make decisions about the quality and quantity of prereading instruction they provide students. Certainly, if teachers know that students possess a vast store of prior knowledge about a topic under study, it is less necessary to spend great amounts of time in prereading. On the other hand, if students know little about a topic, it would benefit teachers to spend time activating and building background knowledge.

We have already suggested a number of prereading vocabulary and comprehension strategies as well as some prewriting strategies that teachers can use to initiate instruction in the content areas. Though instructional in scope, each of these strategies can provide teachers with relevant knowledge about what students know and do not know about a topic. However, we would like to suggest two techniques for assessing prior knowledge that are easy to implement and can provide teachers with the information necessary for effective instructional planning and teaching: word association and prediction guides.

Word Association

Word association (Zalaluk, Samuels, & Taylor, 1986) is a technique designed to measure students' knowledge about a topic by determining what they associate with that topic. It is both simple to create and score, and it can be administered to a whole class. The reasoning behind this technique is that topics about which students possess considerable knowledge should elicit numerous associations, while those topics about which they possess little or no knowledge should elicit very few, if any, associations. Students simply write down as many words as they can think of in association with a key word. Thus, what is measured is each student's entering knowledge base. Assessing prior knowledge through word association can be accomplished using the following steps:

1. *Prepare the stimulus topic.* The keyword topic is selected and printed at the left margin of every line on a piece of paper. This will insure that students use the keyword to cue associations, not newly generated words.

2. *Provide instructions.* Students are told that their task is to see how many words they can think of and write down related to a keyword they will be provided. They are told that the words they write may be things, places, events, ideas, or whatever comes to their mind when they see the keyword. If word association is a novel task for them, the teacher should model the activity and provide practice and discussion for the students. Students are assured that they are not expected to fill in all the lines on the paper. Finally, they are told that they will be given only three minutes to complete the activity.

3. *Scoring.* Once students have generated their associations, responses are scored quantitatively, one point for each reasonable association. No points are given for unreasonable or erroneous associations. For instance, if the keyword is "mammals," one point would be given to "reptiles" because they are another major class of the animal kingdom, but none for "flowers." An additional point may be given for a superordinate category a student generates, but no more than one extra point can be given for subordinate ideas, no matter how many subordinate words are produced. The reasoning behind this is that the student has begun to use the generated words rather than the keyword as cues. In our example of mammals, one point would be awarded for the superordinate term, "marsupials," but only one more point would be awarded for full cluster of subordinate terms such as "kangaroo, wombat, opossum, and bandicoot." The following key may be used to score students' word associations:

0–2 points	low prior knowledge
3–6 points	average prior knowledge
7+ points	high prior knowledge

Let's say that you want to assess prior knowledge about the keyword topic the "solar system." One student wrote the following list of word associations:

Milky Way
the sun
Big Dipper
planets
Earth
Venus
Mars
Jupiter
Mercury

In this case the student would be awarded four points for the words listed. One point would be given for Milky Way since the solar system is part of it. One point would be awarded for the sun as it is part of the solar system; the same would hold true for planets. However, only one point would be given for all the separate planets named because they are each a subset of planets. Finally, no points would be given for the Big Dipper since it is a constellation separate from the solar system. Four points would indicate that this student possesses average prior knowledge about the solar system and a teacher would have to plan to provide a normal amount of prereading instruction for this student before giving a text assignment.

Prediction Guide

A second means of assessing students' prior knowledge of a topic is the prediction guide (Nichols, 1983). The *prediction guide* is a series of fact-based statements given to students before they encounter a text assignment. The students are to indicate whether or not each statement is true or false. For instance, a teacher about to cover the Cold War in American history might provide students with a series of prediction guide statements on the topic. By examining students' responses to each of the guide statements, the teacher can discover not only how much students might know about the Cold War, but also what particular aspects about the topic are known or not known. In this way the teacher will gain valuable information for instructional planning. Below is an example prediction guide for "bats" and the text from which the statements are drawn (adapted from Webster, 1984).

Prediction Guide: Bats

Directions: Before you read a text passage on "bats," predict which of the statements that follow are true based on what you already know about them. Place a check (✓) on the line next to every true statement.

_____ 1. Bats are the second largest group of mammals.
_____ 2. Some bats are the size of a bumblebee.
_____ 3. Bats transmit disease.
_____ 4. Bats are about as intelligent as dogs.

Bats

Next to the 3,000-odd kinds of rodents, some 900 species of bats make up the second largest order of mammals in the animal kingdom, both in number of species and, by estimation, of individuals alive at any one time. Bats, the order Chiroptera, meaning "winged hand," make up nearly one-fourth of all mammalian species.

They range in size from Kitti's hognosed bat, which is the size of a bumblebee and weighs about as much as a penny, to the large fruit-eating bats called "flying foxes" because of their foxlike faces and their size—they are almost as big as a small fox cub, weighing two pounds and having a wingspan of up to six feet.

Most bats' gargoylelike noses, used for transmitting high-frequency bursts of sound, and their huge ears, used to pick up the echoes from the waves of sound, have contributed to the human perception of bats as eerie, even supernatural, creatures that are probably vicious, filthy, and likely to attack humans and transmit disease.

Recent studies, however, show that bats are gentle; keep themselves meticulously clean; rarely transmit rabies; have a measure of intelligence that scientists equate with that of dogs; can be easily trained; and, in rare cases with a knowledgeable owner, can even become a pet.

Whether or not each statement is actually true and the number of statements should be used in the guide are not at issue here. What matters is that the statements reflect information the teacher thinks is important and that students will need to know after completing the assignment. In this way teachers will know in what areas to provide prereading instruction.

Before we leave this topic, we would like to caution teachers that prediction guides are characterized as a series of fact-based statements that aid you in assessing students' prior knowledge. Please remember that prediction guides are separate and distinct from anticipation guides, which are experience-based statements used to activate students' prior knowledge before they read. You may wish to reread the section on anticipation guides in chapter six if this distinction is unclear.

Assessment by Observation

It must be remembered that any test is a measure of a student's performance at that point in time only. Additionally, the administration of a single test or two does not provide sufficient information for drawing firm conclusions about students' abilities. The teacher still needs to add to information gained from testing and to update that information continually. Certainly, the more information we attain, the more valid an assessment can be of a student's abilities. But, that does not mean administering more cloze tests or content reading inventories. Rather, it requires that teachers be sensitive to the entire instructional situation and the major variables involved in it. This means that the teacher pay attention to the reader, the text, the task required of the reader, and the processes needed to complete that task. In other words, assessment needs to be carried on as students interact with text and deal with their daily reading and writing assignments.

The daily routines of the classroom provide rich sources of diagnostic information, and the thorough teacher makes use of it. What we are calling for here is simply conscious effort on the part of teachers to observe and study their students at work in the classroom. Moore (1986) called this "naturalistic assessment" because it was based on observing students' responses to the naturally occurring activities of the classroom versus assessing them in more contrived testing situations. In observation teachers attempt to make judgments about what they see. They observe students in a variety of circumstances and try to detect patterns of behavior that may signal some difficulty. These sources of information can be tapped regularly, and any findings should be recorded in the form of a checklist, teacher journal, or anecdotal record. This information can then be tied in with that gained from testing.

Observation may be the most reliable and valid means of assessing students' reading and writing abilities. It is highly reliable because teachers avoid a major problem of traditional assessment measure—lack of consistency—by basing any conclusions they make upon many observations over a period of time. And these conclusions are valid because they are based on behavior patterns that have occurred time and time again in real reading and writing situations as a natural part of an instructional lesson. Additionally, teachers can assess not only what has been learned but also how well students apply that learning.

For instance, the instructional strategies described in this text can become rich sources of diagnostic information for teachers if they employ assessment by observation. Readence and Martin (1988) provided one concrete example of this by pointing out that anticipation guides, described in chapter six, can be used for assessment by observation if teachers note how much students do, and do not, know about a topic. Further, teachers can observe how well students (1) pose their own questions; (2) anticipate what is to come in the text; (3) justify their responses to guide statements; (4) cope with potentially conflicting viewpoints as they attempt to make predictions about a topic; and, (5) recognize and reconcile their prior knowledge inaccuracies when they encounter them in their reading.

Assessment by observation is not necessarily an easy task, and it does require the ability to distinguish important from unimportant information. Much of this ability comes with experience, but it will come more readily to teachers who make a conscious effort to use their observational powers to study students at work. Informal testing is important, but only through observation can we update this information. Remember, assessment is a day-to-day occurrence.

Summary

The present chapter has offered numerous suggestions for content teachers to secure appropriate diagnostic information concerning the reading/learning abilities of students. With this information teachers will be able to plan effective instruction in their content areas according to the needs of their students. Purposes for classroom assessment and differences between formal and informal testing have been described. Types of informal tests have been discussed, and suggestions for construction of them have been provided. Finally, it was suggested that teachers use their own observational powers to continue to add new diagnostic information to that gained by testing.

Now go back to the anticipation guide at the beginning of the chapter. React again to the statements, this time recording your answers in the column entitled "Reaction." Compare your answers with those you made in the Anticipation column.

Answers for *A Recipe for Cloze Testing*

A. *Constructing the Cloze Test*
   1. Select passage. From the content textbook, select a passage of approximately three hundred words of continuous text. The passage should be representative of the readability level of the entire *text*. The material must not *have* been previously read by *your* students. Complete paragraphs should *be* used.
   2. Identify words to *be* deleted. Approximately 25 words *should* be left intact as *a* lead-in to the selection. *Lightly* underline every fifth word *until* 50 words have been *selected*. These words will comprise *the* missing words to be *supplied* by the students. Words *remaining* after the fiftieth deletion *should* be left intact.
   3. Prepare *a* stencil. Type the selection *on* a stencil, double-space format, *substituting* blanks for words previously *underlined*. Care should be taken *to* make all blanks of *equal* length.
B. *Administering the Cloze Test*
   Duplicate the test *and* distribute one mimeographed copy *to* each student. Emphasize the *following* oral directions to your *students*.
   1. Supply only one word *for* each blank.
   2. Encourage guessing, *as* students should attempt to *fill* all blanks.
   3. Misspellings will *be* scored as correct as *long* as they are recognizable.

4. *The* cloze test will not *be* timed.

5. Before beginning, silently *read* through the entire test. *I* will then read it *aloud* to you before you *begin.*

C. *Scoring the Cloze Test*

Determine each student's raw *score* in the following manner:

1. *Count* only exact replacements as *correct.* Synonyms are incorrect.

2. Misspellings *are* the only exception to *the* above rule. Do not *penalize* the student for spelling *errors.*

3. Inappropriate word endings are *incorrect.*

4. The raw score will *be* the number of correct *replacements* for each student.

D. *Classifying Student Performance*

It *has* generally been found that *students* who score between 40 *and* 60 percent would benefit *from* use of that textbook. *Students* scoring at this level are said to be performing at their instructional reading level. The textbook might be too difficult for those students scoring below 40 percent. It may be too easy for those scoring above 60 percent.

Answers for *Content Reading Inventory*

Section I: Textual Reading/Study Aids

A. *Internal Aids*

1. Page 40, Learning from Text. (Table of Contents)

2. Page 272 (Index).

3. The glossary.

4. It provides an overview of the chapter. (Chapter Introduction)

5. The student needs help with supporting details, sentence length, and spelling. (Pictorial Information)

6. The preface.

B. *External aids*

7. The card catalog.

8. The reader's guide.

9. Answer open; alphabetically (Encyclopedias)

Section II: Vocabulary Knowledge

10. A word is a pattern of auditory or visual symbols which represent schemata. (Recall)

11. A denotation of a word is its broad meaning, while a connotation of a word is defined by its subtle shades of meaning and its limiting grammatical and semantic conditions. Examples open. (Recall)

12. A corpus is a body, or collection, of recorded utterances used as a basis for the descriptive analysis of a language. (Context)

13. Assimilation is the process by which new information is incorporated into existing schemata. (Recall)

14. Extant means existing. (Context)

Section III: Comprehension

15. Adult language users have a common sensitivity to the concept of a word because they know speakers do not interrupt words with fillers such as "um" or "uh" during speech. (Text-Explicit)

16. Learning new words requires more than a simple explanation because they are not just isolated bits of information. Rather, words are defined by the ways and the extent to which they are related to all other words. (Text-Explicit)

17. The largest vocabularies for literature adults are the listening and reading vocabularies because the schemata required for recognizing word meanings in context are more fully developed. (Text-Explicit)

18. "Crass" is a general vocabulary term which is not specifically associated with a teaching area. "Cold War" is a technical vocabulary term uniquely related to social studies. (Text-Implicit)
19. "Secant" is a technical vocabulary term which requires students to accommodate their schemata by modifying them or creating new ones to learn a novel word. (Text-Implicit)
20. Children enter school with developed listening and speaking vocabularies. Instruction in the school enables these children to be exposed to more and more new concepts. Eventually, this exposure enables the listening vocabulary to further expand and the reading vocabulary to overtake the expressive vocabularies. (Text-Implicit)
21. The "Vocabularies" section is organized around a pattern of comparison-contrast as the types of vocabularies are enumerated and discussed. (Author Organization)

Miniprojects

1. In a small group examine a standardized reading test provided by the teacher. Evaluate each subtest of the instrument for the criteria listed below. Use the following classification system: 1 = Satisfactory; 2 = Unsatisfactory; 3 = Not Clear. Add any other evaluative criteria you deem necessary.
    A. Is the stated purpose of each test reflected in the selection of the test items?
    B. Are the directions standardized and clearly written?
    C. Is the test easy for the teacher and student to follow?
    D. Does the test measure what it purports to measure?
    E. Is adequate time allowed for the completion of each subtest?
2. Select a content text of your choice (or one you are currently using) and design a cloze test or maze test. Follow the guidelines described earlier in the chapter. Administer the test, if possible, to three students to see if an instructional match exists between each student and the text. Gather any other subjective data from the students or from your observation concerning the use of the cloze or the maze procedure as an evaluative tool.
3. Using a content text of your choice, design a content reading inventory. Utilize the procedures described earlier in this chapter. Administer the inventory, if possible, to three students to ascertain their ability to cope with the text. Evaluate the effectiveness of the content inventory as a device for gathering diagnostic information about students.

Additional Recommended Readings

Dishner, E. D., Bean, T. W., Readence, J. E., & Moore, D. W. (Eds.) (1986). *Reading in the content areas: Improving classroom instruction* (2nd ed.). Dubuque, IA: Kendall/Hunt. Chapter 4 of this book presents a series of readings on formal and informal assessment.

Farr, R., & Carey, R. F. (1986). *Reading: What can be measured?* (2nd ed.). Newark, DE: International Reading Association.
A comprehensive discussion of various aspects of reading assessment.

Johnston, P. H. (1983). *Reading comprehension assessment: A cognitive basis*. Newark, DE: International Reading Association.
Discusses reading comprehension and assessment methodology.

Johnston, P. H. (1984). Assessment in reading. In P. D. Pearson (Ed.), *Handbook of reading research* (pp. 147–182). New York: Longman.
Review of the literature on the development and current status of the assessment of reading.

Journal of Reading (1987, April), *40*(8).

The whole issue of this journal is devoted to the "state of reading assessment."

Readence, J. E., & Martin, M. A. (1988). Comprehension assessment: Alternatives to standardized tests. In S. M. Glazer, L. W. Searfoss, & L. M. Gentile (Eds.), *Reexamining reading/writing diagnosis: New trends in procedures for classrooms and clincis.* Newark, DE: International Reading Association.

Discusses the need for alternatives to standardized testing and uses observation during comprehension instruction as an example.

References

Bormuth, J. R. (1968). The cloze readability procedure. *Elementary English, 55,* 429–436.

Bradley, J. M., Ackerson, G., & Ames, W. S. (1978). The reliability of the maze procedure. *Journal of Reading Behavior, 10,* 291–296.

Fry, E. B. (1972). *Reading instruction for classroom and clinic.* New York: McGraw-Hill.

Guthrie, J. T., Seifert, M., Burham, N. A., & Caplan, R. I. (1974). The maze technique to assess, monitor reading comprehension. *The Reading Teacher, 28,* 161–168.

Henk, W. A. (1981). Effects of modified deletion strategies and scoring procedures on cloze test performance. *Journal of Reading Behavior, 13,* 347–357.

Henk, W. A., & Selders, M. L. (1984). A test of synonymic scoring of cloze passages. *The Reading Teacher, 38,* 282–287.

Johns, J. L. (1985). *Basic reading inventory* (3rd ed.). Dubuque, IA: Kendall/Hunt.

Johnston, P. H. (1983). *Reading comprehension assessment: A cognitive basis.* Newark, DE: International Reading Association.

Moore, D. W. (1986). A case for naturalistic assessment of reading comprehension. In E. K. Dishner, T. W. Bean, J. E. Readence, & D. W. Moore (Eds.), *Reading in the content areas: Improving classroom instruction* (2nd ed., pp. 159–170). Dubuque, IA: Kendall/Hunt.

Nelson reading test (1977). Boston: Houghton Mifflin.

Nichols, J. N. (1983). Using prediction to increase content area interest and understanding. *Journal of Reading, 27,* 225–228.

Readence, J. E., & Martin, M. A. (1988). Comprehension assessment: Alternatives to standardized tests. In S. M. Glazer, L. W. Searfoss, & L. M. Gentile (Eds.), *Reexamining reading/writing diagnosis: New trends in procedures for classrooms and clinics.* Newark, DE: International Reading Association.

Readence, J. E., & Moore, D. W. (1986). Why questions? A historical perspective on standardized reading comprehension tests. In E. K. Dishner, T. W. Bean, J. E. Readence, & D. W. Moore (Eds.), *Reading in the content areas: Improving classroom instruction* (2nd ed., pp. 136–144). Dubuque, IA: Kendall/Hunt.

Silvaroli, N. J. (1982). *Classroom reading inventory* (4th ed.). Dubuque, IA: Wm. C. Brown.

Stanford achievement test (1982). New York: Psychological Corp.

Taylor, W. S. (1953). Cloze procedure: A new test for measuring readability. *Journalism Quarterly, 30,* 415–433.

Webster, B. (1984, December 12). Science sheds light on bats. *The Register,* Santa Ana, CA.

Zakaluk, B. L., Samuels, S. J., & Taylor, B. M. (1986). A simple technique for estimating prior knowlege: Word association. *Journal of Reading, 30,* 56–60.

10

Anticipation   **Reaction**

———————— 1.   ———————— 1. Individualizing in the content classroom means providing one-to-one instruction for all students.

———————— 2.   ———————— 2. Individual differences among students become less pronounced the longer they are in school.

———————— 3.   ———————— 3. Learning is an individual matter.

———————— 4.   ———————— 4. Having large numbers of students in class precludes individualization in most classrooms.

———————— 5.   ———————— 5. It doesn't make sense to use the whole group as the predominant instructional format in most content classrooms.

Accommodating Individual Differences

Rationale

"Read chapter five for tomorrow. Be prepared for a quiz on the important points."

"How can anyone ask a question like that? If you'd read the chapter, you wouldn't ask that!"

"Susan, I can't explain it any better than the book. Class, let's re-read the page. I'll read it out loud and you follow along."

Do any of the above statements sound familiar? They are examples of statements that express teacher frustration as students fail in their attempts to use textbooks. They are also examples of some statements that suggest that instruction is geared toward the whole group and not small groups or the individual.

Teaching requires helping individuals to change. Learning occurs by making whatever adjustments are necessary in the learning situation, by accommodating instructional methods to match student abilities, and by guiding students as they try to cope with new learning situations. Yet, if we examine the kinds of instruction that traditionally take place in content classrooms, largely undifferentiated whole-group instruction would be found to be the predominant format and the lecture method the primary means of teaching. Numerous factors may be interacting to inhibit individualization in content classrooms; foremost among these are misconceptions and distortions of the concept of individualization.

While we have not dealt specifically with the concept of accommodating individual differences until now, the preceding nine chapters form a general knowledge base for dealing with individual learning abilities in content classrooms. Necessarily, this knowledge base requires some modification before it will suit the wide range of abilities which characterize students. The intent of this chapter is to describe the necessary modifications.

Chapter Objectives

After reading this chapter, you should be able to:

1. Define individualization as it pertains to the content classroom.
2. Understand general principles behind accommodating individual differences.
3. Implement a variety of instructional modifications designed to vary the reading/learning situation according to individual needs.

Graphic Organizer

The following graphic organizer is provided to give you some advance structure for new vocabulary and concepts that will be presented in this chapter.

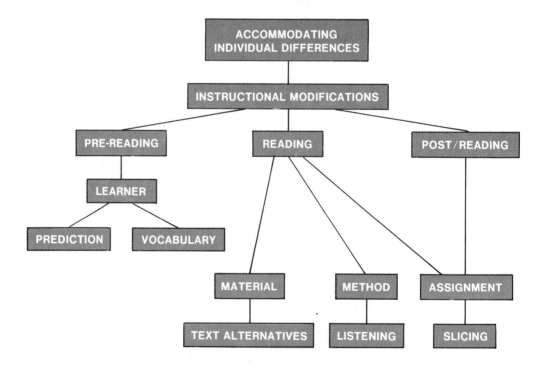

Individual Differences—A Fact of Life

Two ideas should be stressed when discussing the topic of individual differences—its pervasiveness and its multidimensionality. Individual differences are a ubiquitous and enduring fact of life. To deny the existence of individual differences is to deny the essential uniqueness of each human personality. Accepting the reality of individual differences is the precursor to accommodating them in the classroom.

How extensive are these differences? Examining the range of differences in achievement among students provides a very revealing picture. For example, the range of achievement in a typical heterogeneous tenth grade classroom would probably be fifth grade through the fifteenth! Burmeister (1978) has provided the following formula to find the range of achievement:

$$\text{Range} = \text{Grade level} \pm \frac{\text{Chronological Age}}{3}$$

Activity

Directions: Using the formula above, compute the range of achievement in either a class you teach or in a class you have visited. Are individual differences in achievement being dealt with well in this class?

An interesting fact about the range of achievement is that it increases with successively higher grade levels. There are important differences even before students enter school, and these differences increase at an accelerating rate. In fact, the better the teaching, the greater the range of differences that will be found in a particular class. Given equal amounts of good teaching, all students will benefit, but better students will learn more and faster. This is perhaps one reason why all students should not get equal amounts of instruction.

The second major factor of individual differences is its multidimensionality. When we speak of individual differences, we are talking about a plethora of factors, not a single trait. Many cognitive and personality traits seem to have an effect on reading achievement, and this is not to mention the differences that are inherent in exceptional and second language populations. It is not the intent of the authors to explain the psychological intricacies of these individual differences; rather, it is our intent to briefly discuss a few factors to make you aware of the kinds of factors that may affect your students as they attempt to read and learn in your classroom.

In chapter two you learned about two factors, among many, that affect students' ability to learn from text. These were prior knowledge and language knowledge. The quantity and quality of the prior experiences of individuals and their language sophistication vary greatly. In chapter three you learned that attitude, interest, and self-concept are reading-related factors that vary from individual to individual.

Other individual factors that may affect reading achievement as they interact with each other are: (1) physical development, (2) emotional development, (3) rate of learning, (4) mode of learning, (5) motivation, and (6) practice needed. Because of their interactive nature, it might be difficult to speak of each factor singularly. For instance, physical development may influence one's emotional well-being. The same might be said for rate and mode of learning.

If students inadequately develop physically or emotionally, it may have an effect on their ability to function successfully in the total school environment. Such a difference may militate against overall success in school, as well as in reading. With regard to learning, individuals assimilate information at different rates and do it by different means. Learning at different rates or in different manners does not necessarily imply different levels of intelligence. Individuals have special preferences for how they learn new information. i.e., different people have different modes of cognitive functioning and problem-solving behavior.

Additionally, the notion of passive failure, or learned helplessness (Johnston & Winograd, 1985), is another learning difference to be recognized. Students who exhibit *passive failure* may be defined as those students who are resigned to fail and believe they do not have the ability to succeed in their learning. When faced with failure, they do not persist; they give up. On the other hand, when these students do succeed, they usually attribute it to factors other than themselves, such as luck, good teaching, or the ease of the task. The important point to be made about these students is that they don't fail because of lack of ability; rather, they do not, and will not, employ the appropriate strategies necessary for effective learning. Certainly, accommodating the differences of passive failures in the classroom will be different than dealing with the learning difficulties presented by those students who lack the specific skills necessary to complete a learning task successfully.

One last principle regarding individual differences is that sometimes a factor may vary almost as greatly within an individual as it does among individuals. For instance, a student's interest in school may fluctuate dramatically according to subject area. Changing interests, motivations, and life goals are differences that may differ greatly within an individual, especially over time.

A Definition

Accommodating individual differences means many different things to many different people (Marcetti, 1978). Certainly one thing it does not mean is largely undifferentiated, whole-group instruction in which the subject, rather than the student, is the focus of instruction. The problems inherent in such instruction have been recognized for some time. For instance, Hunt and Sheldon (1950) offered that "High school teachers must also realize that much of their frustration is derived from attempting to teach forty pupils as if all the children were able to perform on the same level" (p. 352–353). Nonetheless, the lecture method is still predominant in content area teaching.

At the other extreme is complete individualization in which instruction takes place totally on a one-to-one basis. This may be an ideal to which some educators aspire; however, in the face of the rigors of day-to-day classroom experiences with large numbers of students, complete individualization is an unrealistic and counterproductive goal.

The kind of instructional accommodation to individual differences, or *individualization,* the authors recommend represents a compromise between the two extremes cited above. It does not embrace complete individualization, which requires individual preparation or text material for each student, nor does it call for the abandonment of grouping strategies. Rather, it incorporates the gamut of grouping procedures—whole group, small-group, and individual—and utilizes these grouping procedures within the confines of the traditional instructional plan found in most classrooms.

Grouping is recommended because the authors feel that active student involvement in a group situation provides for productivity in learning (see chapter six), for example, through plays, science experiments, or unit reviews. Students can learn from one another and provide new insight into learning by modeling their thinking for others (Wood, 1987). Feelings of "belonging" cannot be disregarded in grouping situations either. Additionally, teachers can move into their most appropriate role, as facilitators of learning, through the use of different group structures.

For example, numerous different types of small groups exist that teachers might employ. Among them are the following:

1. instruction groups—which allow teachers to teach a specific process or issue with more individual contact than is possible in a large group,
2. research groups—which gather information on a problem and report the results to the large group,
3. debate groups—which present a contest of ideas to the large group, and
4. digressive groups—which use brainstorming to generate creative solutions to a problem.

There are certain essential guidelines that must be considered before teachers can consider trying to accommodate individual differences. First, teachers must have an understanding of the difficulties inherent in learning from text (chapter one). Everyone cannot be expected to read and learn efficiently from subject matter material. Second, teachers must understand the reading process (chapter two). Reading is a complex process involving many factors. Third, teachers need to be aware of how attitude and interest affect learning (chapter three). The affective dimension of learning requires equal consideration in instructional planning. Fourth, teachers must know the materials students are using (chapter four), so they are aware of the text features that may promote or diminish comprehension. Fifth, teachers need to have knowledge of, and use, appropriate instructional strategies (chapters five through eight). In this way students will be able to learn from text more efficiently. Sixth, teachers must know their students (chapter nine). As such, they can promote the instructional match between students and materials.

Finally, teachers need to be aware that the idea of making an overnight transformation from total whole-group instruction to the practices for accommodating individual differences is unrealistic (Earle & Morley, 1986). As with any of the strategies previously described in this text, the authors do not expect a massive, rapid transformation to the ideas we advocate. Rather, we realize that slow, careful adaptation is crucial to the eventual successful implementation of these practices. Accommodating individual differences in the content classroom is no different. Your adaptation to students' individual differences will necessarily be limited by time and resources. At the same time we do recommend that you be aware of the above guidelines before you implement new strategies. After all, you wouldn't want to drive off in your car without filling your gas tank, would you?

Some Suggestions

The suggestions that follow for accommodating individual differences in the content classroom are based upon three assumptions. First, the primary means of instruction in subject matter areas is the **textbook.** The text represents the main vehicle for learning and the pedagogical structure needed by teachers. Second, all teaching revolves around an instructional paradigm that consists of three phases. These are: (1) a pre-reading phase to prepare students for new learning in their text; (2) a reading phase, during which students interact with the text; and (3) a post-reading phase, during which student learning is refined and extended. These three phases mesh in an integrated instructional format and do not necessarily function as independent elements of instruction. Third, in order to realistically consider accommodating students' individual differences, teachers must make modifications in the way they present the textbook within the context of the instructional paradigm. Consequently, you must be willing to make these necessary alerations in order to insure that each student has optimal opportunity to find success in your classroom.

Moore and Readence (1981) suggested modifications for teachers to consider as they employ the instructional paradigm of pre-reading, reading, and post-reading phases. Suggestions to be discussed include: (1) modifying students' prior knowledge, (2) modifying the way in which the material is presented, (3) considering alternatives to the text material, and (4) modifying the assignment made. These suggestions are the authors' attempts to offer you some practical instructional techniques to help you answer the commonly asked question, "What do I do on Monday?"

Modifications in the Pre-reading Phase. The importance of the pre-reading phase was discussed in chapter six, as was the role of prior knowledge in chapter two. The degree to which readers utilize their prior experiences in reading and learning from text will greatly influence their understanding of that material. Students' failure to associate new information with previously known information as they attempt to assimilate text material increases the difficulty of their comprehension task. Additionally, as you are well aware, some students simply do not have the necessary prior knowledge about all the topics they will encounter in text material. (Remember the samples that illustrated the role of prior knowledge in chapters one and two?)

Fortunately, as students prepare to read their texts you can intervene to modify their knowledge of a topic as well as their interest in it. You can provide guided instruction to activate, or modify, students' schemata through the use of pre-reading strategies. Pre-reading strategies serve to activate appropriate schemata and then modify them as new information is entered, thus allowing comprehension to occur. Therefore, using pre-reading strategies to provide guided instruction to enhance the assimilation of new knowledge is one means of accommodating instruction to respond to students' individual differences.

Obviously, this discussion of pre-reading strategies is not new to you; however, the argument for the use of pre-reading strategies is. The wide range of prior experiences students bring to a particular topic needs to be accommodated in order to aid their mastery of new information. This may be accomplished through the use of the vocabulary strategies described in chapter five or the prediction strategies described in chapter six. Certainly approaching pre-reading strategies as a means to accommodate individual differences by modifying students' prior knowledge can only serve to reinforce their use as an essential in facilitating text learning.

Modifications in the Reading Phase. Certainly there is cause to wonder about instruction that presents the same material in the same way to all students. Obviously, in this type of instruction no heed is being paid to the differences in the way students learn or how well individual students deal with the difficulty of the concepts and vocabulary inherent in text. Because of these differences, methods for reducing the difficulty level of the learning material need to be considered. With some students it may be necessary to modify the way the material is presented or even the material itself.

1. *Modifying the Method.* One way to modify the reading phase of an instructional lesson is to change the method. The "reading" phase is really only the name for students' interaction with the information in the text. Implied in its title, though, is the notion that students *must* read to learn the new information. Needless to say, the material can be presented in a different manner and thus may better accommodate some students' learning styles or abilities.

Some students may find the text too difficult to read; others may prefer an alternate means of text presentation. In these situations it would seem to be advantageous to capitalize on students' ability to listen and comprehend the material. Pearson and Fielding (1982) have described the efficacy of using listening as an instructional tool, since both reading and listening are receptive language processes. Listening can be an effective means for student readers to communicate with text authors. Additionally, the use of listening corresponds to the integrated approach to content reading advocated by this text. Thus, much of the same material students can learn through a listening mode. Furthermore, listening might potentially be the *best* means to learn text material for some students because of their differential abilities. It is the opinion of the authors that active listening strategies are utilized too infrequently and that students could benefit extensively from such strategies.

The teacher may read aloud the selected passage from the text after instructing students to listen for particular concepts or other purposes. Students who are able to read the text with ease may be asked to read it to other students who are having difficulty with the reading. Another alternative is use of the tape recorder. Either the teacher or selected students may tape a portion of the text for those experiencing difficulty. These students may follow along as the text is being read, again with specific instructions about what they should be listening for. If a more structured approach is desired as students are listening to a selected passage, *listening guides* (Thomas & Cummings, 1978) are suggested. The listening guide is a skeletal outline of the important concepts in the passage presented in the order and relationship in which they are set out in the passage. Students are asked to write in the desired information as they listen to the selection. The task of filling in the listening guides gives students additional guidance through the outline structure provided. Activities for reinforcement and extension may follow as planned.

An example of a listening guide is given below. If a listening guide was employed with the section of chapter five entitled "Principles of Effective Vocabulary Instruction", it might look like this:

Principle	**Notes**
1. _____	_____
	_____
2. _____	_____
	_____
3. _____	_____
	_____
4. _____	_____
	_____

Another recommended modification that could be used in lieu of reading in this phase of an instructional lesson is a modification of the Guided Reading Procedure called the *Guided Listening Procedure* (GLP). The GLP is procedurally identical to the Guided Reading Procedure, described in chapter six, except that listening is used, instead of reading, to learn from text. In other words, instead of reading to remember everything as the directions specify, you would tell students to "listen to remember everything" in the GLP. Then the teacher or a selected student would read a desired passage to students as they listened. The same person would do the rereading. Otherwise, the steps to the procedure are the same, including the tests for recall purposes. The advantages of using this alternate procedure are similar to those described earlier. The same information can be conveyed by using a listening mode, and it enables the teacher to accommodate students' differential abilities.

2. *Modifying the Material.* Another means to accommodate students' individual differences in the reading phase is to modify the material itself. This can be accomplished by incorporating the use of different material on the same topic before students read the text or, if necessary, in place of it (Readence & Dishner, 1986). The *unit plan* seems to be an appropriate vehicle with which to accomplish the modification of the material. The unit is a plan of instruction in which students explore and respond to a selected topic through their interaction with a variety of integrated activities designed to stimulate and improve their knowledge, information acquisition abilities, and attitudes. Furthermore, the unit plan may serve to enhance students' readiness for new concepts they will encounter.

Central to the success of the unit plan is the identification and incorporation of appropriate supplemental resources and the integration of them to focus on the topic covered by the text. These resources include library books, pamphlets, magazines, high interest-low vocabulary books, and other textbooks. Sources such as audio-visual materials, field trips, and invited speakers should also be considered as well as games, experiments, and puzzles to provide attractive, interesting ways to learn in which reading demands are minimal. The use of such supplementary materials will give you much flexibility in accommodating individual differences of students, yet still enable you to cover the topic under consideration very efficiently. The efficacy of using multiple materials was discussed in chapter three.

Learning centers are suggested as an aid to material modification. The purpose of learning centers is to foster a classroom environment conducive to accommodating individual differences and to encourage self-directed learning behavior on the part of students (Tierney, Readence, & Dishner, 1985). Although often associated only with reading instruction, the concept of learning centers can be adapted for content areas. Centers are organized to accomplish a variety of purposes; however, their purpose in the content area classroom can be to facilitate the utilization of the supplementary materials identified for particular units of study. Materials in the unit can be organized in a variety of ways. One suggestion might be to employ at least one reading center, a listening center, a viewing center, and a games center. Learning centers can provide the necessary organization needed to capitalize on the flexibility provided by the variety of supplementary materials in accommodating individual differences of students.

Modifications in the Post-reading Phase. In addition to modifying students' prior knowledge, the method, and/or the material, assignments required of students may also be modified. Usually the students' comprehension of text material is checked by having them answer a series of questions either found in the chapter's end or in a study guide constructed by the teacher. However, having the whole group of students deal with exactly the same questions is the antithesis of accommodating divergent student abilities.

Earle and Sanders (1986) have suggested some excellent means by which to individualize certain aspects of content assignments. Pearson and Johnson (1978) have also suggested the use of a technique called *slicing* in assigning tasks to students. Specifically, slicing refers to simplifying the complexity of these tasks by reexamining those that are required and recasting them to ease the demands placed on students.

Text assignments may be sliced in a variety of ways. Slicing enables teachers to accommodate individual differences by graduating the learning steps involved in completing assignments and by providing structured guidance in doing so. Slicing may be utilized in the following aspects of text assignments (Readence & Moore, 1980): (1) length of passage, (2) scope of information search, (3) information index, and (4) response mode.

1. *Length of passage.* Though obviously more of a reading task that a post-reading task, length of passage will be discussed here under the umbrella strategy of slicing. Sometimes assigning a chapter at a time for reading represents too sizeable a chunk of text for some students, yet this size assignment is very prevalent. In some cases, poor readers might be overwhelmed by as little as five pages; therefore, it seems appropriate to consider slicing the length of reading task for certain students to accommodate their divergent abilities. Reading assignments should be varied according to the number of concepts assigned to each student. Slicing the length of the passage to even a section or paragraph might be appropriate for certain students to insure their comprehension. Caution is given regarding pictorial aids in text. Authors sometimes use such aids to express what could take large numbers of words. Such aids might be considered a unit of instruction for some students, while other students may focus on the running text elaborating upon a particular aid.

2. *Scope of information search.* Content textbooks, by their very nature, are bursting with information. It is unrealistic to consider teaching all concepts presented; therefore, the teacher must conduct some form of content analysis in order to make decisions regarding the relative importance of the concepts. The *scope of information search* is determined by the number of concepts for which students are then held responsible. As concepts increase in number, the more exhaustive the scope of the search becomes. On the other hand, the fewer the concepts to be mastered, the more limited the search. The less proficient the student's reading ability, the more difficult an exhaustive search will be, and the greater the chance of negative effects on motivation and retention of new learning. Therefore, slicing the scope of information search according to students' individual differences is appropriate.

The number of concepts for which students are responsible should be dependent upon their differential abilities and the importance of the concepts in the chapter. The number of concepts can be varied by adding or subtracting from the number of assigned tasks on students' end-of-chapter or study guide questions. For example, more proficient readers may be responsible for twelve concepts while others need only deal with three or four. It is cautioned that no matter how many concepts are assigned to individual students in the class, whole-group discussion should follow the completion of their work so that all students are exposed to the selected information.

In addition to slicing the number of concepts for which students are responsible on their chapter or study guide questions, two other strategies are recommended for slicing the scope of information search. The Selective Reading Guide, described in chapter six, provides an alternate means of guiding students through their information search. In essence, it may also serve as a means to differentiate instruction either by aiding students in finding desired information in the text, by limiting the amount of information for which they are responsible, or by both. Furthermore, for those students who might still experience difficulty with the reading of the Selective Reading Guide, it is recommended that it be put on tape and students practice using their listening skills.

A second strategy for slicing the scope of the information search is to use a learning centers approach. Used in this way, learning centers become "task" centers. At each center would be a prescribed task for students to complete as part of their assignments. Students may be assigned to certain task stations or may be allowed to select their own tasks to complete the assignment. Teachers can differentiate the number of assigned tasks according to students' abilities. For instance, certain students may be asked to complete only three of six tasks at the centers while others may be asked to do five of six. Tasks at centers may also be graduated in difficulty to help accommodate individual differences.

Two points should be made concerning the scope of information search. First, limiting the search does not necessitate that only text-explicit thinking be involved. It is not the level of thinking that is limited, only the number of concepts. Since all students can think and all students should be involved in higher-level comprehension processes, it is misguided to limit such thinking in an endeavor to reduce the scope of the information search. Second, there is a difference between varying the scope of the search and varying the length of the passage to be read. The number of concepts assigned may be varied while the length of the passage is held constant. For example, in a three-page selection certain students may be responsible for one concept per page while others may be held responsible for numerous concepts.

3. *Information index.* Keying students into the location of important concepts or in some way structuring their search for that information is the intent of using an *information index.* The extent to which the index is used depends on students' differential abilities, the importance of the information, and the depth of understanding required.

Three ways are suggested for teachers to slice the demands of the learning task using the information index. The first method is to intersperse questions throughout the text. Students can be directed to lightly mark question numbers at the appropriate places in the text chapter. In this way questions can be dealt with at the time they are encountered during the reading, thus slicing the search for the information. For some teachers this marking of questions may also serve as a preliminary step to their eventual development and use of study guides (chapter six).

A second method of providing the information index is to provide an actual informational key to the questions. Questions may be keyed to the page, section, paragraph, and/or sentence where students may find the appropriate answer or the information on which the answer is based. This type of information is frequently provided by content teachers when they use study guides with their students. An example of this type of information index is provided below. In this case the students are keyed to the page and paragraph numbers.

What were the causes of the Revolutionary War? (122:2)

A final method for using the information index is really a modification of the listening guide procedure described earlier in this chapter. Instead of providing a guide for the students to fill in while they listen to a selection being read, the guide can be keyed to particular pages or paragraphs through the use of the information index. Students can then search out the information in the text chapter.

4. *Response mode*. A final way to slice the task of students is to change the *response mode* required by their assigned questions. In many cases questions fail to guide students' understanding of text material simply because they are too diffuse. Diffuse questions can be made more specific, in effect slicing the task. What follows is an example of a diffuse question made more specific.

Diffuse: What were the causes of World War II?

Specific: List four reasons for Germany's aggression against other countries.
List four reasons why the Allies wanted to stop the spread of Nazism.

In the case of the first question, it might be argued that the causes of World War II are not stated explicitly in the text, but must be inferred from the lists of reasons for German and Allied actions. Once the sliced statements are answered, students will be more readily able to draw the required inferences for the causes of the war. Thus, recasting diffuse questions requiring higher-level comprehension to specific, literal-level tasks can be an effective means of slicing the assigned task.

Questions may also be sliced by requiring fewer pieces of information. For instance, with the specific directions above concerning World War II, poor readers may be asked to supply only one or two reasons for German aggression or Allied resistance while better readers may be asked to supply all reasons for each. Additionally, the same principle may be applied to higher-level questions as well as text-explicit tasks. The diffuse question on the causes of World War II may be sliced as the literal tasks were by requiring only two or three causes from less proficient readers, for example, and possibly seven from more fluent ones. This strategy slices the task of the assignment as well as the scope of the search.

Still another means to slice the response mode required by a question is to convert recall items to recognition items. Recall tasks demand more on the part of the students because the students receive little guidance and must impose structure themselves. Recognition tasks, on the other hand, are generally easier to answer as they require only verification, not production. It should be noted that converting questions to simplify them in this way does not mean that the questions deal with less important concepts. Rather, the same concepts are learned but in a different manner.

Recognition tasks may be constructed in different formats. Matching tasks are a popular form of the recognition mode. Varying the number of items to be matched in each column increases the demands placed on students. In other words, the use of unequal columns provides students with a greater challenge, while using equal columns slices the assigned task considerably. Another type of recognition format is the multiple-choice format. Again, both multiple-choice and recall questions can deal with identical concepts; however multiple-choice tasks present students considerable structure by dealing with the concepts in more manageable units. The example that follows demonstrates how a recall question may be converted to a multiple-choice item.

Recall: What new problems arose in the United States as a result of the depression?

Multiple Choice: What new problems arose in the United States as a result of the depression? Place a check in the blank next to the correct statements.

   _____ Unemployment rose rapidly.
   _____ Foreign trade deficits grew.
   _____ Money shortages increased.
   _____ Crime rates rose sharply.
   _____ Distrust of the government increased.

Multiple-choice items like the one given previously can be further sliced by utilizing an information index and also by varying the number of items to be verified according to students' differential abilities. Another recognition format that is useful is the true-false question. The previous multiple-choice example can easily be changed to a true-false task by altering the directions as follows: "Place a 'T' for true or an 'F' for false next to each statement." Such directions often increase students' critical attention to each statement.

Activity

Directions: Below is diffuse question requiring a response from recall. Change the question in a variety of ways to slice the task.

What were the causes of the Civil War?

Many questions are constructed in a cloze-type format, in which students are asked to fill in the blank. Such questions can also be sliced. Desired passages may be taken directly from the text or else paraphrased and duplicated with key words deleted. Good readers may be asked to complete the task from recall, while others may be provided a list of the deleted items with some foils added. The poorest readers may just receive a randomly ordered list of correct choices that equal the number of blanks in the passage; thus the complexity of the task is sliced even further.

Finally, questions requiring recall may be sliced by providing possible statements to be verified. Herber and Nelson (1986) have suggested using such statements in lieu of questions to familiarize students with higher-level comprehension processes. Therefore, difficult, diffuse questions might be changed into statements for students' reaction and defense, thus enabling them to experience the thinking processes to be utilized at another time with recall questions. Following is an example of this suggested alternative.

Question: What caused the U.S. to plunge into the depression during President Hoover's administration?

Statement: President Hoover was ignorant of economic policies. He was inexperienced in politics and unable to recognize good advice from bad in economic matters.

Summary

In this chapter we have defined individualization as it pertains to the content classroom and provided a basis for accommodating individual differences. Numerous modifications have been suggested to deal with students' divergent abilities through the use of the traditional lesson format. The chapter presented strategies for modifying the student's prior knowledge, the method, the material, and the assignment. These strategies may be incorporated into the pre-reading, reading, and post-reading phases of an instructional lesson.

Now go back to the anticipation guide at the beginning of this chapter. React to the statements as you did before, this time recording your answers in the column entitled "Reaction." Compare your answers to those made in the Anticipation column.

Miniprojects

1. Choose a chapter from a textbook in your content area and outline how you would attempt to accommodate student differences within the context of the instructional format described in this text.
2. Develop a list of supplementary materials that you might be able to use to augment or to replace a chapter from a textbook in your content area.
3. Examine the study questions at the end of a chapter in a textbook in your content area and slice the questions according to the suggestions discussed in this chapter.

Additional Recommended Readings

Dishner, E. K., Bean, T. W., Readence, J. E., & Moore, D. W. (Eds.) (1986). *Reading in the content areas: Improving classroom instruction* (2nd ed.). Dubuque, IA: Kendall/Hunt. Chapter 8 of this text presents a series of readings on accommodating individual differences.

Marcetti, A. J. (1978). Individualized reading: Current programs in the secondary schools. *Journal of Reading, 22,* 50–54. Presents an overview of various approaches to teaching using an individualized method.

Spiro, R. J., & Myers, A. (1984). Individual differences and underlying cognitive processes in reading. In P. D. Pearson (Ed.), *Handbook of reading research* (pp. 471–501). New York: Longman. Discusses the research on individual differences in reading.

References

Burmeister, L. E. (1978). *Reading strategies for middle and secondary school teachers* (2nd ed.). Reading, MA: Addison-Wesley.

Earle, R. A., & Morley, R. (1986). The half-open classroom: Controlled options in reading. In E. K. Dishner, T. W. Bean, J. E. Readence, & D. W. Moore (Eds.), *Reading in the content areas: Improving classroom instruction* (2nd ed., pp. 319–323). Dubuque, IA: Kendall/Hunt.

Earle, R. A., & Sanders, P. L. (1986). Individualizing reading assignments. In E. K. Dishner, T. W. Bean, J. E. Readence, & D. W. Moore (Eds.), *Reading in the content areas: Improving classroom instruction* (2nd ed., pp. 310–314). Dubuque, IA: Kendall/Hunt.

Herber, H. L., & Nelson, J. B. (1986). Questioning is not the answer. In E. K. Dishner, T. W. Bean, J. E. Readence, & D. W. Moore (Eds.), *Reading in the content areas: Improving classroom instruction* (2nd ed., pp. 210–215). Dubuque, IA: Kendall/Hunt.

Hunt, L. C., Jr., & Sheldon, W. D. Characteristics of the reading of a group of ninth-grade pupils. *School Review, 58,* 348–353.

Johnston, P. H., & Winograd, P. N. (1985). Passive failure in reading. *Journal of Reading Behavior, 17,* 279–301.

Marcetti, A. J. (1978). Individualized reading: Current programs in the secondary schools. *Journal of Reading, 22,* 50–54.

Moore, D. W., & Readence, J. E. (1981). Accommodating individual differences in content classrooms *The High School Journal, 64,* 160–165.

Pearson, P. D., & Fielding, L. (1982). Listening comprehension. *Language Arts, 59,* 617–629.

Pearson, P. D., & Johnson, D. D. (1978). *Teaching reading comprehension.* New York: Holt, Rinehart, and Winston.

Readence, J. E., & Dishner, E. K. (1986). Alternatives to a single textbook approach. In E. K. Dishner, T. W. Bean, J. E. Readence, & D. W. Moore (Eds.), *Reading in the content areas: Improving classroom instruction* (2nd ed., pp. 314–319). Kendall/Hunt.

Readence, J. E., & Moore, D. W. (1980). Differentiating text assignments in content areas. *Reading Horizons, 20,* 112–117.

Thomas, K. J., & Cummings, C. K. (1978). The efficacy of listening guides: Some preliminary findings with tenth and eleventh graders. *Journal of Reading, 21,* 705–709.

Tierney, R. J., Readence, J. E., & Dishner, E. K. (1985). *Reading strategies and practices: A compendium* (2nd ed.). Boston: Allyn & Bacon.

Wood, K. D. (1987). Fostering cooperative learning in middle and secondary classrooms. *Journal of Reading, 31,* 10–18.

Epilogue

In a structure as complex and confusing as the American educational system often appears to be, individuals frequently wonder whether or not they are important in the scheme of things. The authors of this text are convinced that individuals do count, both as teachers and as students, and that it is through the cumulative efforts of large numbers of individuals that the system moves BEST to meet the needs of those it is designed to serve. Moreover, the authors are convinced that content area reading offers a workable approach for classroom teachers, who must cope daily with teaching the issues and concepts of their own specialities. To this end, the text has blended theories and practical strategies in a format that models the intent of the book. Obviously, not all of the theories and strategies will work for every teacher in every content area. Nevertheless, the authors encourage you to discover which techniques best suit the needs of your students. A willingness to try new things guarantees a brighter tomorrow for everyone.

Glossary

Accommodation: the process of adjusting one's existing cognitive structure to accept new information.

Accretion: the accumulation of facts within existing schemata.

Acronym: a word that is formed by combining the intitial letters or segments of a series of words.

Aiming Toward Content: teaching which focuses on content acquisition with no consideration for how to acquire that information.

Analogical Study Guide: a form of study guide in which students use familiar concepts to learn and retain new information.

Anticipation Guide: a pre-reading strategy that activates students' ideas about a topic by asking them to react to a series of guide statements related to that topic.

Assimilation: the process whereby new information is simply added to one's existing cognitive structure.

Attitudes: those feelings that cause a reader to approach or avoid a reading situation.

Bottom-Up Processing: reading that progresses from the surface features of print with little regard for comprehension.

Bound Morpheme: a meaningful language unit that occurs only as an attachment to words or other morphemes, e.g., tele-.

Capacity Limitation: refers to the theory that human beings are capable of attending consciously to only one task at a time.

Cause-Effect: a pattern of text organization linking reasons with results.

Chunking: a type of mental organization in which related bits of information are processed as a single unit.

Closet Clinician Model: attempts to remediate reading deficiencies through phonics and isolated skill drills that are divorced from actual subject matter learning.

Cloze Concept Guide: post-reading cloze exercises designed to cue readers to an author's pattern of organization or to review key concepts.

Cloze Procedure: the systematic deletion and replacement of words from a text selection in order to determine students' reading levels.

Clues and Questions: vocabulary review procedure that centers on student-generated questions and answers.

Cognitive Structure: the interrelated network of our experiences, organized in memory through a system of categories.

Comparison-Contrast: a pattern of text organization that demonstrates likenesses and differences between things or ideas.

Composing: the process of generating and shaping ideas before writing begins and as the actual writing unfolds.

Connotation: subtle shades of meaning that define a word; there can also be specific grammatical and semantic conditions that delimit a word's appropriate usage.

Content Reading Inventory: a teacher-made and text-based test designed to assess students' ability to effectively read and learn from the text.

Context Clues: a decoding technique that consists of utilizing surrounding words and their meanings to identify unfamiliar words.

Contextual: refers to the connotative meaning of words in context.

Contextual Redefinition: a vocabulary strategy in which the teacher places new vocabulary in self-defining or high utility contexts.

Criterion: a relative standard, or score, that implies adequate achievement without reference to the performance of others.

Debriefing: feedback by students in the form of self-reports, introspection, and hindsights.

Decoding: any process whereby a coded message is converted back into thought.

Definitional: refers to the denotative meaning of words.

Denotation: the broad meanings of words.

Depth of Processing: a memory principle that asserts that the likelihood of long-term retention and recall is greater when a mental activity involves close semantic analysis and cognitive attention.

Diagnostic Test: a test employed to determine specific skill strengths and weaknesses of students.

Directed-Reading-Thinking-Activity: a self-questioning process that encourages students to predict oncoming information in text and sets purposes for reading that are personally interesting.

Distributed Practice: rehearsals separated by breaks.

Encoding: any process whereby thought or meaning is converted into a code.

Etymology: study of the history of words and their origins.

Experience-Based: thinking that requires drawing an inference that is not derivable from the text, but rather from one's existing schemata, i.e., reading beyond the lines.

Expressive Vocabulary: words that a person can use properly when speaking or writing.

Extension Activities: pencil and paper exercises designed to reinforce and expand the schemata of newly acquired content area vocabulary.

External Reference: any source of information outside the passage being read.

External Storage: in notetaking, a written substitute for memory.

Fake Pop Quiz: a quiz designed to reinforce, rather than test, recently introduced information.

Feature Analysis: an instructional strategy in which sets of new concepts or vocabulary are defined and discriminated by identifying the unique characteristics of each member of the set.

Formal Tests: standardized, norm-referenced tests used to monitor student progress.

Free Morpheme: a morpheme that can stand by itself, e.g., boy.

Free Response and Opinion-Proof: students read and note in writing points of agreement or dispute for later class discussion.

Frustration Reading Level: the reading level at which the text material may be too difficult for the reader and an especially good job of teaching is required for students to read it.

General Vocabulary: words that are not specifically associated with any one teaching area and are assimilated into existing schemata.

GIST: a teaching strategy designed to foster summary writing and reading comprehension.

Glossary: an alphabetized list of technical words and their definitions used in a textbook or other work.

Graphic Information Lesson: strategy designed to teach students how to interpret graphs

Graphic Literacy: ability to interpret graphs and other visual presentations in text.

Graphic Organizer: a visual aid that defines hierarchical relationships among concepts and that lends itself to the teaching of technical vocabulary.

Group Test: a test administered in a group situation.

Guided Listening Procedure: a comprehension strategy employed on a listening level; the purpose is to enhance recall and organization of text information as well as to promote student self-inquiry.

Guided Reading Procedure: an integrated lesson approach designed to insure that students understand and remember key information from their text.

Guided Writing Procedure: an integrated lesson approach that serves as an alternative to the guided reading procedure by capitalizing on writing as a means to commit information to long-term memory.

Independent Reading Level: the reading level at which the reader may find the text material easy, and perhaps unchallenging, and will need no teacher assistance to read it efficiently.

Index: an alphabetized list of important terms and topics and the page numbers on which they occur in the text.

Individualization: incorporating the gamut of grouping procedures—whole group, small group, and individual—within the confines of a well-developed instructional plan utilizing the textbook and with the teacher acting as facilitator of learning.

Individual Test: a test that may be administered on only an individual basis.

Informal Tests: teacher-made or published tests that employ a criterion to monitor student progress.

Information Index: a device used to structure the information search by keying students into the location of important concepts.

Instructional Reading Level: the reading level at which a reader may effectively learn from text with teacher guidance.

Interests: what students like to read about.

Journal Writing: writing to explore ideas freely without worrying unduly about mechanics.

Key Word Method: a mnemonic strategy for helping students remember new vocabulary.

Learning: a change that occurs in an organism at a particular time as a function of experience.

Learning Centers: organized classroom centers designed to facilitate the acquisition of new information or to reinforce it.

Levels of Text Understanding: the differing levels of thinking involved in reading text material; e.g., text-explicit, text-implicit, experience-based.

Library Power: strategies designed to expand the reading horizons of children by introducing them to the wealth of books in the school library.

Listen-Read-Discuss: an integrated strategy involving students in a guided lecture, independent reading, and summary discussion to ensure in-depth comprehension.

Listening Guide: used to guide listening to an oral presentation; a skeletal outline of the important concepts arranged in the order and relationship in which they occur to aid students as they listen and fill in the appropriate information.

List-Group-Label Lesson: a vocabulary classification technique emphasizing the relationships among words.

Long-Term Memory: an organized store of information based on a person's cumulative experiences.

Macrostructure: the author's pattern of oganization which binds together its complex system of paragraphs.

Maze Technique: a structured alternative to the traditional cloze format for measuring comprehension; students must select from among two alternatives and the correct word to fill in deletions in a text.

Metacognition: awareness of one's own mental processes

Metadiscourse: text intrusions in which the author talks directly to the reader about the information in the text.

Microstructure: the author's ideas and supporting details at the sentence level.

Miscues: observed responses to printed text that do not conform exactly to the print and may preserve (e.g., auto for car) or disrupt meaning (e.g., cat for car).

Mnemonic: a strategy for remembering one thing by associating it with something else.

Modeling: a report by an individual of the mental operations involved in their comprehension process to illustrate its logical steps to others.

Morpheme: the smallest unit of language that has an associated meaning.

Morphemic Analysis: the analysis of affixes and roots to decode unknown words.

Norms: a set of scores against which the test performance of others may be compared.

Options Guide: a form of study guide in which students predict, discuss, and evaluate options available to key political and historical figures.

Organization: the arrangements of parts of a whole in such a manner that the parts are related to each other.

Parallel Notetaking: listening and taking notes at the same time.

Passive Failure: a term describing students who are resigned to fail and believe they do not have the ability to succeed in their learning.

Phonics: a decoding technique that emphasizes the sounds represented by letters in words.

PLAE: guidance strategy for studying which consists of preplanning, listing, activating, and evaluating.

Polar Opposites: a teaching strategy using contrasting words to critique a reading selection.

Possible Sentences: a vocabulary teaching strategy in which students use new vocabulary to create sentences for verification when reading.

Prediction Guide: a means of assessing students' prior knowledge about a topic through a series of fact-based statements that students determine are true or false before reading.

Presenting Content and Processes Concurrently: teaching that provides direct instruction in the processes necessary to acquire content as well as in what content is to be acquired.

Presenting Isolated Skills: teaching that consists of the direct teaching of skills with no consideration for content.

Preview in Context: an informal discovery procedure for teaching new vocabulary by drawing upon students' prior knowledge and the analysis of context.

Prior Knowledge: an individual's background experience.

Probable Passages: a writing strategy in which students predict and create paragraph-length sections of a text.

Problem-Solution: a pattern of text organization exemplified by an interaction of a problem and a potential answer to that problem.

Pseudographics: student- or teacher-made graphs that may or may not be an accurate representation of text material.

Qualitative Factors of Readability: non-measurable variables of text selection that include prior knowledge, text organization, and interest, among others.

Quantitative Factors of Readability: language variables of word length and sentence length as counted and measured in readability estimates.

Raygor Readability Estimate: a readability formula based on word and sentence length; noted for ease of administration and reduced potential for error.

Reaction Guide: a post-reading strategy used to stimulate review of a selection by asking students to react to a series of guide statements related to the selection.

Read-Encode-Annotate-Ponder: a writing strategy in which students annotate and critique expository or narrative text ideas.

Readability Formulas: mathematically derived indices of text difficulty based on an analysis of linguistic variables, the two most common being word length and sentence length.

Readiness Principle: refers to the mental state in which an individual is prepared to derive maximum meaning from a learning situation with a minimum of frustration.

Receptive Vocabulary: words that can be read and comprehended in print or heard and understood in spoken context.

Recoding: any process in which one code is changed into another code.

Rehearsal: the repeating of information for the purpose of retaining the information in memory.

ReQuest: a reciprocal questioning procedure that helps students adopt an active, questioning approach to text reading.

Response Bias: writing down what one believes an examiner wants rather than what the examinee really believes.

Response Mode: the type of response required by students' assigned questions, e.g., recall vs. recognition.

Restructuring: a major modification of existing schemata.

Schemata: a category system of the mind containing information about the surrounding environment; the plural of schema.

Schema Theory: describes the process by which we add to (assimilate) or adjust (accommodate) our existing cognitive structure in the face of new or discordant information.

Scope of Information Search: the number of concepts for which students are held responsible in a given reading assignment.

Selective Reading Guide: a series of teacher-devised guide statements that accompany a reading assignment and provide a model for purposeful, selective reading.

Self-Concept: how one views oneself.

Semantic Map: a diagram that groups related concepts.

Signal Words: the key words that cue a particular pattern of text organization.

Simple Listing: a pattern of text organization characterized by a listing of items or ideas without regard to order.

Short-Term Memory: the "working memory," which holds incoming information temporarily until a decision is made to include this information in long-term memory.

Slicing: simplifying the complexity of learning tasks by reexamining those that are required and recasting them to ease the demands placed on students.

Sociolinguistics: the study of language in a cultural context.

Spaced Notetaking: taking notes during intervals of silence between segments of a lecture.

SQ3R: survey, question, read, recite, review; a technique for improving comprehension of textbook material.

Standard Error of Measurement: the variation, or built-in error, in standardized test scores.

Standardized Test: a formal test instrument utilizing norms as a basis for student comparision of achievement.

Strategy: the planned means to an end.

Study Guide: a strategy that focuses students' attention on the major ideas of a selection at three levels of comprehension.

Study Strategies: the specific strategies that focus on locating, retaining, and recalling information.

Summarization: a succint statement of the main ideas in a reading selection.

Surveying the Text: a pre-reading strategy that involves some form of preliminary look at a reading selection before more intensive reading is undertaken.

Survey Test: usually a standardized test that measures global areas or achievement, such as vocabulary or comprehension.

Sustained Silent Reading: a systematic program that establishes regular reading times for students to practice their reading skills on pleasurable and self-selected content-related materials.

Technical Vocabulary: words uniquely related to particular academic disciplines; the words are accommodated by modifying old schemata or creating new schemata.

Test Ceiling: the upper limit placed on an individual's performance at a particular grade level on a standardized test.

Test Floor: the lower limit placed on an individual's performance at a particular grade level on a standardized test.

Testwiseness: a series of principles that can be applied to exams independently of subject area knowledge.

Text-Explicit: thinking which requires only getting facts as literally stated by an author, i.e., reading the lines.

Text-Implicit: thinking which requires an inference from the text to derive an answer to a question, i.e., reading between the lines.

Text Preview: a teacher devised introductory passage that provides a detailed framework for comprehending a reading selection.

Text Structure: the various organizational patterns writers and readers use to encode and decode thoughts.

Think-Aloud: teacher modeling strategy whereby one's thoughts about how a text is comprehended are verbalized for students.

Time Order: a pattern of text organization exemplifying a sequential relationship between ideas or events over the passage of time.

Top-Down Processing: selectively applying one's conceptual knowledge to the comprehension of content area ideas.

Transcribing: refers to the mechanics of writing including spelling, punctuation, capitalization, handwriting, formatting, and neatness.

Tuning: a gradual modification of existing schemata.

Unit Plan: a plan of instruction in which students explore and respond to a selected topic through their interaction with a variety of integrated activities designed to enhance their knowledge and attitude.

Verbal and Visual Word Association Strategy: a mnemonic strategy in which students associate a word they are trying to learn with personal examples or a concrete drawing.

Verbatim Split Page Procedure: a comprehensive method of taking notes during lectures.

Vocabulary: a corpus of many thousands of words and their associated meanings.

Vocabulary Self-Collection Strategy: a vocabulary acquisition technique designed to teach students how to select the most important vocabulary from reading assignments.

Word: a pattern of auditory or visual symbols that represent schemata, or concepts.

Word Analogies: exercises requiring students to draw inferences and expose subtle word associations.

Word Associations: a technique designed to measure students' knowledge about a topic through association.

Word Map: a visual representation of a definition.

Writing Roulette: a strategy in which students create a simple story containing some of the technical vocabulary they are learning.

Index